BY NORA JOHNSON

Coast to Coast: A Family Romance

Perfect Together

Uncharted Places

Tender Offer

The Two of Us

You Can Go Home Again: An Intimate Journey

Flashback: Nora Johnson on Nunnally Johnson

Pat Loud: A Woman's Story

Love Letter in the Dead-Letter Office

A Step Beyond Innocence

The World of Henry Orient

COAST TO COAST

A FAMILY ROMANCE

NORA JOHNSON

SIMON & SCHUSTER *New York London Toronto Sydney*

The names and other identifying characteristics
of some people have been changed.

SIMON & SCHUSTER
Rockefeller Center
1230 Avenue of the Americas
New York, NY 10020

For information about special discounts for bulk purchases,
please contact Simon & Schuster Special Sales:
1-800-456-6798 or business@simonandschuster.com

Book design by Ellen R. Sasahara

PHOTOS FROM THE AUTHOR'S COLLECTION

Manufactured in the United States of America

10 9 8 7 6 5 4 3 2 1

Library of Congress Cataloging-in-Publication Data

Johnson, Nora.
  Coast to coast : a family romance / Nora Johnson.
    p. cm.
    1. Johnson, Nora—Childhood and youth. 2. Novelists, Ameri-
can—20th century—Biography. 3. Adult children of divorced par-
ents—United States—Biography. 4. Motion picture producers and
directors—United States—Family relationships. 5. Screenwriters—
United States—Family relationships. 6. Hollywood (Los Angeles,
Calif.)—Biography. 7. New York (N.Y.)—Biography. 8. Johnson,
Nunnally—Family. 9. Johnson, Nora—Family. I. Title.

PS3519.O2833Z463 2004
813'.54—dc22
[B]
                                            2004045392

ISBN 978-1-4165-6809-4

For Jon—
who didn't stay around till this was finished

And for Jones—
who got me to write it in the first place

COAST TO COAST

I WAS BORN in the old Hollywood Hospital a few years after the talkies came in. You might even say *because* the talkies came in, since the reason we were there was so my father, Nunnally Johnson—along with hundreds of other writers—could make money writing dialogue for the movies. It was the depths of the Great Depression, the bottom of the birthrate curve, the year Franklin D. Roosevelt took office, the end of Prohibition, the year we went off the gold standard, the day after Hitler came to power . . . but Los Angeles was a boomtown.

The local news was: *Cavalcade* won the Oscar for Best Picture of 1933, and Nathanael West sold *Miss Lonelyhearts* to Zanuck for his new Twentieth Century Pictures. Movies based on my father's first two scripts for Paramount—*Mama Loves Papa* and *A Bedtime Story*—were released, as were *King Kong* and *Dinner at Eight*. It was the year the Screen Writers Guild was founded, the year of drought and the Dust Bowl and the earthquake that cost $40 million and killed 120—in the middle of which my parents picked me up and ran out to the patio of our $175-a-month ranch house in Beverly Hills, the nanny being fast asleep. As they waited for the ground to crack open beneath their feet, I smiled for the first time in my very short life.

My father's first salary, $300 a week, doubled in a year, and went to $2,000 five years and twenty scripts later. Much happened during that time. We moved from Bedford Drive to Maple to Beverly to Camden. Hedy Lamarr's picture *Ecstasy* was seized by the U.S. Customs for indecency. The Farmers Market opened on Fairfax. Nunnally produced *Dimples*, starring Shirley Temple. Bertolt Brecht, Arnold Schoenberg, and other future Hollywood artists fled the darkening political scene in Europe. My father turned down a certain Civil War novel because he thought nobody would go and see a picture about two people named Scarlett and Rhett. Three young actresses, Linda Darnell, Mary Healy, and Dorris Bowdon, arrived from the South in search of stardom.

Among Nunnally's scripts during this period were *The House of Rothschild, Bulldog Drummond Strikes Back, The Prisoner of Shark Island, The Road to Glory,* and *Jesse James.* While his star rose, my mother went to auctions, decorated houses, played polo, and took speech lessons to get the Flushing (Queens) out of her voice. While he talked, laughed, and drank at the Brown Derby and Chasen's with the likes of George Jessel, Ben Hecht, William Faulkner, Herman Mankiewicz, PhilipWylie, Gene Fowler, Harry Ruby, Oscar Hammerstein, Dorothy Parker, Ogden Nash, Jack Benny, George Burns, Groucho Marx, Robert Benchley, Don Stewart, and Dash Hammett, she lunched and played badminton, had facials and massages, and, at one party, held the inebriated Scott Fitzgerald's head in her lap. When beautiful actresses clamored for parts in Nunnally's pictures and solicited further attentions, she wept at home, indulged in some revenge flirting with John O'Hara, or went on extended cruises, one of which led to great disappointment because, though other countries had welcomed her, she was refused a visa to Russia.

In 1938 the rains came, ending the drought. Dorris Bowdon came to Nunnally's office, determined to get a part in *Jesse James.* My mother, the nanny, the Swedish chauffeur, and I packed up the big black Cadillac and drove to New York, leaving California forever. The next year *The Grapes of Wrath* opened with Dorris Bowdon playing

Rosasharn, and in February of 1940 Nunnally and Dorris's marriage was announced on the radio by Walter Winchell. My mother cried, the nanny cried, I cried. In 1941 the Japanese bombed Pearl Harbor, and my mother's new lover, Commander Jo Golinkin, was called to active duty in the Pacific.

After their divorce my parents sent me back and forth twice a year. I was supported by the gold on one coast and schooled on the other, as the British children in India were shipped home to be educated. I and others like me knew the Super Chief menus, the porters on the Twentieth Century, and the Albuquerque train station the way other children know the way to school and the crossing guard. We learned how to have two homes, to drop names of stars and producers and restaurants, to be two people at once. We got used to being taken to "21" and Romanoff's and hearing about the war and the society and how rotten everything was and how poor people were and how we should clean our plates because of the starving Armenians/Chinese/whatever group was currently worse off. We grew up amid contradictions . . . we knew everything and nothing.

PERSEPHONE

EVERY JUNE I went to California and every fall I came back. In 1947, when I was fourteen, my parents decided I was old enough to cross the country alone. My mother—on the East Coast—gave me a pile of books. And my father—on the West—as usual knew somebody in the Business who would be on the same train.

The connection in Chicago between two trains at different stations was considered daunting enough to require help. The man from the William Morris office met me at LaSalle Street Station when I arrived on the Twentieth Century. He saw to my luggage, bought me a hamburger, fries, and a black-and-white milkshake, and told me funny stories about all the kids he picked up and delivered to train stations and airports. He took me to Dearborn Station, found the Chief, and located my roomette. There was one of him in every city of the world, I discovered over the years—a man from the Morris office who turned up and took care of things, a guardian agent of the open road.

And he was trustworthy—more than my own mother. Once, at Grand Central, she had left me in the observation car of the Twentieth Century so I could more fully observe the South Bronx on the way out of town. She kissed me good-bye and left. After over an hour I went outside to find that this observation car had not been attached to the rest of the train, which had departed with the luggage and the accompanying nanny (who was absorbed in *Silver Screen*) but without me. Somehow it got solved—a weeping child and a kind stationmaster were an effective combination, and we were all reunited in Chicago in time to get on the Chief. The man from Morris would never have allowed such a thing to happen.

This trip's celebrity was Miss Lena Horne. She hung on the step of the Chief's silver Pullman car, one hand grasping the steel railing. She was dazzling—the clear silky skin, the big sparkling eyes, and a graceful way of bending slightly backward, causing her ivory cloak to flare behind her. Her smile threw me and the man from the Morris office into half-shadow as she extended one perfect hand, with pale almond nails, toward me.

"Why, hello, sweetheart," she said. "I'm so glad to meetcha!" Moments like this I saved up to tell my school friends, who couldn't hear enough about movie stars. I tried to will my stuck voice into speech, but I was like the tongueless man who sold pencils in front of Bloomingdale's. Miss Horne, wearying of my nonperformance, looked past me to a young man of about my age standing nearby with *his* guardian. The man from William Morris greeted the man from MCA as Miss Horne crooned, "Greg-rey darlin'," and flung her arms around the young man's neck. The two chattered away like old buddies till she told us good-bye and retreated into the train. Through the windows I saw her cloak fluttering after her as she went along the corridor to her compartment.

Gregory and I exchanged greetings, his friendlier than mine, while the two agents took care of the details that we were thought too helpless to take care of. I knew him a little. The son of a director friend of my father's, he and I had been at a couple of dances together. He was nice-enough looking except for a startling cowlick and a too-early beard that had not been skillfully shaved, and his nails looked seriously chewed. Whether there was anything important wrong with him is impossible to say, because I had not yet learned that boys of less than perfect appearance—even the sort that might well improve in a few years—might have very good qualities, and I had the patience of a flea anyway.

Gregory was one of those rare fifteen-year-olds who knew how to talk. The boys I met at school dances, whose looks and fancy footwork rendered me all a-twitter, were something else off the dance floor—they shuffled and mumbled, blurted out football scores or funny stories about dormitory sadism. Since I thought this was mainline male behavior, Gregory's poise made me suspicious. It wasn't masculine—masculine was inarticulate. He was pushy—boys should be cool and self-involved. Their hair should lie flat, and I preferred incipient depression—which I called "soulfulness"—to affability. And he was a terrible dancer. Now he and I would have the pleasure of each other's company for the next forty-eight hours.

I'd logged a lot of time aboard streamliners. I didn't need the typed instructions from my father ("Get to the dining car at the first gong . . . go to the club car if you just want a sandwich," etc.). The Chief's mystique made me happy in a unique, incoherent way—from the starched white antimacassars and scratchy seats and satiny aluminum windowframes to the pull-down steel sinks that emptied out onto the tracks and the tiny linen towels and the tidy ashtrays set into the chair arms and the diesel smell. I loved the dining car with its padded tablecloths and the Santa Fe china with the profile of an Indian chief in full warbonnet . . . and the lamb chops with paper frills and the little oval dishes of peas and mashed potatoes, the Parker House rolls and strawberry shortcake of Fred Harvey, whoever he was, who "Served the Meals."

I knew the light and the landscape. The dusk was long the first evening as we went southwest through Illinois. The green farmland was flat and then rolling as we entered Missouri. Sometimes there were a few houses or the silver shine of a river with a patch of trees bunched up next to it. When the train turned, the whole silver-snake front of it appeared ahead, the rest curving out behind like a reptile's tail, the dim reflections of the diners' faces floating over it like ghosts.

After dinner I went toward the rear, hauling open heavy doors and stepping across the churning metal floors between cars. In the infamous—but attached—observation car, a few people sat in lounge chairs talking in low voices or reading papers, sipping drinks and dropping ashes into the standing ashtrays. The air was hazy with cigarette smoke. After a lot of thought I had decided on Chesterfields. The white package looked sanitary, and the name suggested some handsome country place, perhaps in England, where people rode horses through woods and pastures and jumped them over low stone walls.

Suspended between the two coasts, I felt light and porous, like a trailing fishnet. Neither parental world, so seemingly in accordance but so subtly contradictory, applied here. I was free, my mind could roam at will . . . until Gregory walked in.

He greeted me pleasantly enough and sat down. He'd looked for me in the dining room. Thank God there was somebody to talk to. Then—had school been minimally bearable? How long would I be in Beverly? What was my father shooting? . . . and so forth. Even my sulkiness didn't discourage him. He talked on undeterred about our common background, the world we took for granted. I didn't yet appreciate what rare birds we were, how unique our plumage. We came from the same exotic jungle . . . but he was pleased, even delighted, with his singularity, while all I wanted was to be like everybody else. The two worlds I balanced were flaming balls, burning my fingers if I held one too long.

"I didn't see you on the Century," Gregory said.

"I slept the whole time."

He waved and grandly ordered us each a ginger ale. He was nattily dressed—he even had a watch and a watch fob, or what he said was a watch fob—on a chain.

"Do you usually go alone?"

"I never have before," I said cautiously.

"It's nothing. Listen, I know a girl whose parents went around the world for almost a whole year, when she was *six*. They left her with an aunt in Tarzana. When they got back to New York they only had enough money left for one train fare, so she had to go all the way east on the Chief by herself."

"Was she scared?" I asked.

"Oh, no," Gregory said. "She thinks it's funny."

"Did she miss them during the year?"

"I don't think so," he said.

That made sense. The only time I was away from both my parents at the same time was on the train. It was hard to be with only one parent, though I wasn't sure why. When I first understood why we kept going to New York when I was seven, what I was really furious about was that now they were going to be three thousand miles apart and I had to do all the traveling just to be with them separately. And I hated not being able to say *my parents* the way everybody else could. *My parents* went around the world for a year when I was six. *My parents* starved me and beat me with clubs and locked me in the closet for three days. I wouldn't even care, as long as *they* did it.

"I almost flew this time," Gregory said. "Did you ever fly?"

"Just once and I was terrified."

He settled back in his chair, then reached into his pocket and took out a pack of Camels. He shook it so a couple stuck out and held the pack in front of me, but I shook my head, smelling the nice barnyard smell of the tobacco.

"I'm waiting till I'm sixteen."

"Why?"

"I don't know." I'd never known a boy who asked so many questions. But we were stuck with each other and he was doing all the work.

"How do you know Lena Horne?" I asked.

"She used to come over all the time, she was in a picture of my dad's—they'd work on the script and then we'd all go swimming."

"Is she funny?"

"Not especially."

A familiar tightness gathered in my chest. "She's the only one who isn't. I'm going to spend the whole summer screaming with laughter."

"Is that so bad?"

"No, it's wonderful. It's perfect."

He leaned back and stretched. "We should visit her tomorrow."

"What for?"

"Just for something to do."

"I don't think so," I said. "Tomorrow is Dull Day."

"What?"

"I go so often, I could tell you what we're passing without even looking out the window. Certain things happen at certain times . . . and tomorrow is my day to be bored. I just spend the whole day doing absolutely nothing." He looked skeptical. "The only event tomorrow is when the Super Chief passes us and you can see inside when it goes by. You can look at their steak while you're eating your veal cutlets."

"I don't believe it." He blew a couple of smoke rings. "*You* couldn't spend a whole day just staring out the window. You'd jump out of your skin."

"You're wrong. It's the only time I have to get ready for the summer."

"Why can't you do that at home?"

I laughed. "What home?"

"Well, mine's in Benedict Canyon. If you don't even know where you live you've got a big problem."

"I'll work it out," I said.

"People ought to know where they live."

Night had fallen. There was only a faint tinge of pale gray over the horizon ahead. Now we were really in the plains. You couldn't see, but I knew there was nothing around anywhere—nothing that I understood, anyway. All night and all the next day would be nothing, a washed blackboard, a blank pad of paper, an empty drawer.

"I live in two places," I said.

"You have to choose. It isn't good for you this way."

"Maybe it's very good. Maybe I have everything."

"Well, that's one way to look at it." A way I never had. "I'm crazy about Beverly Hills. That's where the real fun is. New York is okay but it's so damn cold and people can be so mean there."

"They can be pretty mean in California." I stood up. "I think I'll turn in. I'm totally exhausted."

He looked disappointed. "Are you sure? I'm not like you. I'm not crazy about doing nothing."

"Sorry. I'll see you tomorrow probably."

The porter had made up my berth with military tightness. The taut sheets and Santa Fe blanket gave off a faint odor of gravel and engine fuel, the metal smell of the track. I opened the stiff curtain and lay for a long time looking out at the train's window lights running along the ground. The night was dark and clear, starred with batches of tiny lights from distant settlements that flew by like scatterings of fireflies.

The distance between my parents rolled out below me in a carpet of final indifference. I could no more reverse it than I could stop the train itself. Though they were unquestionably through for good, though now they loved other people, I still played this game every trip. At fifty miles there was still a little hope, even at a hundred or two hundred miles it might be reversible, but by morning, well over a thousand, a third of the nails would be in the coffin. Click-click, click-click. Did I get it yet?

But of course I never would.

DULL DAY—drawings on parchment or paper bags, mile after mile of brown land so flat you could see straight to the horizon. There were no towns and the plains had turned to desert, the green had become dry scrub. There was nothing in sight but sagebrush and mesquite and burning heat that you could see in waves through the window. Sometimes there were a couple of shacks and a few dark people stood near them looking at the passing train. Then at Amarillo the West started, and this was where I went through the land change—the visceral pull switched over to where I'd started from, before my mother took me back to New York. Every year I returned to the place I'd been exiled from—like Persephone.

GREGORY found me in the club car.

"I ran into Lena before, coming out of her drawing room."

Of course. "She has a drawing room? All to herself?"

"She's a star. Should she ride in the baggage car?"

"What a waste. Do you know there are people who have to sit up the whole way to California? They can't sleep for three whole days. They take sandwiches in paper bags."

Gregory yawned and stretched. "You're much too serious. Don't you ever have any fun?"

"I have *lots* of fun."

"Well, you sure don't act it. All you seem to like is Bore Day, or whatever you call it." He leaned back and closed his eyes. "How can anybody not like Beverly Hills?"

"Nothing ever happens there. The weather is always just too, too perfect. You're crippled if you don't drive."

"Oh, people drive you, for God's sake. I'm talking about the parties. My dad works at MGM and my parents know everybody there. There are always people at our house swimming, or having drinks around the pool or just chewing the fat. Sometimes we go to Chasen's or the Brown Derby. But a lot of the time they just hang around and talk. Sometimes they get a riff going and they're practically writing the next picture right there—it's called spitballing—and they cast it and think of crazy ideas for other pictures, or talk about which of the old ones to remake. And the stories . . . but you must know all this."

"My dad doesn't go out much. They have little kids, I guess that's why they stay home mostly."

"But they aren't tongue-tied, for God's sake. A lot of the best stories came from your dad in the first place."

My father had been called "Hollywood's No. 1 Wit" in an article in

The Saturday Evening Post. Sometimes he made me laugh till I had tears in my eyes, real tears, till I was crying and laughing at the same time. I didn't know how to make him stop . . . and he didn't know he was doing it.

"People come over sometimes," I said. "Bogey comes with Betty Bacall. Ginger Rogers came once. Groucho comes sometimes."

"But you must have heard all the stories about Harry Cohn and Louis B. Mayer and that whole crew, the old-time guys from the rag business that went out there and made pictures when the place was still practically a pueblo . . . and about the talkies coming in and all. I've had people in New York falling off their *chairs,* I've been to dances where I never even *danced* because nobody'd let me stop talking . . . you might not believe it but girls have called me and *begged* me to take them out because I'm supposed to be the funniest guy in town when all I do is talk about Hollywood. People even want to hear what we eat and what the houses look like and who lives next door." He looked at me. "I know it sounds pretentious but you know I'm not making any of it up. that's why I like you, even though frankly you aren't much fun."

"Damn." It was hard to swallow. I knew every word was true; that was the trouble.

"What's the matter? Jesus, are you crying?"

"Of *course* not. Don't be ridiculous."

The train stopped at Albuquerque for half an hour and we got out and wandered down the platform. The Indians sat cross-legged in the sun with their trays of silver and turquoise jewelry and the same moccasins and beaded belts I remembered from last year. Gregory got his mother some earrings. I didn't know what was wrong with me; usually I was excited about going west but now I was losing my nerve. Maybe it was from being alone.

They put on a second engine to climb the Rockies. The mountains rose up out of the plain in the late afternoon, big and black and red and sienna. Coming the other way everything was mountains anyway, the whole city was dumped over mountains. You wormed your way up through the canyons, but this side was so sharp-edged, so awful, like a warning. I always imagined the backward slide, the two engines quivering, hovering, fighting to get to the top, then braking and sliding back faster and faster into the canyon until the whole silver string of cars crumpled into a tangled heap of metal and smoke and crushed bleeding bodies. The sun was setting over the black peaks and turning the western faces to fire. The chaparral seemed to be burning up and I saw a couple of jackrabbits running as though screaming in pain. Then suddenly it was completely dark, then there was a hot green line, and we were in blackness.

During dinner together—which seemed unavoidable by then, some bond having formed between us—Gregory didn't seem bothered by the climb, though I knew boys would die rather than show fear. At one point he said he was sorry if he'd hurt my feelings before and I said there was no reason to be, envy was one of the deadly sins. I deserved to feel bad. When we went up a particularly steep slope he reached over and took one of my white-knuckled hands in his. His hand felt warm. Mine was a skeleton of ice.

We both had the cherry pie à la mode and then we went to the club car and he got going again about the stars and all that. This time I accepted one of the Camels, took a couple of puffs, and gagged. Gregory asked the waiter for two beers but they wouldn't serve us, and he said he had a couple of cans of Bud in his compartment.

It didn't take any great intelligence to know what was coming but I thought maybe if I let him kiss me some of what he had would permeate me; it would almost be like I had it too. It was stupid not to have it, really. I'd never realized it. It was the least they could do. But they probably didn't take me anywhere because I was such a crabby kid, I *wasn't* any fun. I was better off home with the babies and Nursie. If I went out to Romanoff's with them and Groucho was there and the Bogarts and Coop and Rocky and all the rest, I'd just be a black hole in the bright tapestry anyway.

He had his own compartment, not as big as Lena Horne's but bigger than mine, and I asked how come, they were impossible to get. He said his dad knew people—like mine didn't. I was trying to decide how far to let him go; he was probably wondering the same thing. I was about as innocent as you can get but this was different, something else was going on that was beyond me.

Then he kissed me . . . his beard was prickly and I kept tasting the Camels and feeling his lips and the stubble, and it was awful and I never wanted him to stop. I was drinking in Lena and Louie B. Mayer and Joan Crawford and Clark and Claudette and all the rest of them and trying to picture Cukor's living room and John Huston's set. We both got rather worked up so I told him we'd better stop. It was hard, I wanted to lose myself in it and forget what an ass I was but I couldn't. The poor people were going to California in cattle cars or trucks with their paper bags of stale sandwiches, or no sandwiches, or they weren't going anywhere, and here I was falling apart because I didn't meet enough movie stars. I didn't tell any of this to Gregory, because he'd never believe anybody could be such an idiot.

NEEDLES was the first stop in California. Ten minutes at Needles, where the sun beat down on your head and burned through your clothes into your bones. California was heat and brown dust, the strange fragrance of the desert, and a dumpy little station in the middle of nowhere. California was mountains, stark and bare or else golden-flanked, dotted with green oaks, and miles of orange groves, the clean glossy dark leaves growing out of the dry ground, and hot dry farmland . . . a world away from the white birches, the green hills and crystal rivers of home.

Greg and I had been instructed to get off at Pasadena—staying on the train all the way to Union Station, in downtown L.A., was déclassé. By then we were much the worse for wear. The Chief's amenities didn't include bathtubs. His beard was choppier than ever, and my hair was hanging in strings. I hoped he would suggest meeting during the summer, it would be something to do, but he didn't. Why should he? He'd be having lunch at the MGM commissary every day and going for swims with Kate and Spencer. Even if he had any free time he wouldn't want to spend it with the black hole. I was strictly for the train.

The porters unloaded our baggage at the Pasadena station, where hedges of pink and white oleanders bent in the breeze and palm trees swayed overhead. The air was softer and there was something different about the light, a rough, grainy quality that made everything look like a painting. It was like looking through very fine meshed glass . . . it always took a few days to get used to it.

I made a dash for a tall man in a Hawaiian shirt and pleated trousers, standing with his arms out. He laughed at the violence of my hug. I was ridiculously in love with my father. We both knew it. So were a lot of others—his three wives and four children, his secretaries and maids and movie stars and almost everyone he encountered—which transformed my feeling into a public commodity.

An alto voice called his name, and Miss Horne descended from the train in her pearly clothes, her cape a-flutter. In a moment her graceful hands were in his, and—after peeling me off like a mollusk—he embraced her affectionately and then introduced me.

"We met in Chicago, didn't we, sweetheart?"

Charm . . . it grew on the petticoat palms, flew out of the canyons like flocks of butterflies. It curled around you, crept into your hair and ears. "But we didn't see each other after that, we must have just missed"—leading my father off by the arm to meet some friends, and waving down the platform at blue-jawed Gregory.

To my surprise he was standing alone, looking down the row of chauffeured Cadillacs under the palm trees with a bleary anxiety I had not seen before. When he saw me sitting on the fender while the chauffeur loaded the trunk he gave a distracted little smile, then resumed his worried scrutiny. No car. No Dad . . . no Clark or Claudette.

I ran down the platform. "What's the matter, Greg?"

"He must have gotten held up." His voice didn't hold out much hope.

16

"Oh, they do that. Mine just took off with Lena," I said. "Typical."

That was true too. My beloved dad didn't have great powers of resistance. All my life I'd watched him be scooped up and taken away by women, stars, people. The wife who got fed up with it packed up and left, the one who didn't had him still . . . but as I turned around he was hurrying back along the platform, waving. I had to give him this—he always came back.

"Why don't you come with us?"

"My dad's just a little late, for God's sake. Don't get charitable."

"My father will ask you anyway."

"I'll take a taxi." We both knew there weren't any, or hardly any, and it was an hour's ride.

"Fine," I said. "Stay on the platform. Spend the summer in Pasadena."

Greg wasn't one to pass up an opportunity. In the car on the way I wanted to hold his hand—except that he was telling my dad a great story about Cukor.

GO STRAIGHT TO THE LOCAL LIQUOR STORE

204 East 62nd Street.

Peacock walls, cream satin curtains spilling from ceiling to floor, a white marble fireplace like a frozen meringue. A baroque breakfront in silver and copper, mirror and amber and painted glass, scattering shards of light; a glossy sofa with chocolate stripes, a rose loveseat, a pair of velvet seashell chairs. On the mantel, in glass cases, stood two Japanese dolls in gilt paper costumes, with jet hair, porcelain faces, tiny dots and dashes for features. A coffee table of mirror panels; more mirrors over the fireplace, between the two tall rear windows, and over the Biedermeier table, with its tinkling crystal lamps, in the entrance hall. Our faces were everywhere.

On the console table were very often bottles, glasses, a silver bucket of ice, a jigger, openers and corkscrews and stirrers, a drying lemon with peel scars, a jar of maraschino cherries, little bottles of olives and cocktail onions. Strewn on the mirrored coffee table were cigarette boxes, a chunky silver Ronson lighter, a bowl of matchbooks for when the Ronson didn't work, half-full cocktail glasses, my mother's silver

18

"individual" shaker, hefty on-the-rocks glasses, sometimes with a lip-stick print on the side. A plate of rat cheese and Ritz crackers, a dish of canned sardines, a few celery sticks or nuts, sometimes a nameless pink dip that always ended up full of broken potato chips. Some-body's black suede gloves with a light sprinkle of ashes, and ash-trays—silver, glass, ceramic from European hotels—piled with crushed, burned cigarette butts. Crumpled packs of Chesterfields, Lucky Strikes, Camels, Pall Malls . . . a pleasant odor of smoke and gin and Caron's Fleurs de Rocaille, the odor of home.

Though my mother had quit when we still lived in Beverly Hills, most of her friends smoked, my father smoked, the nanny smoked, the cook and the maid smoked, and in time, I smoked and so did most of my friends. Smoking went with drinking. My father drank his bour-bon and water and then twisted his mouth around an Old Gold, his eyes furrowed in concentration as he clicked his silver lighter. He'd breathe in the smoke, then sit back, take a few puffs while he talked, then crush the long cigarette out impatiently, only to light another immediately. He'd run through half a pack, then get up, shrugging himself into his coat in the vestibule before he left—which he did because they were divorced.

Why was he there at all? Because it had been a friendly divorce. Because they had all the same friends . . . because they were old pals.

"Oh Marion," my mother's friends cooed as they arrived, "isn't this marvelous. It's *lovely*. I *love* it. I told Frank, I don't know how Marion *does* it. Everything is always so *hospitable*, and so *effortless* at the same time."

"I'll make the first drink, then it's every man for himself." She stood before the bar like a figurehead, straight-backed, big-breasted, laugh-ing. ("It's fun to be beautiful," I later found in her diary.)

"Just one of your terrific martinis will do just fine." Then later: "I'll make just a tad more. They're so delicious. Now how much do I put in? Oops—whoops!" Still later—"Oh, I sh . . . shouldn't. Really shouldn't. Is this the right bottle? Don't tell . . ." whatever husband, child, boss's voice of conscience dinned. "Gotta [go to work, be at the doctor, meet Susie's teacher] tomorrow. Just a weeny drop"—a new definition of a drop.

The men were more forthright. "Scotch, Marion, a little ice. Hey, not a whole goddamn glacier! Come on, honey, tilt that bottle, I've had a long day. That's more like it." Slosh slosh. Jovially: "Women can't make drinks. Jesus, I need another. Anybody else?" More talk and laughter, another round.

Cellophane wrappers crumpled, followed by the pungent smell of fresh tobacco. Cigarettes were drawn out and inserted between bloodred lips. Holders were for looks only, for fun. Edith Haggard's gold one, available only at Dunhill's in London, fitted over her middle finger. Some smokers were meticulous about peeling the pack open, some—the ones with a hardcore habit, or no aesthetics—ripped into it impatiently, digging cigarettes out of messy crinkled paper foil. The Ronson usually failed.

"Oh, God, those things never work." Fixing them meant digging into their wet, gaseous intestines. "Anybody got a match? Hey, somebody, I need a match." Someone always had a steel Zippo. "Jesus, it's a flamethrower! They could use that out in the Pacific."

"Oh, Marion. This is . . . marvelous. You are so marvelous to *do* it. I was just saying to Ralph this morning, other people *say* they're going to have you over for drinks, but one thing or another comes up, and they never do. You're the only one that really *does* it. And you always look so *wonderful*. What's your secret?"

"Marion walks around the reservoir every single day, don't you, darling?"

"Almost."

"And facials . . . you must give me the name of your adorable Danish woman."

"Two dead soldiers and we've only been here an hour."

"You're out of J & B, darling. That makes three." (Cough, cough.) God—this is the worst winter for *phlegm*."

Embassy Liquors, around the corner on Sixty-first, delivered in ten minutes. At other times, the "Embassy Boys" cashed checks and even lent money to children of valued customers in need of a nickel for the bus or an ice-cream cone. Twice they had even broken into the house—about as difficult as breaking into a shoebox—when I'd lost my key and nobody was home. My mother once advised me: "Whenever you move into a new neighborhood, go straight to the local liquor store, and then be *loyal*. They'll be your best friends—they'll even cash checks—because they have to make up for not being allowed to charge."

Very soon a smiling Embassy Boy rang the doorbell and handed me a brown paper bag. I gave him the check. Outside the street lamps lit up the spindly plane trees, the sky was the ink blue of sunset. Stores were closing, the lights in other houses were going on. Curtains were mostly open, and I could see people moving around in their living rooms. The whole world was having cocktails, lighting Chesterfields, refilling ice buckets . . . and what a world! None of my friends' houses or apartments were as much fun as mine. Other mothers were stuffier than mine, seemingly older, and rarely divorced—and though I had a few complaints, for plain *gemütlichkeit*, for pure pleasure, nothing was like 204.

"For Lord's sake," Nanny said from behind me, "give me that bottle. Come downstairs, your supper's ready."

The el train rattled by, drowning everything out, then my mother's laugh rose over the voices in the living room. The cascade of crystal pendants on the hall lamps glittered double in the mirror, four times if you looked at them in the fireplace mirror, eight if you craned your neck and peered back again. Fur coats were piled on the creaky newel post and the side chairs, fedoras hung on the hat rack—the womens' hats usually started out, at least, tucked into coiffed hair and pinned in place.

"Marion, that's a riot," someone cried. "Isn't that a riot? Ethel, just listen to this." Murmurs I couldn't hear. "*That's* how far some people will go to get an apartment."

"But I thought they were being thrown out."

"Not anymore." Everyone laughed.

"Where's that bottle? Hey, Nanny's got it! Here, Nanny!" Crunkle, crunkle, unscrew. "There's the White Label. The Red Label. The Black Label. Three cheers for Nanny! A little tipple for you too? Snookie [me, unwillingly] will get some more ice, now, will you, sweetie?"

"Now, sir, she'll cut her hands to pieces, and I'll be rollin' down the steps."

Nanny clumped downstairs, chuckling, me after her. She enjoyed the chaffing. She took the ice pick and chipped at the block of ice in the sink, delivered from the dungeon across the street with the hand-lettered sign saying LOUIE'S ICE COAL WOOD. The icebox only accommodated two icetrays.

"I'll take it up."

"You will not. Sit right down and eat your macaroni."

"I just want to see them one more time."

Up in the front hall, embraces, searches for coats, gloves, handbags. "What did I do with . . . I left it right here . . . I think I'm a little . . . tipsy. Isn't that ridiculous? Why, sweetie—the ice! Look, she's brought the ice! Isn't she a darling? Come here, lovey, let me look at you. How old are you?" (Seven, eight.) "You're so *big!* Tell me, do you like school?" The face in front of me was thickly made up—dark mascara, crimson lipstick, spots of rouge, reddish curls straggling out from under a black bucket hat. "Marion, does she still go to that cute school, with the gorgon principal?"

"She loves it," my mother said. "They do anything the gorgon says, they adore her."

"Let's see, can you do . . . what are those damn things? Lee, lou, loga-rhythms, that's it. Can you do loga-rhythms, sweetie? I'll bet you can."

"Let's go, Lola Loga-rhythm. I'm hungry. Hey, Loga loga loga . . ." A little dance in the hallway, a lurch against the quivering crystal lamps, and the thousand reflections danced. "Oh, Christ. Here, I'll get it. No harm done." The bodies milled around, convivial, saying good-bye . . . only Georges made no move for his coat.

"Where I come from you would long be in bed," he said, putting his arm around me. He was stout, with a black mustache, and once he had brought me a doll from Paris. Sometimes I pretended to play with it. As the others went out the door, he moved over and put one hand on my mother's erect but swaying back. His skin was pink, his wavy black hair was combed straight back. After some thought I had chosen Georges over the others. An importer of wine and cognac, he always arrived with bottles under his arms. He smiled a lot, he made my mother laugh. He was a jolly fellow, a little glamorous, always dashing back and forth to Europe—until France fell.

After my bath, I crept down the three flights—past my mother's bedroom, tousled and fragrant, past the cluttered living room with its stink of stale ashes, down to the basement dining room. Outside the window, at shoulder level, rubber boots and fur-trimmed galoshes kicked blackened snow, umbrellas tapped, little dogs in belted plaid coats trotted by. My mother and Georges sat at the table sipping his special Monnet cognac from fragile balloon glasses.

"Georges, let's play cards. You promised."

"Another time, *ma petite*."

"But you said that before. Just one game." I was addicted to War. He shook his head, but I still hung around the doorway. "Georges, where do you really live?"

"*En France, chérie* . . . but we are in great trouble."

"What kind of trouble?"

"Politics. You are too young to understand."

"I'm not."

"Well, then. There are bad leaders and evil doings these days. One must make difficult choices . . . it is hard to do business."

I thought my mother gave him a watch-what-you-say look. She took me to the stairs. She was always very dressed up, as though life were a party—satin skirt, a cinched waist, a low-cut velvet top. She looked pretty, sexy, and a little blowsy.

"Please, Mama. I'm not sleepy."

"Off to bed, missy. Right this minute."

I gave in easily enough. Georges's presence made me feel safe. I never thought whether he spent the night, but I would have been glad if he did, for I worried that my mother was lonely after the guests left. I climbed back up to Nanny's and my aerie on the top floor. Here bookcases lined the walls, and our fireplace, the only one in the house that worked, was sometimes lit. My tiny room overlooked the little brick backyard, bleak and patched with snow, with its gigantic tree of heaven. Beyond was the city and the Chrysler Building against the night sky.

Nanny had faith. She had only half-persuaded my lapsed-Catholic mother of the benefits of mass, but daily prayer was established. I knelt down on the prayer rug next to my bed, hurtled through an Our Father and a Hail Mary, then showered blessings on great numbers of people—the cocktail guests, a dozen or so school friends, the gorgon teacher I worshiped, every relative I could think of, Mac the grocer, the butcher, the dry cleaner, Louie, the Embassy Boys, and the cocker spaniel, while Nanny dozed in her chair as the radio sputtered softly.

"Nanny, which leaders are bad or good?"

"Who, like Mr. Churchill?"

I hesitated. "I think so."

"He and Mr. Roosevelt are the finest men ever lived."

"Then why . . ."

"Enough talk, now. Did you bless your mother and father?" I heard the scrape of a match, smelled the faint odor of sulphur.

"Of *course*."

"Did you bless . . . you know, *her*?"

"Well, sure."

Nanny didn't believe me. "Bless her again, just to make sure."

"But it isn't fair to bless her twice."

"It isn't a normal situation. The Good Lord will understand."

That made sense. I climbed into bed and lay listening to Gabriel Heatter's mournful tones on the radio. If happiness is the sense of safety, the absence of fear, then I was happy. I didn't know it; I thought the events of my life were ordinary, universal, like the great swells of the ocean, or giant trees, and just as unchanging; that I was neither lucky nor unlucky, that the world was safe, solid, and predictable as the concrete street outside or the falling snow; that it called for no particular gratitude, any more than you thanked the sky for the moon and stars.

REENTRY

WE DROVE ALONG wide blazing boulevards lined with telephone poles, the silver wires whining above, clusters of flimsy pink and blue bungalows flanked by spiky succulent plants and dippy-looking palm trees in their limp hula skirts. I saw the fake-Spanish motels with neon signs pale in the sun, the round drive-in restaurants, the used-car lots fluttering with multicolored pennants, the iron elbows of the oil wells pumping tirelessly up and down in the sand, the petroleum reek, the creeping desert waiting everywhere . . . the shimmer of heat waves, a silver sun, a fierce blue sky.

We came in on the Strip, winding along the base of the Santa Monica Mountains past the Trocadero (pale turquoise) and Ciro's (pale coral), large windowless shapes like beached whales where I longed to go but could never persuade my father to take me, and the Château Marmont, pushed up against the foothills and shrouded in jungle greenery. On the other side of the street the land dropped off sharply into the vast basin that held the city. To the east was Holly-wood—Graumann's Chinese, famous footprints in the concrete, searchlights piercing the night sky, and a place called Carthay Circle (since swallowed up by a freeway) where I imagined movie stars slowly parading, turning this way and that to be admired by adoring crowds.

At the brown-shield Beverly Hills sign, the Strip ended and Sunset straightened out and divided. There was a bridle path down the middle, as there was on Rodeo, where people walked or rode their horses or bicycles in the soft brown dust. It made Sunset a gentler street, a nice place to be at . . . sunset. Beverly Hills is spread out on a plain by the foothills. Not strewn, like some western towns, but planned, as neatly patterned as Manhattan. There the similarity ends. Here I saw space, sunlight, breadth, breeziness; Manhattan was narrow, cramped, cold, with a dark sparkling light.

We went past the Beverly Hills Hotel and up Benedict Canyon, dropping Greg and his luggage at his faux-Tudor mansion. There didn't seem to be anybody around, and no cars were in the driveway, but I figured one rescue was enough. Clark or Joan or Bette would be along any minute.

AS WE CAME back down Sunset, I went back to the rewiring process that had started somewhere in Texas—a little like my mother's wartime electronics. Her dismembered radios, spread out on a card table, were a mass of tangled red and blue wires. I had to complete the switching over, disconnect the red, plug in the blue, turn to a different station. Marion disconnected, Nunnally and Dorris tuned in.

He put his arm around me. "I'm so happy you're here."

"I am too," I whispered, and leaned my head on his shoulder. We wrote back and forth once or twice a week, sometimes more. I told him everything about my life at great length and in great detail. Then when I was with him I was shy and tongue-tied. The best part of me went down my arms and hands, out through the Royal portable onto the paper.

"The kids can't wait. They've been asking about you every day."

The kids. It wasn't possible to forget them. How could I, when most of his letters were about them—how bright they were, how funny and lovable. So they were—it was just that sometimes I wished they didn't exist. And they had a way of always being the center of attention. Had he talked about me the same way?

"To them you're a kind of heroine," he said.

"I am?"

"Yes—and to me too." He squeezed me tightly against him. "I have a great and special love for you," he said.

Sometimes he made me almost cry. Maybe I loved him too much.

THE HOUSE AT 625 Mountain Drive was just north of Sunset, a red brick mansion with white trim and a circular driveway curving up to it. A flight of brick steps, flanked by white azaleas and gardenia bushes, led up to the front door. I followed his palm-tree shirt and two-tone shoes into the house.

The front hall was dramatic, with a sparkling chandelier and a curved staircase designed for a bride or a movie star. White leather doors opened into the living room, a clear green pool where I went while he searched for Dorris. There were chairs with green and gold-threaded upholstery, and a long lipstick-red sofa that curled under a bay window and then snaked out into the middle of the room. Above the bar was the movie screen and over the black marble fireplace was the fake-front bookcase that hid the projector— an arrangement considered a convenience by the natives but seen by easterners as evidence of cultural decay. On either side of the fireplace were the real books, including a shelf with the scripts of Nunnally's pictures bound in fine green and black leather. I'd read all thirty-six; of them, my favorites—*The Grapes of Wrath, The Country Doctor, The Pied Piper, Holy Matrimony, Prisoner of Shark Island, The Road to Glory*—several times. Every summer I spent many hours in this room, lying on the green shag rug, reading my father's dialogue.

I went out to the wide patio and sat in one of the lounge chairs. A few months before, Nunnally and Dorris had thrown a party here that made *Life* magazine. A publicity vehicle for his upcoming picture, *Mr. Peabody and the Mermaid*, it featured a tent that covered most of the backyard, topless starlets with fishtails carefully posed in places where they could be ogled but not groped; ice sculptures of mermaids with bowls of caviar in their laps; a lavish buffet and a guest list of 250 or so that included Kirk Douglas, the Coopers, the Bogarts, the Mercers, Van Johnson, Louis B. Mayer, Lady Elsie Mendl, Deborah Kerr, Edward G. Robinson, Keenan Wynn, Merle Oberon, Ann Todd, Otto Preminger, George Montgomery. The party had lasted till 5 A.M. and went into the annals of Hollywood excess. Pop had sent pictures to me at boarding school, which I hadn't dared to show anyone because of all the bare breasts.

Everything looked the same as last summer except the bright turquoise rectangle of the pool was mostly hidden behind a picket fence. The grass was like emerald wall-to-wall carpeting, and during the war a few chickens ran around clucking in a frustrated search for seeds in the sterilized lawn. The land rose up behind the house and if you walked far enough up the street the clipped lawns stopped. There were brown rocks and dust and scrub and rattlesnakes as you climbed higher and higher, and during the night the coyotes yowled. Now there are tile terraces and driveways and swimming pools, houses with decks that hang high over the canyons. The cliffs are filled, like cracked teeth, with concrete to keep them in place when the rains come. The whole arrangement is fragile, and there are continuous crises as nature threatens to reclaim the earth and turn it back to desert.

NUNNALLY AND DORRIS appeared, holding hands. They were the only couple in my life, the only marriage close enough to watch. They didn't seem to go together. My father was once described (by writer Shana Alexander) as looking like "a small Disney forest animal"—a startled chipmunk with bright blue eyes and thinning hair. But I hardly knew what he looked like. To me he was a force, a searchlight, a backdrop, a set of conflicting principles, an obstacle course, an unattainable life goal . . . a push-me pull-you, images on a screen too close to see.

Dorris was small, with reddish-gold curly hair and big round green eyes. She wore a coral-colored smock and sandals, with golden bangles on her wrists. She looked very young, she *was* very young—closer to my age than to Nunnally's. She gave me a hug, which I only appreciated in retrospect—my mother's embraces consisted of a couple of fingers on each shoulder and a cheek-on-cheek with kissy sounds.

Dorris was a southern girl. There were two in my class and at dances they were always surrounded by boys. I'd spent half an entire evening (when nobody was dancing with me) watching them, and all I could make out was that they talked a lot and sort of crawled up their dates' neckties with their fingers. I tried it with the boy I came with, and he said, "What the hell are you doing? You're ruining my goddamn tie." I explained and he said, "Forget it, *you'll* never be able to do it."

If eighteen years' difference seems too much, if Dorris might be expected to tire of her older husband, wrong on both counts. She and Nunnally were crazy about each other, and they invited the world to appreciate their good fortune. My admiration was tenuous. You're supposed to be happy for the people you love, but it doesn't really work with parents. Occasionally my father told me (in case I didn't know) how much he loved his wife. That was fine for him—it was just that I couldn't join the party. He was branded for good: You are my father. You left my mother. You left me. We have to go on from there. I love you to death, I'll try to love Dorris . . . but don't expect me to dance at your wedding.

THE UMBRELLA TABLE was set for lunch. We sat down and the butler brought out the food and goblets of iced tea.

They asked me about the trip. I stumbled through it all, Chicago and Gallup and the Rio Grande and the two engines and the cherry pie and Gregory—making him somewhat more amorous than he had been and hinting that we would probably see each other over the summer. Somehow the truth never seemed good enough, and the real things, the things I saved up for months to tell him, never seemed worth bringing up when I was with him. His world was so far beyond mine. I knew that he wasn't really so perfect, that he had made mistakes and done foolish things, that once he had only one suit. But I hadn't known him then, and to me he had sprung full-grown from behind his desk at Twentieth Century-Fox or the backseat of the Cadillac.

Dorris was talking about the sprinkler system and what the gardener had said about the grading of the lawn. It was pretty boring but she did much better than my mother, who was reduced to frozen smiles and tense silences during rough patches. Nunnally always ended up doing the talking. He was certainly the most interesting—but when he wasn't the center of attention, he brooded.

I looked at the Italian pottery and bright linen on the glass table. What would my mother have done with this lunch? The shrimp would have been tossed naked into a bowl with chunks of lemon, she wouldn't have bothered to slice the tomatoes, the eggs would arrive in their shells . . . there might even be a Hellmann's jar. She thought watercress was ridiculous and she didn't believe in rolls, but even if she did, she never would have driven all the way to the Farmers Market for freshly baked ones, the way Dorris did. It would have been appealing, but more *paisano,* more carefree—or careless, depending on how you looked at it. Less work for the cook, more for the diner.

I was always comparing the two houses and the two women—the first wife and the second, the northern girl and the southern one, the East and West Coast loves. If there had been a contest—which indeed there had—Dorris had won. And my mom was no slouch—she had men by the bucketful. But Dorris held the winning card.

My mother had an Irish slapdash quality, a good-natured assumption that if she missed something, her good looks or good luck or others' lack of attention or something would make up for it. Dorris left nothing to chance. She was a detail girl, goal-oriented, exact in her choices. She learned from her mistakes. My mother shrugged off wrong choices and moved on with breakneck optimism. Mistakes were the work of leprechauns and we simply lived with them.

They were both pretty and vain, generous and honorable . . . and *both* knew how to crawl up a guy's necktie, my mother having learned in Flushing, where she grew up, and in the city room of the *Brooklyn Daily Eagle*, where she met Nunnally. Both had rather careful, cultivated voices. Dorris, who had been an actress, was as meticulous about her appearance as she was about everything else. In the morning it took her an hour to dress, while my mother did the job in ten minutes, sometimes going out with a curl hanging over one ear or a blob of powder on her nose.

Both were frightened of Hollywood. There had been little in my mother's background to prepare her for it, and she was intimidated, crawling into an icy shell and feeling very sorry for herself. But though Dorris was equally unprepared, she rolled up her sleeves and set about making it work for her.

My mother was the messiest person I have ever known, strewing clothes everywhere, leaving kitchens piled with dinner dishes, sticky pots, and overflowing trash cans. Dorris, my father once said, "could live out of a shoebox." They had opposite metabolisms. My mother was a sportswoman, all bounce and energy, and Dorris moved slowly and sat long. She overestimated herself, was too thorough, started overwhelming projects that she could barely finish—but finish she did. My mother didn't start anything that appeared very difficult and whatever it was had to be done by cocktail hour.

They were both adaptable settlers, skilled in the domestic arts, able to turn a cave into a home in no time flat. Both were great cooks, both gave up their careers at Nunnally's behest, and both were zodiac archetypes—Dorris a persistent Capricorn, Marion a Sagittarius clown.

THE DOOR FROM the house swung open and my two small half sisters appeared on the patio. Behind them came Nursie, intoning "Now stop that, I told you, come down offa there, now you'll get yourself all dirty, don't play rough like that," and so forth. The little girls clung to their parents, staring at me.

"Who's that?" the smaller one asked her mother.

"That's Sissy," Dorris said. "She's visiting here from New York."

They watched me suspiciously, having seemingly forgotten that I was a heroine. I wasn't very good with them. Shy, silent kids I could coax into my lap and read to, but there weren't many of those around—more and more, like these, were nascent comedians.

"But there's already a Sissy," the older one said. Did I mention that there had been a first marriage, that I had an older half sister?

"There are two Sissies," Nunnally said. It was getting awkward. His oldest daughter, Margie, was only a couple of years younger than Dorris. She had helped Dorris get Nunnally so he wouldn't keep going back to Marion, and many tears were shed. That was all in the past, but bits of it kept sticking out from under the rug.

There was a new English croquet set on the lawn, much bigger and heavier than the one I had at home. Now the two little girls were playing with it, a freaky version of the game that involved standing on their heads, rolling balls between each other's legs, turning somersaults, and doing an occasional vaudeville routine. The older one was in charge of things, making faces, suddenly changing the rules, and so forth, while the smaller one ran in desperate circles trying to figure out, usually without success, what she was supposed to do next.

It made me think of *Alice in Wonderland*—flamingo mallets, rolled-up hedgehog balls, and bent-over Soldiers of the Queen wickets, all constantly getting up and wandering off. Fish footmen bearing invitations, white rabbits losing their gloves. It was strange every time, every time it took days, weeks to get used to it. You'd think, after all this time, I'd be a whiz at reentry. But no matter how often I did it, I was clumsy at moving into other people's houses and lives, and poor at mastering their rules. Kings and queens tossed out unfathomable explanations, and ghostly cats grinned in trees.

LUCK

THE DAY I ARRIVED I always called my friends. I didn't have too many in Beverly Hills—just Julie and the Sweethearts next door and one or two others. I called Julie and she appeared within an hour.

I wanted to hug Julie—I did hug Julie, but it was like hugging a clattering skeleton. Her back was a washboard and I could encircle her poor little arm with my hand. I knew enough not to ask her a lot of questions about her weight and all the rest of it. We went into the kitchen and had some chocolate cake, and after she ate hers, Julie went into the bathroom and I knew she was puking. She came back and told me not to worry about it, let's go for a swim.

It was hard to look at her in a bathing suit, and worse when my little half sisters came out with Nursie for their swim. When they went into some awful send-up routine I swam over to where they bobbed in their life vests and told them if they laughed again at her, or made fun of her or anybody else, ever, because of their appearance, I'd hold their heads underwater for ten minutes. I told them they lived in a land of artifice and phoniness and it was disgusting to make fun of people for things they couldn't help—and they weren't all that perfect themselves. They had no idea what I was talking about, but it worked for a while.

The marvel of this speech was that neither I nor Julie had ever, or only rarely, applied its principle to our own lives. We were slaves of artifice. We'd been packaged since childhood, bathed and brought forth by nannies each night in belted robe, bunny slippers, and hair brushed into rigid neatness for Daddy's arrival home. In pictures we are always too dressed up—tailored jackets with matching berets for pony rides in Griffith Park, ruffled pinafores for the La Brea Tar Pits, white sailor dresses and skimmers for lunch at the studio, party dresses with lace for an excursion to Catalina Island, though a band and chorus singing "Welcome to Catalina" did lend the occasion a weird festivity. Nannies whitened our shoes and laid out our Dr. Dentons and ironed our hair ribbons, washed and blocked our sweaters, and sewed up rips—as Nursie did for my sisters—and we, like they, were always being cautioned to keep neat and clean, to be "little ladies."

As we grew older, Julie and I spent most of our time and all of our allowances on pink nail polish, Neet, curlers, tweezers, Bonne Bell lipstick, devices to curl eyelashes and remove zits and make our eyes seem bigger and our ears lie flat. We roamed Saks and I. Magnin, mooning at clothes worn by the stars, and a shopping trip with Dorris or Julie's mother reduced us to jelly joy.

Sometimes we crept into Dorris's dressing room to look into her closets at the clothes hanging on puffy satin hangers. Rows of suits, slacks, and blouses perfectly lined up, an entire closet of new-looking shoes, pumps and sandals and wedgies, sometimes one kind in several different colors, with matching handbags. A whole section of casual clothes, cotton dresses and smocks and peasant skirts and shorts, shelves of sweaters and scarves and bathing suits. There were "afternoon" clothes, silk dresses with jackets and dark-colored "costumes." Best of all were the evening dresses, all satin and glitter and flowing bows and encrustations of pearls and sequins.

We pretended our own more humble closets were much the same, dressing for the smallest occasion, and since there were few, we remained, most of the time, two sloppy little girls in shorts. We thought we were fat—we weren't—and started dieting. I lasted about two days, but Julie never stopped.

"RITA HAYWORTH came for dinner last week," she said now, as we lay on lounge chairs. "She's in Big Ben's new picture." There's a certain kind of kid that can't bear to say Mom and Dad.

"Oh my God," I said. "What did she have on?"

"Well, it was peach chiffon, low in the front and kind of swirling around her bazooms. And a gold-and-pearl necklace you wouldn't believe. And she was very nice."

"Who did she come with?"

"David Selznick."

"Oh my God."

"What's oh God? I've met him a million times. Big Ben's his fair-haired boy. I get so sick of producers. They're the only people we know."

"Well, she had to come with somebody," I said. "She couldn't come alone. What kind of shoes did she have on?"

"Gold high-heeled sandals with about a million little straps and dark purple toenail polish."

"God—you're so lucky."

"Lucky!" she yelled. "Ginger *Rogers* came to your house! Lauren Bacall! Big Ben and Lola have practically never had anybody interesting over before"— except producers.

"She's called Betty."

"I'm *not* lucky. You're the lucky one. You get to live in New York. You have Nunnally. You have Dorris. You don't have a crummy pesty little brother." She rolled into the pool. This was the trouble with Julie, and I never knew what to do about it. She swam around and then surfaced.

"At least Lola and Big Ben are married."

"They might as well not be," Julie said. "I wish they'd get divorced and marry other people who were nice."

"God—you don't know *anything*."

IT WAS TRUE Lola and Big Ben were no picnic. At their house you never knew what was going to happen next. Dinner was a relay race of migrating family members—first Lola was sitting with us, then she wasn't, and then Big Ben came swaying in with his drink and sat down for a minute, then Julie had to run to the bathroom, and her brother Benny would suddenly slither down under the table and make Frankenstein noises. But if this was how real families were, it was okay with me.

Once I'd been there when Big Ben was talking about how he couldn't stand certain people, like half of RKO—and how so-and-so was an ignorant slob and so-and-so was a no-talent liar. Julie was pushing her food around her plate and then Lola came in and took some salad, and started telling a long story about how ridiculous it was to grow up in Oak Park, Illinois, and how she brought all the wrong things to Hollywood, silk blanket covers and antimacassars for the backs of the chairs and little props for the dinner knives so the tablecloth wouldn't get soiled. Now she knew you didn't need anything except a bathing suit and a Cadillac. I thought it was funny but nobody else was even listening, and Benny was pulling his mouth out at the sides and flapping his tongue and crossing his eyes.

Big Ben sat down and finished off a few more so-called friends, occasionally reaching over and taking one of Julie's French fries, and once he even took a piece of her steak she'd cut off.

"What do you need in New York?" I asked Lola.

"A complete black outfit and a lot of money."

Nobody was listening to Big Ben either, so I thought I'd better. He pulled his chair closer to mine, taking a few more fries on the way. He told me how perfect Nunnally and Dorris were, and then how won-

derful I was, and a lot of stuff about how proud Nunnally was of me
and how cute I was and charming and smart, while everybody looked
uninterested except Benny, who gave one of his ghastly giggles. Big
Ben's arm was over the back of my chair and he was squeezing my
shoulder. There was something creepy about the compliments, and I
didn't like the feeling and pulling . . . and when I looked at Julie, she
sprang to her feet.

"Sit down," said Big Ben.

"No." Tears sprang to Julie's eyes.

"Oh, for God's sake. Not this again." .

Julie ran out of the room and we heard her running upstairs and in
a minute there were the sounds of plumbing, then the bedroom door
slammed shut. Lola just sat there and stared at her lap. I thought she
should have gone after her, but she never did, which was why Julie
hated her. My mother wouldn't have either, but it was hard to hate
her, she was so kind of cute and funny, or she thought she was. Lola
was funny but she wasn't cute.

When the maid came in to clear the table everything stood still—
we were a group of statues with the maid picking up plates, and one
empty chair yanked away from the table. Big Ben cleared his throat
and said he was going out, which seemed all right with Lola. Then
Benny went outside to play ball, and Lola said, "Oh, God," in her
deep hoarse voice, and I wanted to laugh again. I sat there with her
and she told me some more about Oak Park, then I heard sounds
from upstairs and I told Lola good night, and went up too.

Julie was lying on her bed facing the wall.

"I'm sorry," I said. There was no reply. "It isn't my fault."

"Of course not," Julie said.

THE CICADAS CHORUSED and leaves from the eucalyptus drifted
slowly down on the surface of the water. Now the chickens were all
gone but the henhouse was still up under the trees. At first I hadn't
understood about the chickens; being a city child I thought they were

some odd kind of pet. Eventually Dorris, who had grown up on a farm somewhere in the South, explained the purpose of chickens in a period of rationing.

Days were longer here, afternoons stretched out into endless dusks and evenings were eternal. The continuous struggle against the elements and other fierce—if less tangible—forces that was the very bone and sinew of New York life didn't exist here. Now when I had all the time in the world, no dishes to dry, homework to do, icy streets to not slip on, buses to run for or subways to negotiate, here where evenings were soft and breezy and light for hours, I was crawling with a nervous energy I dared not let out, as though I were in a very delicate glass cage.

"Lola said your mother hated Hollywood," Julie said.

"How does she know?"

"Because she hates it too."

"Why?" I asked.

"They think New York is more fun," Julie said.

I had only fleeting memories of my mother back then, a dim, sad background figure in a series of elegant houses run by bustling, gossiping servants. I had lived or stayed in eleven houses in Beverly Hills, the first seven in the flats, the rest north of Sunset. The Beverly Drive house, with its antebellum columns and sea of burgundy carpeting, was the last place my parents had lived together. It was here I had first sensed trouble, like a funny smell or a change in the light. Camden Drive was where they spent the summer "trying again," where I first met Dorris . . . so the trying must have been over. Beverly Glen Boulevard was the first home with Dorris.

Rodeo was a dark, shaded pool, full of dead leaves, and a moody father scowling at his afternoon paper, no mother, a fretting Nanny . . . and a pain-in-the-ass kid who kept asking questions. Roxbury was where my friend Jimmy Harris and I threw dribbling ice-cream wrappers into the open convertible of our neighbor Louella Parsons, the gossip columnist, leaving pastel trails snaking down the glossy leather seat. When the enraged queen of the town stood on the sidewalk shouting threats of revenge, public exposure, and ruined reputations, Jimmy disappeared and I was hustled over by my father to apologize to Miss Parsons—who was very grand and forgiving.

We left the Camden house in the big black Cadillac, crossing mountains, deserts, plains . . . my mother and Harold, the Swedish chauffeur in full livery, spelling each other every fifty miles, Nanny muttering "She's crazy to leave him, what kinda life she gonna have?" It was hot, it was hell, the seats were itchy, sweat ran down our faces and backs . . . but it wasn't boring, not crossing the desert and the Rockies, or driving half the night because no hotels were open and being scared we'd be eaten by mountain lions or killed by rattlesnakes or Indians, and everything else I feared and that went wrong.

I spent ten days looking at her back in a sweaty white blouse, tendrils of dark hair trailing down her neck and getting tangled with the catch on her pearls. Why were we doing this? What did she want? How could she hate dressing in beautiful clothes and meeting stars and famous people and going to Ciro's and the Trocadero? Or being married to Nunnally? What was the matter with her?

"THEY THINK Hollywood is boring," Julie said.

"Well, it is."

"It was more fun when we were little," Julie said, "when we went to parties and did more stuff."

The birthday parties. I remembered coming downstairs to a living room full of dressed-up kids and grown-ups, wearing a starched organdy dress with a sash, black patent leather shoes and white socks, and a bow insecurely fastened to my short straight hair. I remember what it was like to look down at a small flat chest, to fasten Mary Janes with a buttonhook, to stand still while somebody tied the sash. The boys' hair was wet and slicked down, and they wore starched shirts, neckties, Eton jackets, and short pants with kneesocks.

There was Pin the Tail on the Donkey, Tag, Giant Steps, Statues, something with water, something with crayons, all supervised by wild-eyed nannies and mothers in hats. There was chicken à la king in patty shells, peas, birthday cake and molded ice cream, party hats and snappers and little paper baskets of candies. There was a mountain of presents. The organdy skirts wilted, sashes came untied, shirts came untucked . . . ice cream dribbled down fronts, blobs of icing fell on patent leather shoes . . . chocolate dribbled everywhere. Pop asked, "Why is it that everything children eat comes out chocolate on their faces?"

The part I remembered best was playing show-me in the bathroom with a couple of the boys—if only I could remember who—till some scandalized adult found us and broke it up. The parties were mostly the same—the waiting Cadillacs, the white-uniformed nannies, the parents' anxious smiles. Sometimes there was a magician or a puppet show or a Disney movie, sometimes there were pool parties, the air full of panicky cries from anxious grown-ups. ("Don't push him . . . give her back that ball . . . if you do that again you're getting right out.")

But the most glamorous ones, the ones I told about in New York, were Shirley Temple's birthday parties at the studio. I still had two of the pictures they sent afterward. In one, Julie's and my chairs sit empty in the front. So desperate were we to wear the right dress and correct hair ribbon that tears and arguments with the attending adults made us too late for the photograph—so we wept some more.

In another photo our tiny heads barely show above one of the tables in a soundstage full of kids. Shirley, a few years older, stands at the top smiling, her mother next to her. We had chicken à la king in patty shells, cake and molded ice cream, there were paper hats, snappers, and a magician with a monkey. Afterward we lined up to greet our hostess and to receive a leather autograph book with her signature in neat round script on the first page. Her mother stood by in a cloche hat, reading the name of each child from a list. Shirley shook each hand and curtseyed. "Thank you, Julie, for coming to my party," she said, handing out an autograph book from the stack. "Thank you, Nora, for being so kind . . ." There were about 150 kids but her manners never flagged, her smile remained bright. "Hello, Susie . . . Danny . . . Ellen . . . it was very nice of you to come."

"Do you remember how much fun swimming used to be?" I slipped into the shallow end.

"We still swim."

"But it was different. Remember how we couldn't wait to get in the water?"

The water was life. The pools . . . the turquoise sparkling ovals and rectangles, cold and clear and purgative. I couldn't get enough, staying in till I was clean through to my bones, my skin puckered and my eyes stinging, gasping and breathless from the diving. It was a religious experience, a daily obsession. And the beach . . . we weren't allowed to get into the ocean because the breakers were too big, so we played along the edge, but it was so exciting and it smelled so salty and good, and it was like being under a wonderful spell, chasing foamy waves for hours until some adult came and grabbed us back and told us it was too dangerous, or too cold, or we were blue or our teeth were chattering, and wrapped us in towels and laid us in the sun to bake like loaves of bread. But now the fun was gone. Last time we'd gone to the Bel-Air Bay Club, all we did was hang around the hamburger place and eat potato chips and drink Cokes and talk about how lonely Lola looked sitting alone on her towel, staring into space.

"We even thought the Tar Pits were a big deal," I said, "and we got a big thrill out of going downtown."

The Tar Pits' bubbling ooze yielded fossils of ancient animals and other evidence of prehistoric life, and if you threw in a stone it would sink straight to the center of the earth. Now only desperate boredom would drive me there. And the long, hot ride to Olvera Street, with its racks of red serapes and staring black-haired dolls and flower-painted banjos and the man in the sombrero wailing and strumming his guitar, and the enchiladas and Union Station where the Chief ended up.

There wasn't much else except an old mission, or much else to do in L.A., but when we were small it was enough.

The Farmers Market, with its white wooden booths and leafy pergolas, was where once I had stood hypnotized by the silver peanut-butter machine that ground the nuts to powder and oil and whose long steel arms kneaded and stretched the silky brown stuff like taffy . . . and the fruits, there was nothing like them back east, enormous oranges and grapefruits and four or five kinds of fragrant melons and peaches and fat grapes, and lettuces with the soil still clinging to them and stiff parsley and peas and beans and bright tomatoes and cucumbers you could smell across the aisle . . . and loaves of fresh bread and cookies and big cheeses they sliced for you, and chickens clucking in cages and eggs stuck with bits of straw, and butter in big chunks.

"There aren't even any good earthquakes anymore." Julie sighed.

Dogs barking, pictures swinging, glasses sliding to the edges of tables, the tremble going right through you and not knowing when it was going to stop . . . and lying in my quivering bed wondering if I was going to die and what it would be like and if *my parents* would weep over me. I loved hearing about the one when I was two months old, and how *they* had taken me out on the patio, which in their untutored state they considered safe.

"Another thing is, now we do everything wrong," Julie said, "like when you messed up with Roddy McDowall."

She had never forgiven me for what she saw as the gross mishandling of a God-given opportunity. Roddy, the winsome kid star of the day, had been in a wartime picture of Nunnally's, *The Pied Piper,* before going on to greater fame in *My Friend Flicka* and *Lassie Come Home.* I was a timid eleven or so when a riding date in Westwood was arranged with him and his sister. We rode on narrow trails along the edges of steep canyons where an occasional snake or lizard slithered, far above a cluster of pink buildings that was the UCLA campus. Afterward, Roddy's mother picked us up and we went by the studio to get Roddy's fan mail, bags and bags of it. We took it to their house and the family went through it. There were not only letters and cards, but poems, paintings, carvings, a Yankee clipper ship made of toothpicks, and more.

"Are you going to see him again?" Julie demanded afterward.

"You've missed the whole point," I said. "It wasn't really a date. It was . . . I don't know, a mail-opening."

"What shirt were you wearing?"

"The plaid one."

She looked at me in disgust. "That rag? Do you know what you're like? It's like if Lana Turner was in Schwab's and the scout comes in and she's wearing an old torn holey shirt and no makeup. You're *stupid.*"

"No I'm not. He doesn't know I'm alive."

"Of course he doesn't if you don't even try. You know what's wrong with you? You have everything and you just mess it all up. It makes me sick."

It did make her sick—she went tearing off to the bathroom, and then she got on her bike and went home. Later her words haunted me, and I phoned her and said I was sorry, though I didn't know what for.

THE LUCITE WALL

IN CALIFORNIA, the quality of the summer had much to do with the quality of the help, with whom I spent a good part of my time. That year it was the Swedish family, Lars, Ingrid, and Katie; Nancy, the cleaning woman; the intrepid Nursie; Hideo, the Japanese gardener; and a few specialists who came to do laundry, floors, or pruning. Nursie had been there longest, following the immaculate children around saying, "Now come down from there, come offa there, don't do that, you'll hurt yourself, you'll get wet, what will your daddy say, I'll tell your mama," in an uninterested voice, sitting up till two and three in the morning squinting as she embroidered minuscule ducks and daisies on tiny dresses and playsuits. (Years later she made dresses for my two small daughters, delicately wrought works of art that I in my peregrinations must not have deserved, for they went down, along with my entire trousseau, in a blazing cargo boat in the Red Sea.)

Hideo was fun till he showed me how to twist the necks of doomed chickens, laughing as they ran headless around the driveway before their terminal convulsions. I didn't know, and didn't want to know, whether the roast chickens we had for dinner were the decapitated creatures I'd seen running headlong, spattering blood, into the garde-

45

nia bushes . . . but they must have been, because we ate the eggs, and the whole operation was a faux poultry farm originally designed to flesh out the wartime household diet.

I know Lars, had he been there, would have protected me from such exhibitions. If William Morris reps handled practical matters, chauffeurs had a finer, subtler talent that equipped them to fill emotional interstices. They were always willing to talk, and I spent a lot of time hanging around garages. Gunter, of a few years before, had been found to be a Nazi, and he and his wife had been duly fired. I'd been too young to understand why being a Nazi was any worse than being, say, a Republican.

The best one was Harold, who drove the black Cadillac across the country . . . his straight back, his unswerving dignity and strength in the company of two unstrung women and one bewildered child, his handsome Swedish profile in his black peaked cap framed against distant mountains in some parched desert, while I was taken down into an arroyo to pee and ask for the fiftieth time, "Why do we have to go to New York?"

LARS TOOK CARE of my father's clothes, brushing his suits, polishing his shoes, and hanging the next day's outfit on the mahogany suit rack, turning down his bed and putting out clean pajamas. On the night table he put a little tray with a silver thermos of ice water and a glass. I followed him around, breathing in Nunnally's Knize Ten cologne. My father was the cleanest person I have ever known, and I liked Lars for respecting and maintaining this condition. He even mimicked Nunnally's habit of leaning down and picking microscopic bits of fuzz from the carpet.

Lars brought the daily papers—there were several—in from the driveway and put them wherever my father was likely to be. In the butler's pantry, a halfway station between kitchen and dining room, he filled cigarette boxes and nut bowls, made sure table lighters were working, made drinks, and organized, without actually arranging, flowers. It was from such small divisions of labor that I formed beliefs about what men and women ought to do. Ingrid did the cooking but Lars made butter balls, rolling lumps of butter between wooden paddles and dropping the little balls into a bowl of ice water. Their daughter Katie was maid, general helper, and "light laundress." Lars was proud of his pretty, accomplished daughter, who would be going back to university after the war was over, though she tended to be something of a "cut-up."

One day he showed me his Lucite—a new invention to which he had the rights, or the franchise, or the intention to do something with. Lucite was like glass but couldn't be broken or scratched; it could be twisted and bent and molded. It was best in pure sparkling transparent sheets. He showed me a few early, rather crude Lucite articles, art deco lamps and little boxes, that I thought very handsome. Someday they would be in the windows of Bloomingdale's and Bullocks Wilshire, and Lars would be rich—at which fantasy he only smiled and gave a little shrug.

But in a way, he already knew how to use the wonderful stuff. There seemed to be a Lucite divider in the car when he was driving, as though it were a real limousine, and Lucite seemed to surround him when he was serving dinner and when he talked to my father. Lucite divided the servants from their employers. But when I helped him set up the croquet wickets, and when he let me sit in the driver's seat and run the motor, just to see how it felt, it wasn't there.

LARS SAID, and everybody else hinted, that Katie and I ought to be friends. I was—still am—at an age to balk at assigned companions, but it was impossible not to like her. She had a winning if undiscriminating delight in everything, and was perfectly friendly to me even though I was five or six years younger than she was—which an American girl would never have been. And she was as pleased, or more pleased, by a picnic in the hills as she was by Hollywood, whose significance escaped her. She was a relief from the dour Nursie and the busy, preoccupied parents and me, the restless stepdaughter, who should, but didn't, have a similarly pleasing and sunny disposition.

She was like an eager puppy, but she was intelligent, she knew we were on different rungs. She hung back, only dispensing little smiles and "Hi-yi's" as she got on with her ironing or her muffin making. But soon we were having little chats when she brought up my laundry, hanging beautifully ironed shirts in the closet. We talked about clothes, school, boys, what to do with our hair. She had a "close friend" at home, they wrote twice a week. She showed me a picture of a sad-looking young man in a black turtleneck.

"He is crazy about my skin," she said. It looked pure and silky and healthy, and free of zits. "Oh, I am lucky, all I do is wash with soap, my mother would kill me if she found me putting anything on it."

Not *my* mother. Both she and Dorris (the two had an uncanny number of things in common) had their "vanities," littered with little pots and bottles, combs and pins and eyelash curlers and tweezers. The Swedes scorned artifice. Beauty was health. Every evening they walked up the mountain and on their days off they went to the beach where they could "really get in the sea and exercise for a couple of hours," as Katie said. The pool only amused her.

"Phooey—I can't even get up to speed." She had been hurtling up and down its length. "Come on, I teach you how to swim."

She grabbed my hand. Katie was a toucher. We walked with arms around each other as everyone did at home or at school or wherever, and held hands. American girls never did that, it was considered "queer." One day I had come upon Katie trying to hug the horrified Nursie, who never touched anyone, the children included, if she could help it. Ingrid only laughed. "Oh, she is very affected, I know." I was pretty sure she meant affectionate.

"I know how to swim." I thought I was pretty good.

"Oh, you are just beginner. Come here, we start in the baby end." She held my arms and legs the right way. "In Sweden by law everyone must learn to swim by age five." She laughed when I believed her.

She set about teaching me to swim properly. Then she tried to institute skinny-dipping at night, which my father banned, until Katie politely asked if the ladies of the house could go on evenings the gentlemen were out or promised not to look, and so Katie, Dorris, Ingrid, and I ended up in the turquoise pool, our white bodies deformed and subdividing in the milky green light. I hadn't dreamed Dorris would join this dreamy saturnalia, and a layer of my complicated resentment of her peeled away that night and floated off with the dead leaves.

"You are beautiful," Katie said one night, as I got out of the pool when the two of us were swimming alone. I grabbed my towel and wrapped up in it fast. "Do you have a boyfriend?"

"Well—not exactly." Besides the Chief business, there had been some awkward little scuffles and a couple of pretty intense necking parties during Christmas vacation, but nothing that seemed to qualify.

"Well, you will, little *flicka.*" I'd thought it meant horse, but it meant little girl. She ran her fingers over my shoulder and down my back.

"Oh, everybody's beautiful here," I said. "Beauty's a big nothing." Considering the amount of time I spent curling my hair and inspecting myself in the mirror, this statement was a big nothing.

She stared, then laughed, and suddenly gave me a hug. "You are completely wrong, it is always something. Relax, what's the matter with you? I have given you fifty hugs, now you act like I don't know what."

SOMETIMES Pop and I played croquet together. It was just about his speed. He was in his late forties, but he slumped and walked slowly, like a much older man. When I asked him about the tennis cups he and my mother had won, and mentioned a reputed fondness for swimming, he sighed as though it had all been in another life.

Around that time, croquet games between the stars and moguls were a kind of institution. Everybody had one of the English sets, with polo-sized mallets and enormous wickets, and the players took turns hosting the matches. So I found myself, one Saturday, eating chicken salad on the patio with three shirtless, suntanned celebrities. Darryl Zanuck, my father's boss, was, to me, just another producer—but the two actors were something else. While the massive Cesar Romero was impressive enough, I was so charmed by Tyrone Power in shorts that I could hardly eat. I had seen him often in movies but offscreen he was even more magnificent, he threw off sparks. I learned that day that the camera, with all its power, can only go so far—stars were stars because they were human searchlights or human magnets, creatures with a magic quality. When they were around, you couldn't look at anything else.

After watching this game of champions for a while I went inside and upstairs to my bedroom. It was cool and clean and white; at night it smelled of jasmine from the garden. From the window I looked down at the sea of rippling male flesh that everybody else took so calmly. I lived surrounded by women—my mother and her friends, a girls' school—and so far the few boys I knew had kept their clothes on. As for my father, once a summer he did a single swipe the length of the pool before getting out, covering up again, and returning to his typewriter. As I stood by the window watching the glossy bodies below, the bedroom door opened and Katie came in with her little handful of laundry. She came and stood next to me. She didn't see many American movies and I tried to explain the importance of the spectacle below.

"That's Tyrone Power. He's a huge star . . . he was in two of my father's movies, *Rose of Washington Square* a long time ago and *Jesse James.* Did you ever see it?"

"Oh, yes. There was much shooting and cowboy stuff, right?"

"Well . . . some. The worst part is when Jesse's up on a ladder straightening a picture on the wall and . . ."

Her arm was draped around my shoulder. "Criminy—why is a cowboy straightening up a picture?"

"The bad guy told him to. Then he says . . ."

She was looking at me, and she suddenly leaned over and kissed me on the cheek. "Little *flicka.* And then what?"

"He . . . shoots Jesse in the back. It's horrible."

"What for?"

"Because he's out for him. It's all . . . you know, part of the story."

Now her hand was slowly stroking my neck and shoulder, then it moved around and traced my collarbone. I kept my eyes riveted on Ty, getting ready to strike. He was hunched over, mallet in both hands. His shorts were very tight and the muscles in his back gleamed in the sun. Katie moved very close to me and her hand moved farther down under my shirt and toward whatever little bit of lacy stuff I importantly called my bra. I was horrified by her nerve but I didn't dare ask her to stop—nor did I want her to. I stood ramrod-straight and squeezed my eyes closed. "Ah, so nice . . . do you feel what is happening to you?" By then she had the other arm around me. She wasn't much taller than me, but she was a strong Nordic girl and I began to wonder if I could get away from her even if I wanted to. I knew it was essential to keep quiet. Her square, pretty face was on top of mine and then she kissed me very gently, once, twice, and my mind was going in circles and I wondered what was going to happen next . . . until there was a sharp rap at the door and a brisk Swedish command.

At Lars's voice Katie froze and spun around. A few more words I didn't need translated sent her running out of the room stiff-lipped, the laundry spilled on the floor. I heard her thumping down the back stairs. Pulling my shirt down I looked at Lars in bewilderment. Probably he knew better than I what had happened. It was the ultimate chauffeur's challenge. I expected some garage wisdom but he did it even better.

He said, gravely, "Excuse me, but I felt it was my duty to intrude. My daughter is sometimes exuberantly affected." Then he backed out and closed the door.

From outside there was a volley of cheers and some yells from the losers. Ty and my father had won. He looked up and my heart stopped as I realized that Katie and I had been standing in front of the open window. I backed away and watched cautiously as Ingrid cleared up glasses and dishes. Then Dorris walked slowly out on the patio, and she and my father stood with their arms around each other.

NOW THERE WAS a Lucite wall dividing me and the Swedish family, who knew, from Nunnally and Dorris and the rest of the world, who didn't. Dinner wasn't very good, though nobody noticed in the postmatch excitement. Ingrid looked glum and Katie was nowhere to be seen. Lars glanced at me a couple of times, trying to read my mind, which was spinning in confusion. All I knew was that I would die with the secret, because I was fourteen and didn't know anything and hardly knew what had happened but assumed somehow it was my fault.

Worse, this wasn't the first time I'd been touched by forbidden fire. At school I had been in love with a girl two classes ahead. I don't remember much about her now except that she was rather hefty and very good at high-jumping, sailing over the four-foot bar like an agile partridge. She knew nothing of my feelings, which lasted all of two weeks, and never would have, except my so-called friends told and everybody thought it was very funny. The current wisdom was that "crushes" were developmental—children went through a stage of dark perversion on the way to a more wholesome world—but I didn't know my father's take on the subject.

And this was different. There had been the possibility of *something happening*—something *had* happened, and the devil knew it. And when something happens, something else usually happens, and then something else, until things are brought to a head one way or another. But this time nothing did. I said nothing . . . nor did anyone. The rest of the world just kept on as usual on the other side of the Lucite. Lars and Ingrid kept glancing at me, Katie avoided me, while I pretended nothing had happened . . . until it was announced that Katie would be going to Minnesota to stay with a cousin.

After she left, the food got even worse and then it came out that Ingrid had never been separated from her daughter before, and was deeply unhappy, and then they all left.

Nunnally tried to find out if I knew anything about it, because Katie and I had been such good friends. I told him I was as surprised as he was but that it had something to do with Ty Power's chest . . . and his legs. When he laughed, as I had known he would, I almost told him what happened but I couldn't guess what he'd say—and I remembered remarks about fairies and queens—and worst of all, he might end up writing about it. So I just said there was something funny about Katie, she wasn't like most girls I knew—and not just because she was Swedish. I must have sounded convincing, because he never asked about it again.

PEARL WHAT?

WHEN I WAS VERY YOUNG, the el train wobbled and clanked along Third, stopping at the little cabin-in-the-sky stations. The trolley clattered along tracks sunk into the cobblestones. There were still a few horse-and-wagon tradesmen—one who sharpened knives, one who sold fruit and vegetables. There was the accordionist with the basso voice that rolled up the street all the way to Second Avenue, and everybody hung out their windows to listen to "Santa Lucia" and "O Solo Mio."

There was the grocer on the corner and the Oriental rug shop and the truss-and-artificial-leg shop and the bridal shop with the dusty dresses in the window, and the Minute Tavern and all the Irish bars called Joe's. There was the surly shoe repairman on Sixty-first who refused to move when they tore down the block. There were the homeless—known as bums or drunks, it was before people were so sensitive and euphemistic—who slept in doorways in the shadow of the el, sometimes clutching bottles of cheap wine. There was the Holmes patrolman and the Sixty-second Street Association that held a carol-sing and an eggnog party at Christmas. Among our neighbors were Jinx Falkenburg, John Gunther, Eleanor Roosevelt, the financier

Otto Kahn, and Mrs. Bergdorf Goodman. Now it seems that there was always snow.

There was the Gorgon School at 43 East Sixty-seventh Street. Miss Gorgon's pince-nez clung to the end of her nose, and her shiny black hair was painted into place. She wore magenta crepe with jet beads hung from her large bosom.

"She has promise," she told my mother, "though she needs to learn patience."

Mama wore a rakish hat with veil, tailored suit, alligator pumps. Handbag and kid gloves. Earrings, upswept hair, crimson lips.

"We think she has *great* promise," she said, her voice increasingly shrill—an effect Miss Gorgon had on her. "And *talent.*"

"Possibly," Miss Gorgon said, with a brief glance at me.

All day long she told us how to live. We should hold our heads up, speak up, look people straight in the eye—shyness was selfishness. We should write clearly and distinctly, pronounce our French *R*'s properly, clean our plates. We should neither bang the piano keys nor read comic books.

We learned that girls were superior to boys, because boys were beaten with a ruler for infractions and girls were not. If I picked a fight with one of the boys when we were playing in the park, he was the one who got punished. "You-will-not-hit-a-girl," Miss Gorgon would howl, purple-faced, pince-nez askew, breaking rulers over the boy's legs and rear as we all watched fascinated. One of the other teachers would comfort the bruised, weeping child afterward. Today the school would be shut down, but that was before people were so delicate and empathetic.

She only struck children whose parents gave permission, which didn't include Tony Perkins. Years later (after making *Psycho*) Tony said that the Gorgon School had provided him with the happiest period of his life. Of course—children love rigidity, predictability, cruelty. We knew where we stood, what was going to happen next, what we were going to have for lunch every day. (Monday: gray meat, mashed potatoes, and peas. Tuesday: gray meat, mashed potatoes, and carrots. Thursday: gray meat, mashed potatoes, and beets. Wednesday and Friday; spaghetti and meatballs.) We knew how to make a smile appear on Miss Gorgon's purple, pockmarked face; we knew we'd be provided with violent spectacle, like the Romans at the Coliseum, or people who watch executions. She never waffled, we knew she'd give it to us straight. From her I learned to detect contaminated judgments—the kind that come of conceit, frivolity, or despair.

Tony was a natural clown, and double-jointed as well. His knickered knees splayed backward, he could cross his ankles behind his neck, he could bend his fingers back almost to his wrists. He had a drollness far beyond his eight years and a glorious, fearless imagination. When he came over to play we became kings and queens, elves and detectives and beggars, pirates and executioners. As famous medics we fought the dread Nippoopiay disease, introduced by my cocker spaniel now quarantined in a flower box, warning passersby that the whole East Side was plague ridden but lives could be saved by our secret vaccine. If they liked we'd give them a free shot.

Half a lifetime later I went backstage after seeing Tony in *Equus*. We hadn't met in decades, but he went right into the old Nippoopiay Pup routine while his wife, Berry, watched in astonishment. He was a fine actor, but I always believed that he was a genius, that he should have done more than speak others' lines, and written or sung or shouted his own instead. Watching him lope gracefully across the stage or down the steps of the Bates Motel took me back to the third floor of Miss Gorgon's brownstone where we skipped in a circle to "Frère Jacques," or to the Christmas pageant where Tony, as Nebuchadnezzar, waved his golden sceptre at a roomful of captive parents. And later when I saw Tony, and then John Kerr, another Gorgon child, in *Tea and Sympathy,* I was proud of both, and knew Miss Gorgon had done something undetectably right.

THE CITY WAS our playground.

There were the double-decker buses on Fifth and the double features with cartoons and newsreels—where, if you weren't careful, you'd end up in the children's section, guarded by a uniformed matron. There was the el ride to Chinatown, with its temple gong and bewildering movies and egg roll shops. There was the bus ride to the Cloisters and the Staten Island Ferry, there were soda fountains and the five-and-ten and the Automat and the Empire State Building and the Planetarium, and the armor room and the Egyptian tomb at the Metropolitan. There was roller-skating on the promenade by the East River and horseback riding around the reservoir, and every afternoon the Gorgon gender wars in the park—the boys on one side, the girls and Tony on the other.

There was skating at Rockefeller Center and hot chocolate at the café, which I had to earn by going around the rink three times without touching the rail. While I slogged along, Ma (in her half of our matching velveteen outfits) twirled and swanned in the middle, sometimes doing a sedate waltz with Mr. Ripley, her skating companion. Later I asked if she was going to marry him, and she only laughed.

"It's like the song, 'They're Either Too Young or Too Old.' He's one of the too-olds."

There was the X-ray machine in the Best's shoe department, where you could look down at your skeleton toes inside prospective new Oxfords. I have been told since that our feet were dangerously irradiated, but nobody knew about that yet and we stayed on much too long, wiggling our toes and soaking up deadly rays till we had to be bodily hauled off.

And the food . . . the sweet sausages at the street fairs on Second Avenue, the macaroni and cheese and the apple pie at the Automat . . . the milkshakes at the drugstore at Madison and Sixty-fourth . . . the chicken Kiev at the Brearley cafeteria. The best hot dogs were on Eighty-sixth Street . . . Lun Far's on Sixth Avenue had the best shrimps with lobster sauce . . . and there was the corned beef hash at Dinty Moore's, where I went with Pop when he was in town, and chicken hash at "21," and the vichyssoise and eggs Benedict at the Plaza, where he always stayed. Frequently after school I stopped at

Mac the grocer's and got a large package of Hydrox cookies, which I took home and ate slowly and happily with most of a quart of milk. It took years to learn which of these things I was supposed to like best.

THE DINING ROOM on the substreet level of 204 had ivy wallpaper and ivy-carved chairs with white leather seats; the white china was edged with a single circle of ivy, among whose green leaves I pushed string beans and drops of gravy. On the buffet in the corner was a copper chafing dish and against one wall was the pine breakfront, with its collection of white ironstone china.

There had been cocktails, of course, up in the living room, and now there were two standing ribs of rare beef, roast potatoes, salad, red wine. Marion was forty-one—which no one knew.

"You look twenty-one. Doesn't she, Frank?"

Marion smiled and preened. She didn't disagree. "With just a little help from Thecla"—the Danish gem who tailored facial potions to her clients. (I can still smell the ether lotion, feel the little jabs as she removed zits from my forehead.) "Thecla tells me she can't get the soothing cream anymore"— but the ether lotion was somehow gotten out of Europe.

"Oh my God . . . I have to have it."

I drifted away from the table. In my mind I moved back and high up, like a cameraman on a boom. Who was there that night? The Duffys, probably, our neighbors from Sixty-first Street. Ann's moon face was free of makeup, her long hair streamed from an untidy knot, she wore paint-spotted smocks. She had put us here—found 204, told my mother to rent it, and decorated it. (Ann decorated everybody's apartments, you could tell as soon as you walked in—the shards of glass and amber, the mirrored tables, the black glass, the jazzy sparkle—and told everybody how to run their lives as well.) Her husband, Eddie, a Pulitzer Prize–winning cartoonist for the *Baltimore Sun,* always wore a three-piece pinstripe suit, a bowler, and boutonniere; they both talked at once, usually about different things. You swung your head back and forth between them as though at a tennis match.

The Sayres might have been there; two writers from across the street, with a daughter whose name, and a corner of whose soul, I shared—unless they were in Hollywood on a movie job . . . small, exquisite Ethel Heyn, a comic among comics, and Ernie, the editor of *Family Circle;* and literary agent Edith Haggard, tiny and elegant with her gold Dunhill cigarette holder and her generosity and her great dirty laugh, and Harrison Smith, editor of the old *Saturday Review*— they could have been there, or Eleanor Hempstead, a Hollywood refugee like my mother, with her long horse face and harlequin glasses, her waggish humor; and *her* daughter Avery; or Dr. Frank McGowan, all charm, fond of the grape, and quiet Ada Ruth, and their daughter, Anne, four days younger than me . . . all of us Depression children, for the most part *only* children, making sisters of each other. Otis Wiese of *McCall's* could have been there . . . Herbert Asbury, town chronicler and author of *Gangs of New York,* and his wife, Edith, a *New York Times* reporter . . . Emily Hahn, *New Yorker* writer and longtime China hand . . . Catherine Bellamy, large, kindly, hoarse-voiced, divorced from the theater, whose son I was supposed to play with, and refused . . . and some capricious name fairy that made all their names start with *E* or *A*.

Except Jo.

Joseph Golinkin was a fine painter of urban watercolors, a commander in the Navy—but he didn't fit into this circle of revelers and he knew it. Not because of shyness or insecurity, for this group, no bastion of mental health, was tolerant of neurotic peculiarities. But Jo's humor was leaden, his timing poor, his sense of what to say when almost nonexistent; he lacked an edge, a sense of himself, that the rest had. He certainly lacked Joel Sayre's brilliant ability to make anything interesting, or Ethel's precision, the way she knew just how to deliver the neat little phrase that brought forth rolling laughter. Jo had no humor, no playfulness; a depressed, solitary man in love with a beautiful woman, in what he saw as a glamorous circle. He'd sailed into uncharted waters.

I was the only one who heard the phone in the hall . . . the small, heavy dial phone on the commode. The wooden seat beside it curved to fit full-sized rear ends, and there I sat, one-third filling it. My clothes for the birthday party, I'll guess, consisted of a white cotton blouse with puffed sleeves and a Lanz of Salzburg skirt with felt suspenders trimmed with red hearts. White socks, brown oxfords that supported the arch, gray knees with small scabs and cuts. Straight hair with plastic barrettes falling out of it, or stiff brown frizz if it was after the permanent wave "on the ends." I looked the way little girls did then, which, like most, I had no great interest in, and largely left up to others.

It was a familiar male voice, hard to hear over the noise in the dining room. To this day I don't know who it was. Not my father. Not Jo, who was among the merry, his small mouth turned up in its little *U* smile . . . someone who'd heard, and knew Marion hadn't. Some prescient person.

"I can't hear you," I said. Now there were hoots of laughter from the dining room, cries for more wine, like a Tudor debauch.

"Tell your mother what I said," the unknown man said firmly.

"What?" I asked, and he repeated something. "They bombed what?"

He said it once more and hung up. We were one on a hurried list. I didn't understand the urgency in his voice. They were always bombing something. We bombed them back. Hitler and Hirohito were made for cartoon drawing and funny imitations. They were the bad guys, but they would lose—Mr. Roosevelt would prevail, the bombing would stop. There would be bluebirds over the white cliffs of Dover, we would come in on a wing and a prayer. The lights would go on again all over the world.

Carrying the information gingerly, like a new soufflé, I walked into the dining room and repeated what I had been told. I had to say it two or three times—they were particularly hilarious. Occasionally one of them would smile at me, or wave, saying, "Hi, sweetie, off to bed?" taking another gulp of wine.

"They bombed Pearl Harbor," I kept saying. "The Japs bombed Pearl Harbor." Finally somebody heard. I remember the woman's face, whoever she was—the made-up, laughing face, brown curls abounce, the boozy eyes that suddenly came into focus.

"Pearl what?" somebody asked. "What's that?"

Then utter silence fell over the table. I must be joking. I shouldn't joke about such things. I went and clung to my mother. "I'm *not* joking." They made me repeat it three or four more times. Then—who had been on the phone? What else had he said, *when* had it happened, how had he found out . . . and where and what the hell was Pearl Harbor? (And how could none of these people have heard news that must have arrived in New York several hours earlier? But this is what I remember.)

Ma kept patting me absently, her eyes moving to Jo in alarm. I watched the tableful of adults fall apart. Some muttered, looked at their watches, ran upstairs to turn on the living room radio. "It's in Hawaii. It's *ours*"—which had to be explained to those—almost all— who had never heard of the place. Three of the men sprang to their feet to use the phone; Jo's call to the Brooklyn Navy Yard took priority. I followed his dark-blue uniformed back and shiny black hair out into the hallway, watched him dial, but I couldn't hear what he said. Others lined up to phone editors or agents, to check children. Somebody called the hospital . . . as though the casualties were coming in already.

At the table one woman cried on another's shoulder. "We're in the war," somebody said. "Oh, God help us. Oh, it's so terrible . . . so awful."

It seems to be that evening that Jo and Marion kissed passionately and tearfully in the vestibule, murmuring things I couldn't hear, but which had to do with Jo going to his battleship, the *Montana* . . . which made me feel very admiring of Jo, and thrilled at his courage. On the eve of his departure, I liked him very much . . . more so when someone said that the war might go on for a very long time.

THEY'LL NEVER BOMB
THIS PLACE

THE WAR: coffee cans of cold grease, large balls of crinkled aluminum foil packed tight, piles of newspapers for . . . something. Tangled khaki knitting hanging from fat needles, green ration books. The green of one cigarette pack turned white ("Lucky Strike Goes to War!"). Fabric shortages sent women's skirts ever higher, silk stockings turned into parachutes and were replaced by rayon, rubber scrapers by plastic. Meat, butter, and sugar were rationed. As it seems now, the natural materials, steel and silk and rubber and leather, went to war, leaving the synthetics. People dreamed of silk stockings and huge steel cars and thick juicy steaks.

Our food changed. After watching my mother squeeze a blob of vermillion coloring onto a white, lardlike brick, I refused oleo. Instead I took pieces of Wonder Bread, pulled off the crust, and pressed the middles into sticky white balls that I rolled in salt and ate slowly, with great pleasure, from the palm of my hand. There were war cakes made with bacon grease or canned tomato soup, there was war casserole and war soup of a strange dingy gray. Spam appeared.

The can was such a cute shape, and it was so trustworthy, always the same, a kind of hamlike, salty blob of American cold cut. Frying, it smelled a little like bacon, and turned into brown rectangles, which were good with a baked potato, and it made a nourishing, stick-to-the-ribs war casserole. Nobody complained much—a holy sense of sacrifice prevailed.

Travel accommodations were scarce, cars scarcer, and fuel was rationed. We took the train to our cottage on Long Island, where we rode strangely light, mostly plastic war bicycles a mile to the store and carried bags of groceries home in the baskets. We had a Victory garden—apple and pear trees, berry patches and grape arbors and herbs, and half an acre of vegetables—which seems too ambitious for a city woman whose day stopped at the cocktail hour. But as my father produced Morris agents, my mother came up with small, barrel-chested Italians named Louie—so some Louie or other must have done most of the work.

Then she wangled a car from somewhere, a comic SUV called a Jeep station wagon. It had a canvas tent for a roof, and backseat passengers were blown, splashed, or burned by the weather as we bounced along Northern Boulevard—which we thought was funny and all part of the adventure of war.

Pearl Harbor . . . the azure bay I imagined with a few bombs dropping silently into it changed our sensibilities. The adults were graver, their voices lower, sometimes falling into silence when I appeared. Newsboys hawked more papers than ever—three or four, with banner headlines, came into our house every day. The radio murmured continually. Walter Winchell and Gabriel Heatter were like two uncles, one waspish and one mournful, ceaselessly talking across the room. Everything stopped—dinner, homework—when Mr. Roosevelt was on. And at least once, perhaps more often, the airwaves picked up the babble of the distant madman, ranting through the static.

Unknown to my mother, Nanny and I were addicted to war movies. The evil armies marching in goose step, the good Americans striding forth straight and true. Grim-faced *commandants*, the Nazi salute, the shiny clicking boots . . . depraved scientists with small round glasses, rubbing their hands. Embraces in airports, on docks and train platforms, tearful girls with belted coats and upswept curls going home to their shared apartments with Murphy beds, stockings hanging over the bathtub, percolator bubbling on the stove . . . a hand poised over a ringing phone or ripping open a tiny V-mail envelope. Frightened soldiers in their bunks, Varga girls pinned up on the wall, happy to have a cigarette or a bottle of soda and a little jitterbugging . . . and the air battles, prop bombers with brave cartoons painted on the side, bombs falling out of their bellies like eggs to land with little puffs of smoke, planes going down in a haze of flame and twisted metal; the tail gunner in his glass shell riddled with bullets before our eyes.

MY MOTHER'S FLIRTY cocktail-hour persona gave way to a new, sharp authority. When the air-raid siren wailed, she was firm about the blackout curtains—the tiniest beam of light could bring bombs raining on Sixty-second Street. Leaving Nanny and me on the kitchen floor to listen for bombers and antiaircraft fire, she put on her warden's cape and flashlight and paced the street till the all-clear. She belonged, besides, to the City Patrol Corps (belted khaki with lots of brass buttons, a peaked de Gaulle cap atop her dark curls), whose mission was to spot enemy submarines in the East River. This was not funny at the time. Playing prison ball on the Brearley pier by the river, I kept an eye on the surface of the dark oily water for periscopes, on the sky for stray Messerschmitts.

Newly purposeful women in uniform, in business suits, in overalls came and went constantly. Ann Duffy arrived from around the corner in her spotty smock, Gertrude Sayre strode across the street in her bathrobe and slippers, smiling around her cigarette. Edith Haggard dropped by after work in her tailor-made, her little John Frederics hat with a puff of veiling, the Dunhill holder on her finger. Dottie Anderson, our wartime tenant, and a couple of others were in uniform.

There were usually one or two for dinner, friends from my mother's electronics class, or the Red Cross, or her job as a "technical writer"—composing instructions for rifle assembly. The men were gone. Frank McGowan and Ernie Heyn were in the army. Joel Sayre was in Persia writing for *The New Yorker.* Jo was in the Pacific.

LATE IN THE WAR, Ma's friend Florence came from London. A black hat, blond curls, purple lipstick, a fur coat, valises. Lots of trilling and greeting and hugging. She'd managed to get her sons to Canada—I knew the English kids had been evacuated at the beginning of the war while their parents stayed behind. Florence got out because she was American. She told us about the Blitz.

"There we'd be at somebody's flat, and the V-2's would come, the rockets you know, the whistle and then that horrible silence, you don't know where it's going to strike. We'd fling ourselves facedown on the floor trying not to spill our drinks." Like my mother, Florence's default condition was a cocktail party.

"What happened when it hit?"

"Well, when the whine stopped you started counting, and tried to gauge how far away it was, like thunder after lightning, to tell how far away the storm is. The nearest one went off half a block away, just along the Embankment. That was very bad. I'd say to myself, the children are safe, I've had a wonderful life, I've been blessed."

FLORENCE AND MA had been best friends at Flushing High, and gone on to live what I thought glamorous lives. An earnest Catholic father and stern suffragette mother had driven Ma straight to flapper frivolity. The idea, she and Florence explained, was to collect beaux like charms on a bracelet. The thing was to have fun, and money never hurt. Life was a game, a giggle. Florence married a Scottish playboy, and Marion, working as a stringer on the *Brooklyn Daily Eagle,* met a cub reporter named Nunnally Johnson.

Here's what I was told: It was instant love. They met over a crossword puzzle. He proposed on the first date, she demurred. Marion was engaged to someone else and Nunnally had a wife and small daughter, and a girlfriend as well, but none of that seemed to matter.

There were career changes—Nunnally went to the *Herald Tribune,* Marion (after a brief stint in a chorus line) to *Success Magazine.* There were life changes. His divorce became final; her family, with whom she lived, moved away—leaving her open to an impulsive elopement in 1926. "We had entirely too much to drink," she told me, "and we took a taxi to Portchester." They returned to Nunnally's walk-up apartment at 11 West Fiftieth Street (now Rockefeller Center.) But he awoke the next morning and declared the whole thing a terrible mistake.

Both report that he gave her a bad time. They were still drinking entirely too much. After a few months she quit her job and joined her family in California. Letters followed, begging her to return, and such were his powers of persuasion that she came back and they married again in 1927—this time in Hackensack, by bus: "cold sober. I wore a fur-trimmed maroon velveteen suit I'd bought for forty-five dollars. It was very becoming."

The Hackensack marriage worked better—arguably because Marion stopped working: "I couldn't have held a job anyway, we were out at speakeasies until four in the morning." By then, she said, "it was obvious that Nunnally was going to make it." Besides his column in the New York *Evening Post,* he had over the years sold dozens of short stories in the rich market of those plummy days to *Smart Set, American Mercury, The Saturday Evening Post,* and others.

New York in the twenties has been called the nothing-sacred age of journalism, the paradise of the newspaperman. Mistakes aside, my parents had either the luck or the enviable ability to be in the right places at the best times. They hung out at Bleeck's and Texas Guinan's with writers and editors such as Frank Sullivan, James Thurber, Harold Ross, Herman Mankiewicz, Gene Fowler, Stanley Walker, Faith Baldwin, Finley Peter Dunne, Heywood Broun, the Sayres . . .

and in Europe every year with Florence and her husband, they played at being Scott and Zelda and the Murphys. They drank champagne at the Brasserie Lipp, and my mother, I'm told, danced the Charleston on top of a café table on Bastille Day. Left to his own devices, my father chose to sit with American cronies Austin Parker, Julian Street, Cam Rogers, Eddie Duffy.

In 1930 the best of Nunnally's short stories were collected in a book, *There Ought to Be a Law.* He quit the *Post* to be a freelance writer and he and my mother moved to Great Neck, though he still worked in a hotel room in town. But by 1932 the Depression caught up with them. The magazines had shrunk to half size, and the competition—J. P. Marquand, Lardner, Fitzgerald, Sinclair Lewis—was fierce. *The Saturday Evening Post,* his prime market (he told me once), didn't protect their writers during the Depression as *The New Yorker* did, with advances and drawing accounts—which was why *The New Yorker* kept their best writers (O'Hara, E. B. White, Thurber, S. J. Perelman) and the *SEP* lost theirs to Hollywood. My father and dozens of other New York freelancers, frequently persuaded by Herman Mankiewicz (scriptwriter of *Citizen Kane*), went west to write for the movies.

"OH, WE LOVED champagne. And strawberries, and soufflés . . . things with fringe, cloche hats," Florence told me.

She stayed for several weeks in the other tiny bedroom on the top floor. I sat on her bed while she creamed her face and put up her hair in curlers. "And then what did you do?" I'd ask. "And then where did you go? Is it true that Pop got counterfeit money at a bank in Spain? What did you eat? What did you wear?"

"We rolled our stockings. Tommy wore plus-fours and sometimes a kilt. And Nunnally knew everybody. He held court at the Deux Magots or the Lipp while your mother and I went shopping. Oh, we laughed and laughed, we had such fun. It was a marvelous world, you know—we knew it every day when we woke up."

One morning, brushing her teeth, she gurgled, "You know Jo will be off his battleship before long."

My heart sank. "Is the war almost over?"

"Nobody knows, lovey. Oh, one can't believe the trouble caused by that awful little man."

"If he's so awful why does she like him?"

She stared at me for a moment and then laughed. "I meant Hitler, silly. As for Jo, you must try to like him, for her sake. He isn't *so* bad if you give him half a chance. Not half as amusing as your father, but then nobody is. You mustn't compare them," she said, spitting Listerine into the sink.

"Oh, I don't." Even the idea was shocking. I swallowed. "But then why did Mama leave him?"

"Oh, darling, surely she's explained." I shook my head. "You ought to know. They were on and off for years, then he met Dorris and it got even more complicated. There were misunderstandings and lost letters and frantic telegrams . . . and your mother has a bad habit of skipping out when she can't cope, just as he was coming to town she'd manage to be on a cruise or in the hospital or something. Oh, it was Shakespearean, it was like the ending of *Romeo and Juliet.* I can't tell you how furious I was with her, he was the love of her life."

PUT IT IN THE CAN

DOWN TO BEVERLY, out Santa Monica . . . a left turn into what is now Century City, which was then part of the Twentieth Century-Fox lot. Past a flinty-eyed guard into a village of little stucco buildings and vast windowless soundstages fringed with pink oleander flapping in the hot wind. I had never been to such a private place. Nobody was there who didn't belong, nothing went on that didn't have to do with the Business. (Dhahran, the American company town in the Middle East where I later lived for a while, reminded me so much of Fox that I kept calling it "the lot." Same little buildings, same oleander . . . same flinty-eyed gate guard, that one wearing a *gutra* . . . in one place they made pictures, the other oil.)

I followed my father there when I was small, drove him when I was grown. I loved the backlot; the Western street with the saloon, the Manhattan street with the row of brownstones, the little café on the Rive Gauche. (A "fairyland," Scott Fitzgerald wrote in *The Last Tycoon,* "not because the locations really looked like African jungles and French châteaux and schooners at anchor and Broadway by night, but because they looked like the torn picture books of childhood, like fragments of stories dancing in an open fire.") Nunnally was surprised that I wasn't as charmed as he by the props holding them up from behind. He delighted in the workings of make-believe, but I wanted to be fooled. I had never taken a watch apart to see what made it work. He took me to a place where they were burning up a tiny dollhouse that, on the screen, would look life-sized, and to another place where a man was clopping two rubber cups on a surface in a way that sounded like hoofbeats.

We visited sets—picking our way over coils and black snakes in a dark soundstage to the brightly lit corner where confusion was canned as fairy tales. When I was young the process was hard to understand. What did it all have to do with a camera, how did the camera take pictures that moved? (A thousand pictures, flipping quickly by.) What did the cutter—the editor—do? (Reshaped the ragged strips of film so that it all made sense and looked smooth, and more . . . using hot splicers, working on a flatbed.) How could sound be part of it? (It was recorded on a track that moved along next to the flipping pictures.) Where did the music come from? (It was recorded separately, later, on another track, and was written especially for the picture, unless it was Rachmaninoff or Stravinsky.) What about pictures that had been made in France, but the actors spoke English? (That was dubbing, done afterward.)

Why did those people sit up on cranes . . . booms? (To see better.) Why did it cost a lot of money when a plane went overhead or somebody coughed or a director's chair—like the one I was sitting in—squeaked and ruined the take? (Because—I was told as I was packed off the set in ignominy—all those people had to be paid union wages, because time is money, because they'd go over budget, and Mr. Skouras—the head of the studio—would be mad.) What did the director do? Set up the scene, told the actors how to act and the cameraman how to film, saying "Action" or "Roll 'em" or "Put it in the can."

The stars were made out of some superior stuff. Tyrone Power and Alice Faye, Ginger Rogers, Groucho Marx, Bogie, Betty—you couldn't keep your eyes off them. One evening on Mountain Drive I had looked up to see Judy Garland standing in front of me, her eyes ablaze, her small swaying body lit up with some tragic fire. Her silent presence threw everything else into shadow. On the set they were treated like precious dolls. Minions combed their hair and straightened their clothes and touched up their makeup while they talked to the director about the next scene.

What did the producer do?

"He decides to make the picture," Nunnally said.

Pop was a born scriptwriter. He even had script-sized ideas, with scenes three pages long. An unwilling producer, he appeared to avoid the set—when I went to the studio I always found him in his office. We walked over together, watched the shooting for a while, and then he left. And he minimized his role in preproduction by turning out scripts so finished that rewrites were rarely needed, nor other writers, nor anything that took him away from where he wanted to be—in front of his typewriter.

Then how did it all connect? What became of the scripts, those slender volumes of dialogue? They were not real books, but temporary storage places for words to be brought to life by actors, who memorized them to say in front of the camera. Never, like some writers, did he feel diminished by the transitional nature of his work, nor did he ever doubt that the script was the most important factor in the equation. Later, he was exasperated by auteur directors and their fixation on power. He knew where the power really was.

At Martindale's bookstore on Little Santa Monica, there was a ritual. Salesladies greeted him, asking if they could help. Well, he wanted so-and-so . . . did they have any ideas? With seeming carelessness they produced their favorite new novels. He listened carefully to what they had to say. A shrug from Miss W., a little moue from Mrs. S., and the book might go back on the table or the shelf. But a nod, a couple of meaningful taps, sent it on its way. We always left with an armload and within an hour he'd be home in his corner armchair cracking the first glossy cover, a scotch and ice on the table next to him, a new pack of Old Golds.

As we walked around the lot, people—mostly little short men—appeared through doors, out of cars, from behind palm trees. They pumped his hand, cigar smoke circling their bald heads. I think of him looking down on a ring of producers, agents, and studio honchos in sport shirts, high-cut trousers, and two-tone shoes. Inside the building, permed, flame-lipped secretaries flocked around with memos, reminders of meetings with VIPs, urgent phone messages from stars, production stills of lovely hopefuls, freshly typed script pages that these women turned out with lightning speed while new ones were being painfully gestated in the next office. In the commissary he was greeted by cowboys, mole-cheeked ladies of the French court, Nazi generals with monocles, leading men with gleaming teeth and lifts in their shoes, heavily made-up stars in head scarves with throaty voices and twining arms. "Nunn-ley. Don't tell me this here's your little daw-ter." And more producers, ever-alert agents, script girls in slacks, harassed cutters, depressed writers, and agitated directors.

At the end of the day the rushes were shown in a sleek, silent gray room like a tiny movie theater. The director, the cutter, the producer, perhaps the writer (whose importance was diminishing rapidly) sat together in front, while lesser members and hangers-on sat behind. The day's work was scrappy and uncut, the snapboard announcing the take number, the director's voice saying "Cut. Try it again," or "Put it in the can," or an occasional yowl of laughter. When the film was on, the room was dead quiet. Sometimes the director or the producer said loudly, "Let's lighten that background" or "Can we do something about her hair?" or "Look here, he's half out of the frame." When it was over, everyone sat in silence for two or three minutes, deep in thought, then went into a huddle in the front row. These sessions confirmed the importance of the cutter. She—usually a woman in slacks and a head scarf knotted on top—wrote down all the comments and then went and organized the whole mess into coherency.

So I learned that without any member of the team there would be nothing. Making pictures called for team spirit, a huddle that produced a winning play so smooth that the fights, the compromises, the shortcuts, the hirings and firings, the props behind were all invisible, and all you saw was the moon over Miami, and Fred and Ginger dancing.

TALENT

JO WAS TALENTED. He illustrated books—*The American Sporting Scene,* with text by John Kieran, featured his watercolors of horseracing, hockey and polo, golf and tennis and sailing. He did drawings and paintings of the docks, the el, the trolleys, the saloons and fire escapes and subway stations in the slummy corners of the city.

He painted the portrait of my mother that hung in the dining room of 204. She sits on a Manhattan terrace in a midriff dress, a couple of inches of stomach showing and a Rosalind Russell hairdo whose popularity was mercifully brief. She looks similar to but not quite like herself—some earthier Marion, a peasant woman on a penthouse.

I thought of artists as sensitive souls who were deeply moved by sunsets and sad-faced children. But Jo was ingrown and secretive; his soul seemed dull and frozen. That he saw meaning and excitement in the slumped figures of dockworkers and the straight, cocky spines of jockeys, that he understood city light as it fell on the rivers and the streets and sifted through the latticed el, was a double insult . . . all this sentient awareness was rationed, saved for his art, leaving none for the people in his life. I didn't know that all artists are like that, and wouldn't have cared if I did. All I knew was that his oval, swarthy face was a closed gate, dark as his commander's uniform.

"Your mother wants to marry Jo," Nunnally said one night after dinner.

It was late in the summer of 1945, the war in Europe was over. Our beloved Mr. Roosevelt had died in the spring. We were playing double solitaire in the Beverly Glen house—the one before Mountain Drive, the first house with Dorris, the house atop a hill with a curving driveway lined with yellow rose-trees.

In the den there was a brick fireplace, over which hung a large Confederate flag. Questions about the small number of stars always led to a little history lesson. My father's hometown in Georgia, Columbus, had been mostly demolished by General Sherman. I had learned "Marching Through Georgia" and "Le Marseillaise" at school—Miss Gorgon's taste in music ran to the martial-inspirational—but when I sang it to my southern grandparents, thinking they'd be pleased I knew a song about their state, I had been hushed and scolded.

On another wall was a large framed drawing called *Life's Choice.* It showed two parallel roads—a wide one lined with taverns, brothels, burlesque theaters, seedy bars, sloe-eyed women in slit skirts, lustful men, falling-down drunks clutching bottles, shifty Svengalis making shady deals in dark doorways. At the end was a conflagration of roasting humans, their faces contorted in agony. The other road was straight and narrow. Along its edges were churches, tidy houses with gardens, children walking to school, families with dogs, pairs of nuns carrying Bibles, and so forth. At the end were pearly gates and flocks of angels playing harps.

"But why?" I asked, alarmed.

He put down his cards.

Because she was lonely. Because a woman needed a man. Because she deserved some happiness—there was no reason she shouldn't be as happy as he was with Dorris. Jo would be home as soon as the war was over and expected an answer. This must have been just before Hiroshima. He'd been waiting for one ever since Pearl Harbor. He was usually overseas—I had half forgotten about him.

I asked my father if he knew Jo. (A little.) If he liked him. (Beside the point.)

I said I didn't like Jo and I was pretty sure he didn't like me, because once he'd brought a Christmas present for the dog but nothing for me.

My father pushed on. "Some people, especially men, aren't very good with children. Jo is shy, Marion tells me. He finds it hard to show his feelings. It isn't that he doesn't like you, it's more that . . ." He leaned back, lighting a cigarette. "He just doesn't know what to say."

I knew he hated this conversation as much as I did, and that he was trying not to lose his temper, which made me nervous. I was at a wretched age. I had stringy hair and zits, I had glasses for nearsightedness, braces on my teeth. I didn't know what I was, where I was going.

Nunnally soldiered on. "Remember Jo has no children of his own. In time he'll learn what to say. You and he can become friends if you'll let him. He isn't a bad man—just different from the kind of people you're used to," and so forth, condemning Jo more with every word. He didn't look at me. Then suddenly he exploded: "Damn it, she deserves some happiness!"

Cards slammed down, a few onto the floor, ashes and sparks swirled up from the ashtray. He was on his feet, striding past the Confederate flag to the door into the hall. Up the steps, along the upstairs hall to Dorris's room.

I sat there trying to make sense out of this statement, then, because I didn't know what else to do, I finished the game for both of us.

He had been practically there. If he'd just stayed he would have won—he had all the right cards.

SOME LITTLE INDIE

"Where are the stars?"

Gregory didn't actually say it, but it was written across his face, along with "You actually dragged me over here for *this?*" Then an expression of weary resignation: "All right—who are these peripheral people I have to endure all evening?"

I was having a party. Days of work, weeks of thought and planning and agonizing over the guest list, yeoman's work by Dorris to turn Julie's and my sow's ear social lives into something silkier. At one point Julie went to bed for three days, at another I got hysterical and threw a tuna-fish sandwich at her. Nunnally threatened to move to the Beverly Hills Hotel till it was over.

It was nobody's fault—the problem was inherent in the situation. It was like starting principal photography with only your aunt Millie and a couple of dirtbag cousins to carry a high-budget film that the studio's whole financial future hangs on. It was going to be like one of those little indies from Iran with no plot and everybody standing around staring at the camera.

The guest list was: Julie. Gregory. The Sweethearts, Sylvia and Lily, and their older brother, Don. Kim, my oldest friend in Beverly Hills, whom I'd been avoiding. The Jacobson boys, some director's kids who had come to my fifth birthday party, and a girl nobody had ever met that Dorris thought was about the right age.

Julie wanted Roddy McDowall. I said no, never—he'd be bored, he'd be miserable, he didn't know I was alive. Julie said if we didn't have Roddy McDowall she wouldn't come and she'd never speak to me again. I said that suited me fine. Dorris suggested we invite him to shut Julie up and hope he refused. So we did and he did. This A-list had been put together with blood and superhuman patience, like the Treaty of Versailles—but it had the durability of some fragile Middle East so-called agreement forged in a hail of bullets.

The Sweethearts lived next door, in an enormous Gothic house with squeaking doors, beamed ceilings, pools of light from ancient windows, dusty recesses, massive furniture, echoes. Inside, the Sweethearts, a family of sweet frail people, stole around like good fairies in a haunted castle. Mr. Sweetheart was an executive with a record company, not on the plumb line of the Business, and the family's marginal status showed in details like Mrs. Sweetheart, who didn't drive, waiting among the maids at the bus stop on Sunset. To me, the girls' sweetness and good manners rescued their name from mockery, and testified to strict upbringing and patriarchy of the highest order, but their innocence about Hollywood made them seem lost at this soigné gathering.

Don Sweetheart went to UC Santa Barbara. He wore jeans, a bolo tie, belts with silver buckles, and tooled-leather boots, and he walked with a subtle cowboy swing. He never came through the hedge, at most allowing his sisters and me to go over and listen to his jazz records, and on special occasions to give back rubs to him and a friend. This led to teasing and giggling and on to playful but proper wrestling matches, more exciting for us than the boys, who presumably out of desperate boredom were reduced to rolling around on the floor with little sisters. It was almost worse that Don had come to the party, because now I had to worry about what he thought, as well as Gregory, on top of my hostess responsibilities.

Kim had bitten me regularly when we were three. I remembered her teeth marks in my arm, two matching half circles evenly dented. Her father sold lawnmowers, which today would relegate him to a modest subdivision two hours' drive into the desert, but at that time it seemed to easily support a Spanish-style house next door on Maple and a cottage at Lake Arrowhead where, when we were ten or eleven, Kim invited her friends over for necking parties, while I sat down on the dock and slapped mosquitoes. She was a big, fearless girl who could step barefoot on red ants and stay underwater for what seemed like an eternity, and now she got swimming cups and prizes and was training for the Olympics instead of finishing high school and talking about getting married soon and how New York was an evil place . . . but we needed guests.

The Jacobson boys looked miserable, and the girl of the right age, the daughter of a high honcho at Paramount, turned out to be sixteen and sexy . . . so there went Don Sweetheart, who had half-promised to teach me how to drive.

The cars brought them one by one except the Sweethearts, who came through the hedge. When the silence in the front hall became unbearable, I took them around and showed them the moving book-shelves, the built-in Capehart, the mural on the dining room wall, the sleek deco study, and the fairy-tale nursery—as Dorris or my mother always did, even if the guests had been there fifty times. ("Nice house," Gregory said.) Then we went into the living room and Max, Lars's successor, passed Cokes and pretzels and pushed the furniture around and pulled down the screen, and we watched a newly released Bette Davis picture.

Don Sweetheart was sitting next to the Paramount daughter, I was between Gregory and a Jacobson boy, in a fever of speculation over whether my new dress, which had a Greek-key neckline, had been a good idea or was going to ruin the party out of sheer ugliness. Greg was playing do-you-know with the Paramount daughter, Shirley (wouldn't you know). Kim was laughing in all the wrong places, and during the long fadeout I saw the nearest Jacobson boy slowly stroking the gold-threaded upholstery.

"Not Bette's best," Greg said to me.

"I thought it was terrific."

"You would. It's just the sort of thing you like."

"How do you know what I like?"

"I just do. So the movie's over—now what?"

Why had I invited him? Because he was a boy. The only other party I had given, in New York, had been a disaster—six very dressed-up girls and one short, shy boy—a second boy, we heard later, had come up the front steps, taken a look through the window, and fled. The shy boy danced with each of us while the stack of 78 records plopped down, one by one. The rest sat in a circle staring. After they left I cried. This was going to be my life.

THE TABLE WAS set up by the pool, with bright summer linens, hurricane candles, crystal goblets of Coke. We all trooped over and sat down. Kim, who had a lisp, said "Goth." Julie, in a droopy yellow dress, sent me a nervous look, and the Jacobsons sank into ever more sullen silence.

"I see it's just the kids," Gregory said.

"Well, Betty and Clark couldn't come. And the Andrews Sisters all have strep throats."

As Gregory looked annoyed, Don Sweetheart fixed me with a blue stare and laughed.

"I think it's nice," Shirley said. "My parents are *always* around. They don't give me room to *breathe.*"

"Do you hate your parents?" Julie asked. This was her usual party conversation. "Which one do you hate more?"

"I can't stand my father," said one of the Jacobson boys, and his brother cuffed him pretty hard and snapped, "Stop, or I'll tell him you said it."

"I tell them leaving young people alone is a sign of trust," Shirley said.

"Or complete neglect," Julie said.

"You're the hostess of the mad tea party," Don Sweetheart said to me. "Make a joke."

"Her jokes are terrible," Gregory said.

"You're so rude. I thought the line about the Andrews Sisters was cute."

"Oh, that was good, Nora. They'll sign you right up."

"You talk," I said. "*You're* so smart. You're so funny."

"All right." Gregory suddenly turned to a Jacobson boy. "If you don't mind my asking, are you planning to steal the silver?" Irv, his name was, dropped the fork he was examining.

"I was just looking at it," he said in a low voice.

"Get a good look?" A ghastly silence fell as Max served the hamburgers and fries.

"I wanted to see what kind it is."

"It's Gorham sterling," Gregory said, and I kicked him under the table. "You wanted me to talk."

The Sweetheart girls began to giggle, and Don said, "You know what, I'll put on some records. Maybe somebody wants to dance." There was an outdoor speaker.

I smiled gratefully, until it turned out he meant him and Shirley. He didn't dance very well. You could tell he came from California—his shoulders jiggled around and he kept pumping her arm up and down. The rest of us sat watching, the boys twisting in their seats, the girls waiting to be asked.

Gregory leaned over and said in a low voice, "He's a communist."

"What?"

"I'm not going to say it again."

"I *heard* you. I just don't understand you."

"You don't? Where's the dictionary?"

"I *understand* you. I just don't . . ."

"Oh, God," Greg said, then asked Kim to dance. She was bigger than him and she jiggled and joggled her boobs around à la Lake Arrowhead. She was wearing an awful pink sundress. Then Julie got that expression on her face and went into the bathhouse. She was good at it, it was just as though she was going off to pee, and nobody noticed.

Then Nunnally and Dorris appeared, in a carefully planned casual stroll across the lawn. They were charming, they knew exactly what to say. They pretended we were civilized. They even danced—my father's annual dance, like his annual swim. (My mother had once said, "No man worth his salt knows how to dance.") He did all right but he looked as though there were a lot of other things he'd rather be doing. Shortly Gregory looked at his watch, dropped Kim's hand, and came back to where I was sitting.

"God, Greg, did you just leave her there?" Kim was by the lemon tree, looking large and helpless.

"She can walk." He leaned over and went on, "I want you to understand this. The whole family is."

"Is what? What family?"

"The father has been called in front of the Committee. Why are they here?"

"I don't know. Why are you here?"

"I was invited. Is he a friend of Nunnally's?"

"I don't know. I suppose so."

Then several things happened. Dorris and Nunnally left, which was like the exiting of the ward nurses. Everybody went a little crazy. Kim threw her fries at Gregory, who kept saying, "Is this really happening, or am I dreaming?" When Julie's hamburger went into the pool, the Sweetheart girls collapsed in giggles, and then everybody regressed and started pitching fries and pickles around. Don Sweetheart asked me to dance. He said, to the strains of "Blue Moon," "Well, this didn't work out very well."

"What didn't?"

"The party, dope."

"Don't joke about it," I wailed.

"You have to take charge."

"I don't know how."

"All right, I will." He turned and went back to the table. It was the evening for getting left in the middle of the dance floor. "All right—time for a swim," he said firmly. Everybody stared at him. "You heard me, go put on your suits."

"Who put him in charge?" Greg asked loudly.

"I did."

"Why?"

It was because I was a born follower, but I wasn't about to tell him that. We changed into our bathing suits while Max and the maid cleaned up the French fries and pickles and spilled Coke. By the time we were floating around in the milky green water the change in mood was so marked that I decided Don was some kind of genius, until it occurred to me that since he was twenty he looked on the rest of us as a bunch of ridiculous infants. It was amazing he'd come at all, which he told me later in the summer he'd only done to shut his sisters up. He sat on the diving board swinging his legs, the avuncular chaperone, while we played dopey swimming pool games . . . or most of us did.

Julie was in the bathhouse, still in her dress.

"I look fat. I can't bear to go out there."

"Yes you can. It's dark."

"Not that dark."

"They don't care, they'll think you're thin. Get in the water fast and stay there."

Slowly she got into her bathing suit. "I wish I could die."

"Oh, stop it."

She ran out of the bathhouse and jumped into the pool. Under water you couldn't tell anything because bodies looked as though they were dissolving and coming apart and floating around in sections anyway. We kept going underwater to stare at each other but everybody looked surreal, you couldn't even tell girls from boys. Gregory swam over and began talking to Julie, which I thought was very nice of him, but in a few minutes he swam to the shallow end and told me he had to leave.

"If you go everybody will go."

"No they won't. They have to wait for their cars."

"Well, so do you."

"Erique is there right now."

He put on his shirt and grabbed the rest of his clothes. "Walk me to the driveway."

"What's the big rush?" I asked, as we walked dripping through the rose garden.

"I have another engagement."

"What?"

"Well . . ." He sighed. "All right. Promise to keep your mouth shut."

"Of course." I'd promise anything.

"I'm having a . . . thing."

"What?"

"A thing, you know, with . . ." He whispered the name of a well-known actress.

I laughed. "You wish."

"No—I'm serious. Her husband's on location. Erique is totally discreet."

Either he was really good or it was true. "But that's terrible." He was only a year or two older than me. She had to be thirty. Thirty-five.

He laughed. "You don't know anything about anything."

"But how did it happen?"

"It just happened, dope. They were over for dinner one night and at the end I took her up to the room where she'd left her coat."

"Do you mean you actually . . ."

He laughed. "I've said enough. But never mind that, the main thing is for you to get rid of those Communist creeps. I doubt if Nunnally knows about the father."

"If so, he doesn't care, Greg."

"Have you ever heard of guilt by association?" Erique drove up and Gregory threw the rest of his clothes in back. "He could get into serious trouble. I know. A lot of people have."

"Aren't you going to get dressed?"

"What for?" he asked, grinning. "Thanks for the party."

He slammed the door and the car rolled over the concrete to the street. I felt like throwing rocks at it, bricks, chunks of pavement. I didn't know whether it was because of what he had told me or because he hadn't told me more. It was true, I didn't know anything. Still worse, I didn't know how to find out.

A couple of chauffeured cars rolled up the driveway and I ran back through the rose garden to the other party guests. It was a crazy climate, hot in the daytime and then suddenly freezing when the sun went down. Now everybody was dressing and putting on sweaters.

Don shepherded his sisters back through the hedge. Shirley got in one car, Julie in another, and Kim, risking arrest by the local police, said she would walk. The last car was an old Chevy driven by a man who introduced himself as Irv Senior. The two boys managed a couple of dismal thank-you's, but I was still wound up.

"Listen, it was really fun to see you again," I said. It had to be me saying it, nobody else was standing there. "Come over again for a swim, okay? I'll call you." It sounded like my voice.

They looked surprised, but Irv Senior smiled, so I must have sounded as though I meant it. Later I knew that for some reason—which was not apparent at the time—I really had.

THE GIRL IN THE
BLUE VELVET DRESS

IN SHARP CONTRAST, the parties at 204 were glorious.

The buffet table was down in the dining room, the Christmas tree in front of the living room window, the cards standing on the mantel, mistletoe hanging in the front doorway. We had one every year, and the previous Christmas Steve Merrill, the closest thing I had to a boyfriend, had come with his mother.

Among the forty or fifty guests was a thin-lipped blond woman in a turban who was talking about the Red Cross, and her pale abashed son saying he was glad to meet me. We had talked about school, which was all anybody ever talked about to you if you were thirteen. When I offered him some smoked turkey, he said he might puke.

The smoked turkey was black with very white meat. My father sent one every year, a symbolic presence, that and the Royal Riviera pears you could eat with a spoon. The turkey was sliced into slivers that went on pieces of pumpernickel wth dots of mayonnaise. There was always a bowl of red caviar and sour cream, and potato chips, and celery stuffed with Roquefort, and little meatballs in the copper chafing dish.

There were three bars, if a bar is a cluster of bottles and glasses, and a silver bowl of eggnog in a ring of holly, and every once in a while somebody popped open another bottle of champagne.

"Oh, Marion," the voices chorused, "you've done it again. It's perfect . . . the house looks adorable . . . the turkey is marvelous, how sweet of Nunnally to still . . . is that the doorbell? You look divine, oh, the dress is heaven, where did you get it . . . not the Heyns! the Sayres! the McKayes! the Asburys!" Cries of greeting. "I just finished my shopping . . . you wouldn't believe the mobs in Lord & Taylor . . . I couldn't find anything for Ed, for Ned, for Ted . . . the women all get nylons . . . fruitcakes for the teachers . . . money for the maid."

I loved these parties, I wanted them to go on all night. They were so lush, so beautiful and warm and so crammed with sensory joys. Sometimes I just stood in one spot and breathed it all in, wishing it would never stop. That Steve Merrill threatened to puke was a bad sign right from the start, that and a certain musing look that flitted across his mother's face. (Look at this. Isn't it cute. But the turquoise walls . . . and the doggie-spot on the rug . . . and half of these people are drunk.)

I forgot then remembered months later when I went to the Merrills' apartment for dinner. Ginger ale for us, little glasses of sherry for the parents. Lace place mats, cloth napkins, table polished like a mirror. Mrs. Merrill spoke of balls and benefits, Mr. Merrill recounted news from his club. They asked me where our country house was. *Divorce* passed without comment, the movie business drew amused interest—they saw it as an outrageous hobby. Silence as Steve and I stole glances at each other, silence when Mrs. Merrill rang her tinkly little bell for the butler to clear the table. Mr. Merrill told staid little jokes over the meringue glacé. They were the real thing. Nunnally and Dorris could put it on if they chose, but that was Hollywood, where everybody was playing games. The Merrills were diamond-hard authentic.

Steve and his mother left our party before the carol singing and—fortunately—before I got totally drunk. It crept up on me via a glass of champagne that turned into three glasses and some eggnog and a Manhattan mixed by one of two or three male guests who were keeping an eye on me. ("I'll keep an eye on her, Marion, you have enough to do.") One was a terrible son-of-friends, younger than me, whom I ordinarily avoided, and now through the swaying mists his lecherous evil little face winked as he twisted champagne-cork wires into rings for my fingers, and for my friend Anne, who was not far behind. The watchdog adults were helping.

As Anne and I squealed and giggled and flung ourselves around disgracefully, my mother loomed up before me with fire in her eyes. I'd stepped over the line. And we'd crossed swords before the party—I'd archly told her I thought I'd get drunk like everybody else, and to my amazement she turned pale and said if I did she'd never give another party at 204, ever. Anne was by then pushing her way upstairs toward the bathroom to throw up and the room was spinning along with my furious mother and the creepy male guests and the whole party, the more polite members of whom were pretending not to notice.

Anne and I collapsed into bed in our party dresses like two tattered dolls, and woke up with massive hangovers. Anne, whose parents drank too much anyway, was horrified at herself, but I brushed it off as nothing. It was a growing-up ritual, a passage to adulthood. I actually thought—for an unnaturally long time—that there was something smart about it, and even my mother's ongoing, uncharacteristic anger didn't penetrate. While Anne wept with guilt, I made a speech about how the whole thing was learning *how* to drink, the sooner the better. French children had wine with their school lunches . . . and so forth. It was a skill—like learning how to ride a bike, how to smoke. I wasn't entirely wrong, it was just that I completely missed the point.

After the holidays, Steve began writing me from his boarding school.

Dear Nora,

You might not remember but we met at your mom's party. I was slightly green in the face because I had flu and felt like I was going to flash the hash any minute. So you probably managed to forget me.

The other time we met was New Year's Eve at your friend's apartment at the Carlyle. Well your friends parents apartment. A bunch of us were at the Vanguard and the Gate and a few other places. Then somebody said these girls from Hewitts were having a party on 72nd street. So we all got into taxis and went uptown losing a few people in the process and picking up a few more. By then everybody was pretty tanked. The party was full of college people and these guys from Yale kept trying to start fights. It started getting messy and somebody said it was getting close to midnight and he knew a girl who was having a party at the Carlyle.

So we went tearing over even though somebody said he knew her and her parents always locked up the booze, but when we got there your friend had picked the lock of the liquor closet and the lights were out in the living room. A few people were making out in there. Some of us went in to see what was going on. You couldn't see much except the glowing cigarettes and these terrific jazz piano records were playing. We were all kind of groping around and some people lost their dates and found other people by mistake. I ended up on the couch with this girl in a blue velvet dress and you know who that was.

So it's that guy in the dark that's writing you. The one you were with at midnight. The one you got up and left at 12:30. Remember?

It's a little embarrassing to write a girl you've only known under *certain circumstances*. But New Year's Eve gets crazy and my God there was more booze than I ever saw in my life.

I wasn't exactly stone cold sober but I wasn't drunk or anything, I can remember everything . . . the lights from the city shining on your hair and that's why I'm writing.

If you wonder where my date was, I couldn't find her when I left the other party, and later it turned out she left with one of the Yale guys. Nice, huh?

I hope you answer this, Nora, because you're pretty hard to forget.

Sincerely,

Steve Merrill

Dear Nora,

Yesterday was my big day—I got your letter!!!!

Frankly I wasn't sure you were going to answer me. After all, I was just this guy you met in the dark (har, har) I've been trying to remember what we talked about though the time we spent together wasn't mostly talking if you know what I mean (har de har har)

I don't know why I sound so stupid and self-conscious whenever I like a girl.

First I want to explain something you might not understand. Just because we met the way we did doesn't mean I thought you were somebody else. What I meant is, even though it was dark I knew you weren't my date because I lost Debbie at the other party. Of course I didn't know who you were but I knew you were different . . . I always thought she was a nice girl but after that night my whole opinion of her changed. Now we aren't seeing each other any more. I saw her a couple of times to make sure she understood. She cried and said she was drunk New Year's Eve and now the thing with the ass from Yale was over.

I can't believe the way I'm going on and on to a girl I don't even know. I guess I want to be sure you know I want to get to know you as a person and not just somebody on the sofa in the dark. That sounds terrible but I hope you know what I mean, we were all kind of crazy that night. Do your eyes match your dress?

Write soon,

Steve

There had been a hiatus while I brooded over the tangled, subliminal message about the girlfriend. I suspected she wasn't gone, she'd keep turning up crying and apologizing and for some reason he wouldn't be able to tell her to take a walk, he'd go back to her in the end. I wondered how you got to be the kind of girl boys went back to. Some girls had boyfriends they could count on, but I had a feeling I never would, I'd always be wandering and waiting and not understanding anything, and having to take chances all the time. And the girls with boyfriends were the kind of girls who never had to worry about anything anyway, grades or looks or money or anything else, things just fell into place for them. I wondered if there was anything you could do to turn into that sort of a person or if you were just born one way or the other, either always safe or always lost, like being left- or right-handed . . . and it was so complicated I wondered how I'd get through life if everything was going to be like this.

But finally I did answer his letter and we ended up going out over spring vacation. I got a new dress. Ma let me have a facial from her Danish gem. I'd never had a real date before and I made around fifty phone calls to find out what you should wear to the movies and a hamburger afterward, and what you should talk about (him) and how you should act (be yourself).

I arrived under the clock at the Biltmore with advice written on my frontal lobes as though I were going into a final exam. If I'd been wiser I would have known that he was almost as frightened as I was, but I assumed, in spite of evidence to the contrary, that he was some kind of emotional rubberman—fear and complex feelings just bounced off him. We walked along the street in glum silence, our heels tapping loudly on the pavement. My brain was rocketing around in frantic orbits but my tongue was in spasm. I'd followed the dress and hair codes but the idea of presenting my humanity to this stranger was laughably hopeless. How could I be myself, when I didn't know what I was? When we got into the movie I was so relieved I could have wept, and when he dutifully held my hand I grimly thought that this was probably the only way to communicate, these little fleshly joinings. I liked words, loved them, believed in them, but now they had deserted me, even threatened me, because I was afraid that they might turn around and attack both of us.

The movie was at the Sutton on Fifty-seventh Street—we had met at the Biltmore out of sheer ineptitude—and when we came out the western sky was pink and the lights were starting to go on. An opal moon hung on top of the Chrysler Building. New York at dusk has never failed me yet and that day it was like stepping into a better enchantment than other people ever have, a more powerful magic.

Steve and I glanced at each other. He was a ruddy-faced, husky young man with straight brown hair, about my height, given to sniff-ing and clearing his throat. But at that moment he must have felt the same electric quiver as I did, seen the same dancing sparks, for we both broke into broad unjustified smiles and then, finally, stumbled our way into shy sentences. I suspect his heart sprang up too—not from love, about which we knew nothing, but from hope . . . if not this dusk, then some other one.

DRIVE

NOW I WONDERED, every morning as I woke up on Mountain Drive, how I would get through the day. Lacking any real obligations, I made some up. I thought it was necessary to:

Put my hair in metal rollers every night even though it all came out in the pool.

Read more scripts—leather-bound, with glossy stills—which disturbed my father and encouraged him to supply me with better literature from Martindale's—Hemingway and Maugham and Sinclair Lewis, which I read along with *Jesse James* and *Tobacco Road.*

Every day, count the number of boys I had danced with (twelve) or kissed (two). Sometimes I read Steve's letters over. I thought about our date and reexamined it for flecks of sparkle and romance.

Count the number of nice dresses I had (three) in case anybody asked me anywhere. Make sure they were clean and ironed and didn't have any holes in them, and hang them up neatly. Check shoes, handbag, and white angora bolero, underwear and stockings—a readiness idea I got from reading about preparation for earthquakes or atomic war.

Write my friends in New York every week and tell them what a fabulous summer I was having. I improved Brian, the biweekly diving teacher, increasing his bit parts in two pictures to speaking parts in three, slicing twenty years off his age, and hinting that he'd taken me out—I didn't say to a swim meet at a local high school so I could enter the diving contest, which I didn't win. The truth was I hated Brian, his Chiclet teeth and his bronze-blue color and what I was almost sure was toenail polish. When he thought I wasn't looking, he yawned.

I WANDERED THROUGH one silent, sunlit room after another, looking for somebody to talk to. The kitchen was a pretty good bet, Nursie and the cook were often there drinking coffee and discussing their employers sotto voce, eyes darting about. Nursie liked to talk about her Bradfords, the richer, far superior family where she'd worked before.

"*Those* children never could get away with what goes on around here, climbing around and yelling, they had respect or else they heard about it. *She,* Mrs. Bradford, was a real lady, you know." Eyebrows raised. "From a *certain* kind of background. There was simply no discussion, things were always done *correctly.*" And Madam's scarcely worn clothes fitted Nursie exactly—unlike Dorris's, which were too small.

And the cook: "My last place, Mr. W. wasn't such a picky eater and the missus left me alone to do my work. *Some* people, I hate to mention names, are always finding something wrong. And the idea of feeding children all day long . . . the W. children ate the good food that was put in front of them and didn't talk back."

I missed the Swedish family, Lars and hot little Katie. But I'd learned not to get too fond of the help, who came and went so unpredictably. A black couple I'd loved disappeared without explanation, a cleaning woman I had always been glad to see was discovered to be a liar and summarily fired. Pop wrote me about the difficulty of finding good servants, and often I arrived in June to find new faces in the kitchen and pantry. Only thin, dour Nursie remained a fixture.

There were my little sisters to play with. Late in the afternoon when they were already a mess it was fine, but if it was after-bath time any games were accompanied by Nursie's "Don't get her all excited, I just got her dressed. She threw her toys around and I don't want to pick up again. I just braided her hair laced her shoes tied her hair ribbon." When the girls were babies it had pleased me to remove whichever one I found shackled to a potty seat and set her free—which meant being collared and scolded later by Nursie, but I was never sorry.

THEN ONE DAY came an invitation from the Jacobsons, or the older one (not the one who stroked the golden threads and inspected the silver) for Julie and me to go over for dinner. I accepted immediately, then had to argue with Julie, who first considered the whole thing below her, then above her because she was such a loser, then I can't remember what else, but ended up in dizzy delight when Lola said she'd spring for a new dress from Bullocks. I didn't want a new dress. The Jacobsons were in a different loop, I wanted to have a look at it—but I thought I'd better discuss it with my father.

"Gregory Miles says they're Communists," I said. "Is that okay?"

"Why not?"

"It might get you in trouble because of guilt by association."

He chuckled with delight. "That's very funny, darling. I'll tell the Committee."

"What Committee?"

"The one that's perpetrating this foolishness, and driving everybody crazy."

There is a story about Nunnally, possibly apocryphal, that when a Committee member came to his office and asked prying questions, he pulled up his collar, glanced furtively over his shoulder, and hissed, "We're not allowed to tell."

"It isn't so funny," Dorris said.

He lit an Old Gold. "The worst possible thing to do is take them seriously."

"We have to take them seriously."

She told a couple of stories about things that were not funny— people who'd lost jobs, people nobody would hire—but I couldn't get them to tell me what a communist actually was; they kept going back to what had happened to people because they were suspected of being communists. My impressions were largely from a movie called *Song of Russia,* in which happy peasants sang and danced on the steppes. There were close-ups of muscular arms and girls with fat blond braids. It seemed to be meant seriously but I thought it was very funny. Abbott and Costello and *The Great Dictator* had sharpened my eye for the ridiculous—perhaps exactly what my father had been talking about. He was, after all, of the Mencken generation.

CULVER CITY. There were a lot of drive-in hamburger places and used-car lots and the hokey little apartments called dingbats, barren little hills and oil wells. The houses were mostly small one-story bungalows and small cheap ranches. Max parked in front of a yellow bungalow with a couple of fat palm trees like elephants' legs in the front yard.

We rarely went east or south of Beverly, and this could have been another country. We had discussed our wardrobe re our hosts' political sensibilities, and Julie's new dress went into the closet with her other new dresses. Julie said that communists were poor, they *loved* being poor and not owning anything, and they shared everything, even toothbrushes—so we decided to be plain as plain could be, two drab Raggedy Anns.

David, the older one, gave a start as he opened the front door. There was no front hall; you went straight into the living room. It reminded me of the waiting room of Nanny's chiropodist on Second Avenue—plain, beige, boring, but with more books. David invited us to sit down while he brought drinks. The kitchen was nearby and I could hear him cracking icetrays and opening Coke bottles. I was used to the sturdy dwellings of harsher climates and this house felt like a shoebox, as though I could easily punch a hole through the wall. It was not a house to get angry in or tell secrets in, or even to love much—it looked neglected, unimportant to its inhabitants.

It looked the way Julie and I had tried to dress and the way Mrs. Jacobson, who appeared shortly, had succeeded in dressing, as though she didn't care what she had on because she had more important things on her mind—as did Mr. Jacobson, in chinos and an old sweater. From David's appraising glances I was afraid we'd slid over into caricature. The Jacobson men were polite and Irv Junior, of the curious fingers, pulled out Julie's chair at the dinner table—where we went immediately, because the Jacobsons didn't have cocktail hour.

Irv Senior did most of the talking. He said he knew Nunnally a little and admired him because he was one of the few people in town with any principles at all. And it wasn't so easy these days when everybody was walking on eggs and all the rumors were flying around. Mrs. Jacobson said they'd been in Hollywood for a long time and she'd never seen anything like this . . . and more. It was serious talk—no jokes or one-liners, no radar for absurdity that made up conversation as I knew it.

Mrs. Jacobson had cooked the dinner, which was ordinary but serious roast chicken. I was on the verge of repeating Nunnally's admonition to expect borscht or blinis, lox or blintzes, when a warning light went on in my head. Something told me that my father might be able to get away with saying something like that, but I couldn't. I didn't understand about Jews anyway, I didn't know who was and who wasn't, or what being Russian or German had to do with it—not to say who ate what. At that time the secrets of Auschwitz and Dachau (known now—though not then—as the Holocaust) were just beginning to seep out. If I had heard them I didn't understand why anybody would want to torture or kill Jews, which my mother said included most of our friends. The occasional scrap of anti-Semitism that I parroted had been dealt with quickly and sharply by one parent or the other, leaving my conscience clean and me in confusion. And I certainly didn't know what Jews had to do with Communism, which I still didn't understand either. Were the Jacobsons Jews? Did I know, did I care?

When we were finished, the boys cleared the table and Mr. and Mrs. Jacobson disappeared, leaving the four of us sitting there staring at each other. Then David went over to the record player and put on some Bach.

"You look different." He sounded disappointed.

"Do I?"

"At your house, you seemed more like . . ." He cleared his throat. "Like a typical Hollywood girl. That's what all of you seemed like."

"There wasn't a single typical Hollywood girl there except maybe Shirley. I don't even know what a typical Hollywood girl is," I rattled on. "I only live here part of the time. I go to school in New York."

"Well, I had you all wrong, I guess." He collapsed into a chair. The East didn't impress him either.

Now his younger brother took off the Bach and put on Glenn Miller, and he and Julie started to dance. I thought it was very brave and polite of Irv Junior, because she really looked terrible, skinny legs and arms sticking out of a dingy brown dress she'd had for years . . . but then I didn't look any better.

As David drummed on the arm of his chair I began to feel embarrassed. How had we gotten out of the house looking like this? Because Nunnally and Dorris were out and Lola was away and Julie was staying over. There had been nobody around to check us out except Nursie, who said, "Well, that dress don't fit, it's droopy, you better comb your hair, it's all knots, let me polish those shoes for you, that's too plain, why don't you put on a necklace, that thing has spots, what are you wearing those socks for, your father wouldn't like your going out that way," her usual who-cares, talk-to-kids litany that nobody paid any attention to. My little sisters had screamed "YUCK" at the sight of us, but they said it all the time and I paid no attention. David sat in the chair staring woefully at the other two.

"David, where's the bathroom?"

It was a certain kind of vintage L.A. bathroom, with shiny black-and-orange tiles and a five-watt lightbulb. Peering in the little mirror I put on the lipstick I found in the bottom of my purse, along with an old necklace from the Santa Monica Pier. Combed my hair . . . yanked down the neckline of Julie's old dress . . . scratched my cheeks, wiped the look of sad deprivation from my face . . . took off Nunnally's old black socks, which had reminded me of some children's book about Romanian orphans, and stuffed them into my bra.

"Got dressed in such a hurry . . . the brats hid my comb and brush," I said as I came out.

David looked surprised, and Julie looked at me in pained betrayal. But it worked. I got to dance to Hoagy Carmichael.

After a while we went through the kitchen and out into the little square backyard, enclosed with chain-link fencing. Part of it was tiled and all around the edge were bush roses and leggy zinnias and half-dead bird-of-paradise, and growing out of the straggly lawn were the obligatory lemon and lime trees. The people next door were having a cookout and we could hear everything they said. One of them called and asked if we cared to join them, and we thanked him and refused. We could smell the burgers cooking and there was a table with paper plates and ketchup and potato chips and pickles and bottles of Coke and beer.

"Not like your place," David said.

It sure wasn't. "Well, so what."

"I didn't want to ask you here," he said. "I thought you were, you know, a typical . . . "

". . . Hollywood girl."

"That's right. Glamorous."

"Well . . ." It was almost dark. "I wasn't so sure about coming. Because I thought you were communists."

The silence hung over the yard, the house, all the other yards, Culver City. I'd spoken too loudly.

"Where did you get that idea?" he whispered.

"Gregory Miles said so."

"You mean that creep at your house?"

"He's very smart."

"He's not. He's an ass."

"He's an ass too."

It was horrible whispering so we went back inside, but in that house you felt like people could hear you no matter where you were. That's what money could buy, space, thick walls, privacy.

David said, "My parents aren't communists. But so what if they were?"

"So nothing. Why should I care?"

"I think the whole thing is stupid."

"I don't exactly know what a communist is," I said, "but please don't explain, I mean, not now. Maybe another time." I envisioned an hour of lecturing.

"Why not now?" he demanded.

"It always seems to take so long and I never understand, and then I feel stupid . . . and it's all so grim." The dishes were still in the sink and out of habit, as though I were in New York, I began washing them and putting them in the dishrack.

"People say things about my dad. People like your friend."

"So what?"

"So . . . are you serious?"

"I think so," I said. "Why do you listen? Why should he care? Your dad is a real nice guy." I ran water into the sink while David stared at me.

"Well, he's afraid somebody might say something about him, that he's disloyal."

"So what if they do?"

"Because people are scared to death of losing their jobs. This committee investigates anybody who doesn't think the way they do . . . and they think the Russians are evil."

"Well, why doesn't your father do a remake of *Song of Russia,* and show how terrific they really are . . . if they are?"

He stared at me. "Nobody'd produce it, that's why. You really don't get it," he said sadly, almost fondly—and then the door swung open and Irv and Julie came in. I was sure they'd been necking, they had that pink bruised look. I threw Julie a dish towel.

"She's a more typical Hollywood girl," I said. "She's hardly even seen a dish towel. Julie—what's this for?" She'd need to know if she was going to be poor.

"It's for wrapping up rolls."

"We have to go soon." Max was coming back at ten.

"You put lipstick on," Julie whispered, as the boys finished up the dishes.

"You've been necking."

"I hate that word. It's so cheap and juvenile." Her eyes were misty, and she looked almost pretty—which she had been before she got so thin. I rolled my eyes. "You won't believe what we've been talking about."

The cookout neighbors stood in the driveway as we said good night to the Jacobsons, and waved good-bye along with them. They all watched us get into the car. As the big Cadillac rolled down the street I sensed an audience—lights seemed to go on in windows as we went by, unless I was dreaming. It sure was different from Beverly Hills— whether better or worse I couldn't tell.

We went back via Motor Avenue, which was a little out of the way, but Max, who was an okay guy, knew I loved Motor Avenue. It was perfectly straight but it rolled up and down in soft even waves across a golf course, like a long floating ribbon. I have never seen a street like it before or since. I asked Max if I could drive just for a minute, I'd never tell a soul. Lars had let me drive around the block and I'd never mentioned it to anybody till now, but Max said he didn't work for me but for my father and he didn't want to get fired.

Julie was whispering, "Communism is *wonderful*. It's the only hope for the future . . . everybody is equal and happy and you don't have to share toothbrushes. Irv thought that was funny. He's going to give me some books to read, Karl Marx and somebody Lenin. And guess what, I kept part of the dinner down and it was okay."

"It sounds okay," I said. It wasn't for me. I couldn't even get through one evening without lipstick.

"Irv says they all sit around, whole families, talking about ideas and stuff," Julie said, rather wistfully.

"Listen, Jules. You'd better learn to drive. Otherwise you can't see him. Your father hates communists, and Jews too. I heard him say they should all be shipped back to where they came from."

"I'll go on my bike."

"Ten miles to Culver City?"

"It isn't ten miles."

"It's more."

"Lola will take me," she said. She looked happy in the flickering lights, and usually she never looked happy.

WHEN I WAS SMALL there was the concrete . . . white, hot in the sun like a lava flow, hissing with steam when it was hosed. I lay face-down on its rough surface, breathing its raw rocky scent, begging the gardener to spray me all over so I could lie in white clouds until the ground heated up again.

The white streets were divided by a line of black tar, just the opposite from streets in the East, just as the license plates, for a period, were mirror images of each other, the New York one orange with blue letters, the California one blue with orange. Cars in California were kinder, friendlier, almost like pets, rolling in closer to the houses, sometimes grander than the houses; they were cleaner, they smelled better. People loved them more, sometimes they even lived in them for a while. I wanted to drive one badly.

I hung around the garage where Don Sweetheart was painstakingly renovating an ancient forgotten truck—and only the Sweethearts would have trucks or rooms or furniture lying around forgotten. I went over every day and handed him wrenches and oily rags, dropping hints about how terrible life was if you couldn't drive.

"How old are you?" he asked from under the truck.

First I just saw bare feet sticking out of dirty chinos, then part of the rest of him writhed out. I told him fifteen, staring at his bare white chest, with about a dozen blond hairs on it. There hadn't been any wrestling on the floor that year. Self-consciousness had emerged over the winter, along with breasts, though Don didn't appear to notice them.

"You could get a learner's permit, I suppose. Well—okay."

I was stunned at his ready agreement. "When?"

"In a few days, doll, soon as I'm done here." Half a grinning face appeared next to the dusty tire. "It isn't the doing—it's the anticipation."

"No it isn't. The whole idea is, if I could drive, I could take the girls all the places you won't take us." It wasn't really the whole idea.

"Life is about process—not product. The good stuff never comes when you're looking for it."

"PICTURE AN *H* where your right hand is," Don said.

The *H* represented the positions of the gear shift, rising from the floor in a quaint arrangement, which, according to the cognoscenti, gave the driver—or all drivers but me—total control. As I failed to synchronize the clutch, the accelerator, and the gear shift, we screeched out of the driveway accompanied by my gleeful screams and Don's dismayed yells.

At first I thought it was hilarious when dried-out paint cans, ancient tools, and other Sweetheart trash rolled and rattled around the back as we jerked along Sunset. We were surrounded by shiny Caddies, Pontiacs, Packards driven by chauffeurs or very glamorous people in sunglasses, the occasional smooth delivery truck bearing flowers, dry cleaning, groceries, ten-gallon bottles of Arrowhead water. We drove halfway to the beach and back again.

It wasn't easy. The truck would have challenged an experienced driver, and I was young, nervous, nearsighted, and distracted by Don's blue eyes and good-natured chuckle. I started off badly. He was patient with all my mistakes, joking or talking about his geology major while I fought with the clutch. I wondered why he had agreed to this at all. It was probably like the wrestling, he was just bored.

I could not, of course, be closed up in a car with a boy two or three times a week without great explosions of the imagination—nor perhaps could he, nor perhaps anybody—and soon Don began to carefully, subtly come on. First he kept his left arm on the back of the seat. Then on me. Hand on neck—I pretended not to notice. We drove up to Mulholland Drive, which goes along the mountain ridge, at night—so I could learn to do hills and darkness—and then there was some serious neck business. When we pulled over to one of the view spots and looked down at the sparkling city, I thought something was going to happen, but there was only some hand-holding, and I supposed he was in mortal conflict about my age.

Then one day he said, "I want to show you something."

He got in behind the wheel and drove up into the mountains. There were the main canyons, Coldwater and Benedict, that went through to the Valley, but there were also small ones that forked and wound and split into even smaller ones as you went higher, and then trailed off into little pockets of heat and silence and nothing. Don steered around tiny corners and dirt lanes till he got to a certain place where he turned in and parked the truck—which he pretty well had to—and we got out into one of the miniature canyons.

The air was hot, still, fragrant, dangerously quiet. The canyon walls rose sheer and almost vertical. They looked fierce and dry, and it made me dizzy to look up at them, but trees grew right through the rock, and chaparral from the mountain grew down in tufts. It was like being at the bottom of a well, looking up at a patch of blue sky.

It was so dry you could hear the air baking. It was very still, then the silence fragmented as though it were made of a million little dots. Everything separated out—cicadas, crickets, distant bird chatter, far-away traffic, the rustle of small creatures in the dry leaves, the slow dripping of water from somewhere high above—a chorus of minus-cule sounds. A concrete culvert ran down next to the road below, and a tiny stream of water trickled down and a few bright red flowers bloomed in it, seemingly right out of the concrete. There was a very faint, occasional clickety-click, and Don said he had seen pebbles and rocks dancing along in their ordained path, like some giant game of bowls . . . and that this tiny stream had cut the canyon in the first place, eroding it drop by drop over thousands or millions of years into the place where we were standing. Sometimes when it rained the trickle became a torrent, and the culverts, which were all over the mountains, turned into white-water rapids—sometimes bringing down boulders and hunks of mountain and depositing them at the bottom.

After a few minutes we got back in the truck. As we drove down the mountain, I felt as though I were leaving some lost memory or dream . . . and I wondered why certain things here, the land, the light, the smells, the things that grew, had such a potent familiarity, and why 625 Mountain Drive, comfortable and charming to its inhabitants, was, to me, only a dull pleasant hotel where I was assigned to put in time.

"Why did you take me there?" I asked, as we came down to rooftops and familiar streets.

"Because I'm a geology major," he said, "and because I get tired of hearing you bitch about California."

"But I don't."

"You do all the time."

Maybe I did. Usually I didn't take the place seriously, I thought the whole state was like the back lot . . . but I was a native, in me was a col-lective California unconscious that mostly slept but awoke every once in a while and reminded me where I had come from.

The strangest thing was that when we were in the canyon I hadn't thought once of hands on necks, or whatever was between Don and me (virtually nothing except what I made up), though now that we were down again my mind was going back into the same old soup. If I could only keep it on the mystic canyon I'd be a better person—and maybe that was why he took me there. I thanked him till he said, "Oh, *please*," grinning, and I got out of the car and ran home before I spoiled it.

SALLY . . . cute Sally, who hung from rings upside-down. Who had pierced ears. The kind of blonde who gets a good tan. She lived on Doheny . . . she was studying acting. So dense was he, or so immune did he think I was from ordinary human responses, that he never tried to hide her existence. When he began bringing her up as a topic of general interest, like D-Day, my driving dropped back badly. We backed into a palm tree; I almost stripped the brakes.

"What's the matter with you?" he yelled. "You were doing all right."

"It's this awful truck," I said crossly.

"Don't you realize that if you can drive this thing, you can drive anything?"

"I only want to drive an ordinary car."

"You'll thank me someday, doll." He twisted a piece of my hair.

"Did you ever take Sally to the magic canyon?" I asked. Silence—the kiss of death.

In front of the Beverly Hills Hotel is a traffic light where Benedict Canyon, Beverly, and Cañon Drives all cross Sunset. As I looked at Don, stricken, the light turned red and there was a mean crack as we went into the back of a sleek café-au-lait Cadillac. There were no seat belts or straps; by then we were used to grabbing the wheel or each other. As the horror sank in, the café-au-lait chauffeur jumped out and, doing a little hysterical dance, assessed the damage, and then traffic police appeared. One waved the traffic by in the other lane, and one got out of his car, swaggered over, and put a foot on the running board. The stern face of the law appeared in the window.

"Well"—looking around at the rolling junk shop and smiling evenly. "Well"—holding out his hand for our papers and my learner's permit.

"Oh, man." Don was digging through the crammed glove compartment.

"It might interest you to know that you've just slammed into the rear bumper of Mr. Sam Goldwyn."

"Oh, I'm so sorry," I wailed. "I'll tell him how sorry I am."

"I doubt he cares a patooty whether you're sorry."

I needed Lars, I needed the guardian agent . . . anybody who could talk us out of this. Don and I were too stunned, or too innocent or stupid to drop Nunnally's name, which would have gone a long way toward erasing the whole business. I was a novice (and ever remained) at the delicate art of "pull" and was afraid of using the wrong tone of voice and further infuriating the cop, or sending him off into peals of laughter. "And my mother is Judy Garland," he'd hoot.

Besides, I didn't understand the range of this kind of power. I thought it was strictly limited and assumed that name-dropping wouldn't apply here, because Nunnally and Sam Goldwyn were at different studios. Everything I'd heard about the tightness of studio management, about actors being "borrowed" and "loaned," had sunk in deeply. Fox, MGM, Paramount, and the rest had their own laws and police, and I suppose I thought of them as small political entities, little Balkan countries within the city of Los Angeles. My father would only shrug and say, "What can I do? That's how they do it over at MGM." And so I said nothing.

Don was badly shaken—he had a pink-eyed rabbity look as he frantically fished in the back for documents, and when I thought of Mr. Sweetheart, I didn't blame him. The Beverly Hills cop was kicking the truck fender and saying, "Where'd this thing come from, anyway?" There was a little genial back-and-forth but when I said I lived in New York he seemed annoyed, more so when the dog-eared documents Don finally came up with turned out to be badly out of date.

The real punishment of a car accident is the tedium of mopping up.

We signed things, wrote down names and phone numbers, and were made to get out and inspect the damage so Mr. Goldwyn's dented bumper would be engraved on our lawless minds forever. Through the window I saw a straw hat and a pair of broad shoulders in a pale jacket, very still and straight.

Don insisted on driving home, while I sat blubbering apologies. I kept telling myself that if I could drive this truck I could drive anything, but it didn't help.

"I'll pay for it," I said.

"The insurance pays, you jerk," he said. "That isn't the point." He dropped me off without a word.

"I feel terrible. I'm sorry, I'm sorry."

When I told my father that evening he said, "Why didn't you tell Sam who you were?"

"But he doesn't know me."

"He knows who I am, for God's sake." He had passed the time in his life where he was truly responsible for life's minor miseries, and I suppose the teaching opportunity escaped him.

But Mr. Sweetheart had given Don hell and grounded him, his sisters told me—and now Don behaved as though it were all my fault, which it was only partly—he was the one who let the papers get out of date. He acted as though I had typhoid—and nothing his sisters said could get him to even talk about it. But I was beginning to see that boys never talked about anything, you just had to figure things out for yourself.

Then I thought I had and I went over one day when everybody seemed to be out, and only Don's car—his real car, the one he wouldn't let me drive—was in the driveway. I went in the side door and found him in the baronial living room playing Meade Lux Lewis records, and I sat next to him on the floor.

"Listen, it was all my fault," I said. "I should have told the cop who I was and they would have just let us go home."

"What do you mean, who you were?"

"Am. Who I am. Nunnally's daughter. I should have told him."

Don stared at me. "Don't go on with this."

"Kiss me," I said. To my amazement he did—maybe he couldn't think of anything to say so he did this instead. So that was three.

"That didn't mean anything," he said when we'd finished.

"I don't care."

"It was kind of a mistake."

I looked at his bare feet on the Oriental rug, the bolo tie around his neck. "Why?"

"You're just a kid," he said. "You don't know anything. You add two and two and get five or three and a half. I keep waiting for you to do just one thing that's right—just one. It's going to take you forever to understand *anything,* and I don't feel like hanging around."

ONE FOR MY BABY

JULIE SAID on the phone, "They're leaving the country. Mr. Jacobson can't get work here . . . they can't even pay the rent on that stupid little house. Irv and I are going to be parted forever."

I always listened patiently to Julie. Every kiss, how the state was going to wither away, how everybody was going to be equal and happy. How *fat* she was—which meant looking at her in the nude and swearing that she was *thin*. Lola drove her to Culver City and left her with Irv while she had lunch with some disaffected friend, then picked her up later. After a couple of martinis Lola didn't care what was going on—which wasn't much in the thin-walled little house with unemployed parents wandering in and out. The full-body inspection was for some misty future time when she would sweep in somewhere looking like Rita Hayworth—and Irv would tenderly remove her Adrian gown and go mad at the sight of her beauty.

"Listen, Julie. We're having a party, do you want to come?"

"They're going to England. Why don't you invite a boy?"

"There isn't one."

"You're better off. Maybe I'll come just for a few minutes," Julie said.

"You'd better, they don't do this very often. Dorris says giving parties is worse than major surgery."

It was like Carthay Circle.

The Cadillacs turned into the driveway, the chauffeurs hopped out and opened the car doors . . . the stars descended. Lit by the blue lights under the shrubbery, they moved up the front steps, past the azaleas and the gardenias, through the door into the hall—the Humphrey Bogarts, the David Nivens, the James Masons, the Johnny Mercers, the Dave Chasens, and the Gene Fowler Jrs.; my older half sister, Marge, and her husband.

There were joyful cries of greeting and a lot of kissing and embracing. It was before mass hugging started. In New York people pecked you on the cheek or just stood there, pulling their gloves off and talking about the weather. These embraces were floating and tentative, the greetings of delicate, careful butterflies—couture and coifs came first.

I'd expected beauty, confidence, amour propre, but not such oceans of affection. *My* party guests had been close to hostile. These people appeared to be happily married—at my party not a single boy had paid more than three seconds' attention to any girl. Did such fondness of heart come of fame, beauty, talent, wealth—or was it something else entirely? Why were they all so happy? But then, what was there for them to be unhappy about?

You'd never have guessed that Dorris had spent the previous three weeks in a kind of extended anxiety attack, a combination of frayed nerves, stubborn persistence, and occasional tears that in some miraculous way merged into an iron fist of efficiency. Now, in a golden satin dress that almost matched her hair, she was dazzling . . . prettier than my mother, I had to admit, and without the insolent vanity common to beautiful women. My mother preened and purred at herself in the mirror; Dorris was serious and critical about her image.

She took her guests on the customary house tour. It was quite a sight, this flock of peacocks in long sweeping skirts of chiffon and taffeta, ivory and pale green and buttercup yellow and crimson; graceful arms and necks decked with dazzling jewelry; silky hair swept up in curls, falling over shoulders, or pulled back in shiny buns. Julie and I straggled along, following the stars into powder rooms (there were two) to see who yanked at girdles and pulled up stockings, who reapplied what makeup, who picked her teeth and who surreptitiously sniffed her armpits, who took an incredibly long time on the toilet.

In the living room, Max passed glasses of champagne while my little sisters, in bathrobes and bunny slippers, followed with nuts and canapés. Hjordis Niven and Betty Bacall lounged on the serpentine sofa, Pamela Mason held forth in the middle of the shag rug. James, seemingly a little shy, stood by the piano. Ginger Mercer and Maude Chasen were in a corner with their carefully curled heads together, Bogey, Nunnally, Marjorie, and Gene stood laughing by the bar. Ice clinked against glasses, lighters clicked, matches scratched, smoke billowed from red mouths, and laughter burst forth in joyous peals.

Then the best-looking man in the room, in the best-tailored tux, left his beautiful Swedish wife and came in my direction . . . David Niven! And he found something interesting to talk about for ten minutes or so, fixing me firmly with big, intelligent eyes and a beguiling smile, in an accent not *so* British as to be incomprehensible, and appearing to listen attentively. He neither turned his profile, nor glanced into the mirror over the bar. I would go through the next year or two comparing him to every male person I encountered: "*He* isn't like David Niven," and I would always be right.

On the dining room table were candelabra, gardenias floating in crystal bowls, silver ashtrays and cigarettes in tiny silver cups and initialed matchbooks, English china and Danish silver. I had been afraid nobody would talk to us, but Betty Bogart turned out to be a smart, nervy girl from Brooklyn, willing to joke with me, and Julie had James Mason next to her and Johnny Mercer just across . . . which would have made up for being ignored by the rest. But we were not, and we had squab and asparagus with hollandaise sauce and chocolate mousse.

After dinner the men settled back with snifters of brandy and cigars while the women went upstairs and sat around Dorris's bedroom seraglio-style. The maid served demitasse while Max Factor was reapplied, hair was touched up, cigarettes were lit with golden lighters, stocking seams straightened and garters adjusted—revealing who wore garter belts and who wore girdles. There was a lot of rustling in and out of the dressing room and the bathroom, with accompanying sound effects—running water, plumbing gasps and gulps, the clink-clink of jars and bottles, and the snap of handbag clasps. After a while, everybody moved on to the nursery to admire the sleeping children and the skill of Nursie, doing her microscopic needlework on little sunsuits and matching bonnets.

BACK IN THE living room, the guests were . . . well, mushier. Previously straight backs curved and hunched, clear voices got raspy and loud. Tuxes hunched up and shirtfronts bulged. After-dinner decay had set in—loaded ashtrays, sticky brandy snifters and watery highballs, half-eaten mints on little monogrammed napkins, bent matchbooks. The noise level was high; there was a burst of laughter every minute or so. Essential as it was to be comely, it was the raconteur who held the room still—for Hollywood was really a golden encampment of storytellers. During one of the lulls came a low voice near the fireplace:

"Who dug that thing up?"

Johnny Mercer—bald, glassy-eyed, sprawled in an armchair—was addressing Julie, standing by the mantel in a clingy black dress. First she didn't hear, then she did.

"It's a skeleton on a diet."

Drunks, in my experience, were usually cheerful and silly, putting lampshades on their heads, or else rubber-legged like my father. Johnny Mercer was the first bad one I'd seen in action. With fearful accuracy he'd zoned in on the most fragile person in the room. Julie gasped, cringed, looked around for escape . . . but the door to the hall was a mile away. I moved carefully toward her, though in truth I was afraid of the man.

Julie's puckered, tight look, the one that previewed tears, and the abrasiveness of Mercer's voice began to attract attention. People turned, voices dropped to a murmur . . . there were glances and a couple of quick whispers. A savior was assigned—a supersavior with an odd-looking smile and horsey teeth. Bogey went over to the armchair and said something inaudible to Mercer, then moved on to Julie, who by then was reaching blindly for the fire tongs—why, I wasn't sure, but there were worse things she could have been doing. She looked at Bogey—I waited for "Do you hate your father? Do you love your mother?"

He said something to her, I couldn't hear what, and her face lit up. She never told me what it was, but later she said he made her forget the Jacobsons, as well as forgive me the ten minutes of undivided attention from David Niven (which had not gone unnoticed), and best of all he made her feel lovely without actually saying so. Well, sure; this was, after all, Humphrey Bogart.

People working on a picture had to be at the studio at seven, so Hollywood parties usually ended early. People got up and started moving toward the door, all but the figure in the armchair. He was nodding, tapping on his knee, humming . . . a hum that started aimless, like an engine starting, then turned into a gravelly voice singing his own "One for My Baby and One More for the Road." Everyone turned to listen to the beguiling boozy croak. I thought I'd hate it, coming out of this man, and I waited for flat notes and unfunny lyrics. But it was irresistible, it was like honey.

Maybe it was all about talent. If you had it, you would be forgiven anything.

AND ONE MORE FOR THE ROAD

ERIQUE SAID, "I am required to ask of you to remove your shoes not to soil the fur rug." I looked down. So it was. Naturally.

"Sure," I said, prying off each sandal with the opposite toe. This was going out the driveway. By the time we were on the Strip I'd been told not to spill Coke on the upholstery.

"Anything else?" I asked.

"Nothing furthermore," he replied. He had some kind of weird accent.

"Does Mr. Gregory go a lot of places?" I asked.

"It is not for me to reply, Miss."

I sank down in my seat and stared out the window. The price for this was high, but I'd been desperate. I'd asked Don Sweetheart if he could take me but he was still grounded. He'd been lying on the living room floor with his bare feet tangled in the record albums strewn around him on the Persian rug. They hung open, the records falling out of their slots, and Don's bare toes stuck through two of the circle holes. He was beating out Glenn Miller on his bare pale chest. When I told him where I wanted to go he looked amazed. The Sweethearts were unlikely to be in such a situation and even if they were, nobody would know about it. But on my side of the hedge it was different. It was painful, I'd be going back east soon and he wouldn't even notice I was gone.

"Have you ever known anybody who went to Rancho Tranquillo?" I asked Erique.

"It wouldn't be my place to reply to that, Miss."

Of course he'd been there, merely by chance, a dozen times. It was a wonderful place, everybody in the Business went there. He would recommend it for his own family. And so forth. We rattled through Fullerton and Yorba Linda. The fabled desert was a bleak moonscape with occasional strings of matching bungalows. Dust and sand blew across the road and into the car window and onto the fur rug. I'd thought Greg might come along for moral support or just for laughs, but oh alas, he was going to the Bel-Air Bay Club with "people." I couldn't avoid explaining the whole thing to him, which brought forth a lecture on the quality of my friends and how if I wanted to improve myself I'd find better ones. Communists, psychotics, and campus dolts (Don) would get me nowhere; no wonder I couldn't adjust to Beverly Hills. But I could borrow Erique, Erique who had to be back by six-thirty because Greg had a reservation at Romanoff's.

If you blinked you'd miss the tiny golden RANCHO TRANQUILLO sign buried in a grove of eucalyptus. The road burrowed through scrubby woods and wound through the foothills as we approached the mountains that separate Los Angeles from the rest of the world. Then we climbed through clumps of trees and scrub, nimbly rounding hairpin turns till the road spread out and flattened into a vast parking lot with a mountain view. Beyond was what appeared to be a resort hotel, a complex of pseudo-adobe buildings tangled in the trees like a trompe l'oeil.

Erique parked and I went inside. There was a big white room with leatherette seats and a woman with platinum hair sitting behind a desk. She looked me over and asked who I wanted to see, then told me to go out to the Patio Grande and turn left.

Julie was sprawled in a lounge chair near a century plant like the ones that flank Beverly Hills garages. They were big, weird succulents, and when we were little we'd break off big hunks and drip the clear jelly sap onto our arms and legs, then rub it in . . . God knows why. There was a huge lawn with a fence all around and little round beds of cactus and begonias, and people were slumped in lounge chairs or seated in patio chairs smoking. The visitors sat up very straight and brisk, holding fruit baskets and boxes of cookies. At first it looked like a summer outing or reunion of some sort, then you saw the staring into space and picking at the grass.

Julie looked pale and skinnier than ever, and her dirty blond hair was straight and dull, as though the color had been leached out of it. A cigarette hung out of her mouth. She was wearing an old pair of white shorts and a man's shirt, and let's be charitable and say I'd seen her look better.

"I can't believe you came," she said.

"Of course I did."

She pulled out a pack of Luckies and began digging into it. The place was pretty nice. Beyond the wide lawn was a swimming pool and some empty tennis courts. A few people in chaps and ten-gallon hats were riding horses slowly around a ring. The only anomaly was the occasional nurse wandering by.

She went through the whole smoking thing, scrunched out one cigarette in an overflowing ashtray, dug another out of the pack, and lit it and blew out the match. "How did you get here?"

"Gregory Miles's chauffeur brought me."

"What?"

"Well, Max couldn't come because Dorris is pregnant and she needs him every day, and . . ."

"She's pregnant?" Julie's eyes widened.

"Well, so what? She's always pregnant."

"God. Why does she want so *many*?"

"How should I know?" I shrugged. "I guess she likes kids."

"Lola can't even stand having two."

"My mother wanted six but something was wrong with her, and she could only have me. Or that's what she said, anyway." She could have made it all up. It was hard to know what any of them really meant.

"You'll never believe who's here." Julie named three major stars, all ravishing, talented, and, according to *Photoplay,* happy as humans could be. "They brought V. here in a straitjacket. She was screaming and saying she had to get in here *fast* because the barbarians are at the gate. And you know what—she's right." S. couldn't stop crying and was given insulin shock treatments, which Julie described in detail. "You wouldn't believe what she wears to dinner. She has this kind of Turkish outfit, balloon pants and floaty top, all purples and reds, and a fez hat. And bare feet. And her hair's growing out and there's about three inches of gray."

"Gray?" I screamed.

"Ugly frizzy gray . . . she's much older than you'd think. About forty-five." She smiled wanly. "She doesn't wear any makeup here."

There was a silence and then I said, "When are they leaving?"

"They've already gone."

"If he can't get a job there, will they come back?"

"How the hell should I know?" She was staring at her palm, twisting her hand slowly back and forth.

She jumped to her feet and began walking away very fast, me at her heels. I could hardly keep up with her. We were going around the lawn like a couple of trotters for the second time when she threw over her shoulder, "I took a whole bunch of Lola's pills. Benny found me."

Tears came into my eyes. "Why didn't you throw up?"

"I don't know. The one time . . . I don't want to talk about it." There was a long silence, then, "If they were staying I'd be okay . . . I'd stop barfing. I'd . . . stop . . . barfing." She was almost chanting. "I'd stop being such a bitch. It's just that I get so lonely. I wish I was Dorris, she's so lucky."

I wanted to say I wasn't so sure, but it wasn't the time to go into all that. I looked across the lawn to the main building where an odd figure, in pale gray cap and uniform, stood waving its arms and flapping its hands.

"That's Erique," I said. "I have to go."

Julie grabbed my arms, a peculiar gesture for her—like the rest of her family she wasn't a toucher. Her big hazel eyes were dark.

"Thanks for coming. I'm sorry I'm like this. I'm so, so sorry. That business at the party . . . that was almost my favorite song."

"He was just drunk, Julie."

"Oh, right. *Just* drunk."

I felt almost sick. Erique's gestures indicated imminent departure: *if you aren't in the car in two minutes you can take a hike.* I was almost glad; she was starting to burn up.

"I have to go, Julie."

"Maybe they'll come back." Her eyes shone with lunatic hope. "You're so lucky to have Nunnally. He's per-fect." She was still hanging on my arm. "Things like this don't happen in your family."

"Other things do."

"But somebody fixes them." She licked her dry lips. "I'm scared I'm going to lose it again."

"You won't. You're going to be fine."

I turned and ran across the lawn after Erique. Julie stood by the cactus on her little stick legs, smoke rising from her cigarette. She would have looked about eight years old if her eyes hadn't been so dark and desperate. After I looked once I didn't look back again.

Erique had had a great time with the other chauffeurs. He'd found things out I wouldn't believe, not that he was at liberty to tell. Things were not always what they seemed. People had problems you'd never suspect. Respectable families—Erique thought movie people were respectable—didn't let such things out. But he always knew they were there, and he knew which ones were going to get worse. Alcohol was usually part of the trouble. But there were some families that just didn't have the will to make things better. And they pulled everybody down with them, even those who tried to help.

WITH THE GREATEST OF EASE

I WROTE TO Steve Merrill and told him I was giddy from the parties I was going to in L.A. and that I'd never had such a terrific suntan, and he wrote back about what a great time he was having sailing on the Cape. His letter was mostly about jib sheets and spinnakers, but it ended:

> There's a certain *girl in a blue velvet dress* I haven't seen in three months. I can't believe I'm actually looking forward to the beginning of school!!!!! Not that boarding schools let people have a normal social life but your school has a *calling hour* and you can bet I'll come to see you. So if there's a big drooling hairy beast howling at the front gate you can tell the headmistress it's a friend of yours (har, har) and she better let him in OR ELSE!!!!!!!!!
> All my love,
> Steve Merrill

There was a visceral thrill to *all my love,* and I'd carried his letter around for a week and read it three or four times a day. I had a serious problem about answering, which had to do with sailing and Center Island and the war ending and Jo.

It had started four years before with the cottage. The idea, my mother had said, was to remodel it and sell it at a profit. At ten, I didn't really grasp the last part, but I liked the idea of home improvement and I wanted to be in on it. I said I didn't want to go to California that year, not really expecting anybody to listen, but to my surprise they agreed.

But instead of letting me stencil walls and grow herbs in pots, my mother sent me to the nearby Seawanhaka Junior Yacht Club to learn sailing and improve my social skills. It was not a success. I was terrified of the young Roosevelts and Rockefellers and their Seabirds, I hated the filthy clubhouse with wet towels and old sneakers everywhere and the sour-smelling kitchen where we made peanut-butter-and-jelly sandwiches, the rocky Sound beach and the August tides of jellyfish, the barnacle-encrusted pier that bloodied your legs. I was not a sailor. I made so many mistakes that nobody took me out except for ballast. The *only* thing I learned that summer was many, many four-letter words, most of which I had never heard. In some cases it took years . . . decades . . . to find out their meanings.

When I tried to compose a reply to Steve about sailing, to demonstrate how much we had in common, I couldn't get past all that or the bottom-line truth that we didn't really belong to Seawanhaka, because there was no father in a yachting cap, and any attempt to hide these essentials would reek of falsehood. I had told Steve that my father was in the movie *business,* trying to make it sound more reputable. Steve showed only polite interest. His circle had nothing to do with the entertainment world—Dad was a banker.

• • •

I HAD A POOR GRASP of our place in the world. I didn't know whether we were rich or poor or medium . . . or what. Nunnally was rich, but Ma was a puzzle. Our brownstone off Third Avenue seemed several notches below my classmates' apartments, with their doormen and elevators and marble hallways. Oh, 204 was cute. It was fun. I loved it, everybody loved it, but it was ragtag—things creaked and squeaked, they broke and fell apart. You loved it for its puppy-dog charm. But Third Avenue had the el noise and drunks curled up in doorways and scuzzy Irish bars. It didn't have class . . . *we* didn't have class. We had a Jeep and a tumbledown shack in the country, with homemade curtains and hand-painted walls. We didn't do things right. We never got the dog spayed, we were always giving away puppies. We rode to town on plastic bikes. I had the privations of war mixed up with wealth and poverty and class and cute. And it was hard to know what my mother meant by remarks like, "Oh, damn, I'm broke again," which appeared to be apocryphal, since nothing changed much.

THEN SHE REALLY DID sell the cottage and bought another house, and then traded that for another, and by the end of the war we had Windswept—a refurbished stable on a hill with gardens and a long curving driveway and great oaks and maples. The living room had ceiling beams and a fireplace and refinished oat bins and three rooms that had been the stalls. At the north end was a glassed-in porch that looked out over the woods and the lawn sweeping down to the Sound and the Seabirds rocking on their moorings.

The houses came and went almost soundlessly—my mother was, after all, picking her way between my Hallmark heart and the bottom line. I had wept over each sale. But Windswept, I believed, would be forever. She couldn't sell this one, this Chesterfield home that no one could ever disapprove of. Windswept gave us a chance, except . . . except Jo was there and he was half-owner. And he set up his easels and canvases in one of the stalls, and Ma looked frozen the way she did when I was making it obvious I didn't like him.

So every time I unfolded the increasingly grubby *all my love* I wondered whether I could ever invite Steve Merrill there and show him that we were okay . . . in case he was wondering. Jo was dark and saturnine, he wore no yachting cap. How would I introduce him, how would he behave? And he wasn't even a naval officer anymore, he was just a bad-tempered guy painting pictures in the bedroom.

I'd call him "our houseguest."

THE ONLY OTHER THING to tell had to do with my half sister Marjorie, who was thirteen years older than me. (Nunnally and his first two wives, Alice and Marion, had all been together on the *Brooklyn Daily Eagle* in the twenties.) Marge and Gene Fowler Jr. were film editors, then known as cutters. She had edited two of Nunnally's pictures, and Gene was associate producer of another two. At that time they were both well on their way to the top of their field.

My father had longed for his children to be close, or at least to get along. But Marge and I were too far apart in age, and too rarely together—and she and Ma were contentious. To me Marge was an enviable free spirit, bold and fiercely honest, even a daredevil. From my early years I remembered green nail polish, loud singing in the shower, disreputable boyfriends with motorcycles, and some disgraceful escapade—she had run away and been brought back by the police. Then she had wanted to be a nightclub singer, and practiced in front of the mirror to radio music—Veronica Lake hair flopping, hips swinging, fingers snapping.

She never had much use for me, but for Nunnally's sake she did her best, and usually took me somewhere when I was in California. This time it was to the airport, where she and Gene, who had been in the air force, did stunt flying for fun.

Gene took me up in a two-seater tandem plane. He sat in front and

I sat behind. We were strapped in, wearing goggles; there was no roof. He had a one-way phone, and he'd say "Now we're doing a snap roll" or "Get ready for a barrel roll," while I hung on and screamed. The scenery went spinning around—the ocean was on top and the mountains were upside down, the ground was all over the place. The last thing was gliding upside down. When the plane landed I was so dizzy I could hardly walk. I got out of the cockpit and staggered over to a corner and retched and retched some more.

First Margie and Gene thought it was funny, though when I actually threw up they stopped laughing. They put me in the backseat of the car where I curled up in a sick heap. Back at the house they took me inside and dumped me on the bed, where I pressed my face into the pillow and didn't dare open my eyes because everything was still heaving. Marge sat on the bed and talked about Jo and how he was a perfectly nice guy and I shouldn't stand in the way of my mother's future, and if I loved her I'd want her to be happy. I said she had it all wrong, Pop had been the love of her life. Then Pop came home. He came in and took a look at me, then gave Marge hell out in the hall. I wished he wouldn't because she didn't like me much anyway, and this would only make it worse.

"ALAMOGORDO is up that way, on the mesa," Gregory said.

I'd slunk out of town. Pop was at the studio, the kids and Nursie were out somewhere. I'd gone to Dorris's room to say good-bye. She was in bed—white as porcelain, her spun copper hair in a delicate curtain over half her face, her green eyes wide. I asked what was wrong and she shrugged. Just pregnancy. And she was tired, sometimes everything got to be too much. The house . . . the children . . . the undependable help . . . the social obligations . . . all the responsibilities of being a Hollywood wife, it was like running a corporation. And for Nunnally everything had to be perfect. He wouldn't eat this, he wouldn't eat that—what he really wanted was his mother's cooking. And she always had to look her best, look at the competition—which meant constant trips to the hairdresser and shopping and endless fittings, and facials and massages and all that. And the obligations were piling up again, they'd have to entertain again soon, and even the idea made her want to crawl under the bed and never come out.

The room was gold and mossy green, fragrant and quiet. I liked it when she talked like this, it made her more human and fallible. I told her she did everything perfectly—but she only sighed and smiled ironically, as if to say, "Thanks for trying, but we both know everything around here is out of control and you're just trying to be polite." We had an exchange like this every once in a while and I never knew what to say. She had no idea how puzzled I was at her dissatisfaction. I thought she did everything flawlessly. So I ended up thanking her and saying I'd had a wonderful summer—which Pop had told me to do, which I hated because it proved that I wasn't family.

I had to leave from Union Station; Max had an errand to do downtown. And then guess who got on at Pasadena . . . and so what?

"What's Alamogordo?"

He put down his fork. "Don't you read the papers?"

"No."

"It's where they tested the atom bomb, you moron. The land of the mushroom cloud."

"I don't want to hear about it."

He said, "Don't tell me you've picked up that terrible stuff from those awful people."

"What people?"

"The ones you hang around with."

"I don't know what you mean. It scares me, that's all. Tell me about your summer, Greg. M. must be drowning in tears."

He froze. "Don't mention her name." I made a face, and his eyes blazed. "I don't want to discuss it."

We'd made it over the Sierras and now we were heading into the Rockies. The high desert was violet in the setting sun, with tones of red and gold and green flooding it like plumes of dye.

"I wish to God we could order a bottle of wine. A Médoc would be nice—something unpretentious. Do you know anything about wine?"

"No. Why should I? I'm having the steak," I said. "I can tell this is really going to be fun."

"What do you mean, *this*?"

"The trip. Us back on the train together."

"It isn't supposed to be fun. There isn't any *us.* It isn't a *date*—it's an accident. I was hoping I'd be alone, the office was sure nobody else would be on board . . . except Claudette. And I don't feel like talking."

"Then why are you sitting here?"

"Because I ran into you while you were waiting for a table and didn't think I could politely get out of it."

I crossed my eyes and stuck my tongue out, while Gregory stared out the window pretending he didn't know me. We ate in sulky silence and after I'd finished my strawberry shortcake I got up and left. I didn't see him till the middle of Dull Day in the observation car, where I was writing a long, very bad poem.

"Sorry." He told me he and M. had parted for reasons beyond my ability to comprehend, which he wasn't about to explain.

"Gregory, why are you like this?"

"Like what?"

"Critical. Big chip on your shoulder all the time."

"I'm none of those things but if I'm not Happy Hooligan it's probably because I'm going back to school, which will be complete torture."

"What's the matter with school?"

"I'm not the type."

"Well, that's the truth. I can't wait to get to Andover. To be honest I was bored to death all summer."

He pulled a Camel out of the pack and lit it slowly. "Poor baby. Didn't anything interest you at all?"

"Well . . . there was one dinner party." I reeled off the cast, told him all about it. When he looked envious I was delighted.

"That's the stuff of history," he said.

"It was just Hollywood."

"What you don't understand is that *Hollywood is history.*"

Out the back window the track whipped out from under us like a casting line. We were swinging down some low hills somewhere in the middle of the country. It was almost dark; heading east the time rushed in toward us, crumpling up like the contents of a file. I wondered if we'd end up in his compartment again and if so why I would be unable to say no, and why I usually never said no to people.

Gregory said, "I don't get it. On one coast you have a life and a family some people would die for. On the other you have a divorced mother and her boozy friends and the Third Avenue el."

"You don't know anything about it!" I said furiously.

"I have a working brain." He looked surprised when I stood up. "Where are you going?"

"I don't have to listen to this."

"Has she got a boyfriend?"

"Dozens!"

"Hurray for Mom." He was sitting there with cigarette smoke curling out of his lips, up into the unruly brown hair falling over his forehead. He looked profoundly unhappy.

"For your information, we have a fabulous house on Long Island with lawns and stables and yachts and rose gardens, it's gorgeous, but you'll never know because you'll never see it. Other people will, all my other friends are going to be invited to Windswept for weekends, but *you never will.*" I turned to flounce out.

"Go ahead, go stick your head in the ground. You just can't stand hearing the truth," he said loudly, as the five other people in the car looked up from their newspapers and magazines.

I went through six cars as fast as I could. He could come and pound on the door of my roomette, shouting eternal truths, and I'd never open it.

As I was standing there a door at the end opened and a man and a woman came out of their compartment. The woman was slender with short curly hair . . . it was Claudette Colbert and her husband, Dr. Joel Pressman. They came toward me, single-file, which was the only way you could walk through the train corridor. She was wearing an outfit like the one she had on in *It Happened One Night.* You could see why Clark Gable was crazy about her and why the sight of her legs brought the passing cars to a screeching halt. She was pretty and smart the way girls were in a certain kind of movie, and when they played dumb everybody knew it was kind of a game or a joke.

Oh, how much better I could have been! Gregory was like Clark or one of those smart newspaper guys—they were rude and bossy and they thought they knew everything—but if you were Claudette or Myrna Loy or Bette Davis you could spin one around on the palm of your hand, smile and say something clever and charming, and the guy wouldn't have a chance. And the last thing you did was brag about your country house. And it wouldn't hurt to have a smile like that. Before I knew it she was looking at me and saying, "You aren't Nora, are you? Nunnally said you'd be aboard." She took my hand and so did he, and we stood there while she exuded charm and I admired her . . . and I wished I could do whatever it was she did that made everything seem so easy, and that made the whole car light up.

MA WAS RIGHT INSIDE the waiting room at Grand Central. She looked very good—people said she resembled Myrna Loy—in a blue suit and hat with a tall feather and spectator pumps and white gloves. It was before Labor Day, at which time she'd have to move on to tweed and alligator and calf. I was the usual mass of wrinkle and stringy hair and brown skin. We hugged in our polite fashion; Nunnally's hugs were better. She'd gotten a redcap and he piled the luggage into a cart. She seemed glad enough to see me but I thought she seemed a little low.

Back at the house, bags unloaded, the rewiring was almost completed. Comparisons weren't fair; 204 looked scruffy and tumbledown, dusty and worn. It always did after California, and it took me a couple of days to be okay about it again. I wandered around inhaling its musty smell, looking at my many reflections. Everything shook and trembled. The stairs creaked as I started up.

She said, "We can't go to Windswept."

"What?"

She had to repeat it a couple more times. She and Jo were finished. In those unenlightened times, she didn't hesitate to say that a lot of the problem was that he and I didn't get along. She'd done it for me, I came first. I was all she had. She'd find somebody else. Feeling both pleased and guilty, I assured her that she'd certainly find somebody much better. I'd help her, I'd ask all my friends. I didn't dare show the massive relief I felt—so massive I forgot to ask about Windswept until later. What did Windswept have to do with it?

"Well, Jo owns half of it. I would never have the money for a house like that. So now we have to make other arrangements."

It took many years to find out that she got stiffed. I never knew how or why. She had sold the previous house and put the money into Windswept. He had contributed half. Somehow he ended up with all of it and ended up living there with the woman he married instead. She missed him, she was sorry about the house, but she never blamed him. It was a wrong decision, the leprechauns had been at it again. She never cried over spilt milk.

A CAUCUS RACE

When I was sixteen, I finally asked my mother what had happened between her and my father. She divorced him, she said, because he wasn't true to her.

Her eyes dropped to her lap, like a hurt child, as though she had only found out last week. I was lying on the end of her blond-wood deco bed with the cream satin quilt and the purple afghan she'd knitted during the war.

"Did he have other girls?"

Slowly she took off her reading glasses. "It was Hollywood. I was very unhappy there."

She was tapping her fingers on the book cover. I looked at my still fairly glamorous mother in her silk nightgown and lacy bed jacket, sitting stiff as a doll against the bank of pillows, smiling angrily.

"How could you possibly be?"

She looked through me into the past, as though I were a gypsy's globe.

"Nunnally was very successful. People are attracted to it like bees to honey. The wives were dragged along like old bags of groceries . . . people didn't talk to me at parties . . . nobody paid any attention to me. Your father didn't hold his liquor very well. Other women were always after him, for parts or whatever else they could get. I didn't want to bring you up there. God knows how you would have turned out." She sighed, then her eyes fell again.

"So you left him."

"Yes." Long pause. "I tried and tried. After a while I gave up and we came back here. I wanted to be with my family."

That meant Gobbie, my crotchety grandmother in New Rochelle, and my Aunt Margaret and Uncle George and my boy cousins. Margaret and George liked to sit on their balcony overlooking University Place and count the mixed couples, which meant a black person and a white or beige person. George worked for the Anti-Defamation League and he was a Jew, which they thought was a big deal.

"Did you have a lover?" I asked, almost in a whisper.

"I'd rather not say." So she had.

"Do you think you'll ever get married again, Ma?"

"My first job is to see you off on the road of life."

We had reached a tandem point in our singular caucus race. We had dates, we got dressed up and went to parties about equally, considering that I was away at school most of the time. We were agreeable contestants, we rooted for each other. I didn't dare ask her if she missed Jo.

"Thank God *that* broke up," Aunt Margaret had said, sotto voce, shaking her head. "You were right all along. All the people who told you how fine Jo was were lying through their teeth."

Unlike my mother, my aunt always spoke with unshakable authority. She had been taken by Gobbie to march in suffragette parades when she was a child. She had run Macy's book department in the twenties when it meant something. Now she worked for the Fertility Department of the Margaret Sanger Foundation. I might not believe it, she said, but more women wanted to have babies than didn't, and her office addressed both needs.

"The trouble is she never got over Nunnally," she said firmly. "Women never do."

. . .

ORDINARILY Olivia Price's living room was closed off by a red velvet rope. But on special occasions, such as supper before the ball, they unhooked it and let people in to sit on the brocade sofa and silken chairs. And there we sat—three girls and nine boys, dressed to the teeth.

I wore a strapless dress of pale pink taffeta strewn with satin roses, silver sandals, and short white kid gloves, and I carried a tiny sequinned bag. My hair was permanented into little curls and I wore too much pinkish makeup. I was sprinkled with Yardley's Lavender.

The boys (including my escort, Steve Merrill) mostly slouched and writhed or stared at their feet, the girls sat up stiff and bright. The silences were long. Steve winked whenever he caught my eye, and Olivia and a toothy boy with glasses put their heads together and snickered. Then Olivia's mother arrived in a long crepe dress and strings of pearls.

"Well," she said. "Well." She had black shiny upswept hair and sharp dark eyes. "Ah, here's my stag line"—the reason for the oversupply of boys. Sometimes the invitation required four escorts, but I was not deeply into these matters. I was hovering on the edge, testing the waters. I was thinking it over.

Ma had said, "If you really want to come out, I *think* I can manage it." Coming out at that time meant a young girl's entrance into society, first at a ball and then, traditionally but not really, at parties every single night for a year—by which time an engagement could be reasonably expected. An ideal debutante would have been born to the right people at the right address and gone to the right schools, but since the war things had loosened up and you could usually buy your way in, even if you were a showbiz kid.

I was touched by my mother's words, but—not for the first time—I sensed precarious finances. And that wasn't all.

"I don't think we have what it takes, Ma."

"What do you mean?" she asked, looking relieved.

"We aren't blue-blooded enough."

But we were! Nunnally's family could be traced back to Jamestown, possibly even the *Mayflower,* and her own people were, if not aristocratic, solid and respectable. I could hold up my head anywhere. I could probably join the DAR, if that interested me.

It didn't, and that wasn't the point anyway. We lacked the touch. I didn't think my mother, jolly as she was with a houseful of drunk adults, had the iron confidence to steer a dozen squirming, embarrassed youths into a discussion—as Mrs. Price had—of the merits of Mrs. Hubbel's dancing class or the intricacies of choosing a boarding school, or as deftly maneuver them into signing a dance card. I knew I could never be Olivia, who became ever more a little duplicate of her mother, cocking her head at the same angle and giving identical bright little nods.

And—the old problem—we lacked a father figure. The appearance of balding Mr. Price in his reading glasses brought the boys to their feet, made them shake hands and behave like normal human beings. The older Prices kept us afloat until Olivia announced that they were going out and we were going to dine all by ourselves.

Mrs. Price put on her mink, Mr. Price his British warm, and they left. In the dining room we sat at an enormous polished table, grandly, if oddly, set with English flatware, Spode serving plates, silver butter plates, and place cards on plastic place mats, with paper napkins. The chandelier was lit as were the candles in their crystal holders, but the glow was sepulchral, and the only sound was the clink of glasses and spoons on soup plates.

I was beginning to understand that conversation didn't fall from the sky like snowflakes but must be made, if only to avoid tedious recitals of football scores. Jokes were the coin of the realm in my family, and the only one I could think of was a well-known line of my father's about his picture *Tobacco Road,* and how—when asked if his Georgia kinfolk were anything like the dirtbag Joads—he replied, "Where I come from we call that crowd the country club set."

I laughed heartily at this family chestnut and so did loyal Steve, but nobody else did. I doubt that anybody understood it except Olivia, who asked sharply if anybody had seen any good plays or movies. That got us through the roast lamb. During the next leaden silence, one of the boys, a little one with red hair, said that he'd been to a party a few nights before where everybody did this stupid thing with butter, you put a little piece on the fold of your paper napkin and ripped it apart fast and it flew up and stuck on the ceiling.

Immediately paper napkins ripped and the air was filled with dabs of flying butter. Wee blobs flew up and clung to the ceiling and the Venetian glass chandelier, sometimes dripping or dropping down into the wax-fruit centerpiece while everybody howled with laughter and Olivia screamed, "STOP, STOP, STOP!" She was gazing at the chandelier, her eyes like shiny brown buttons. "Oh, Mummy will *kill* me. It's an *antique* and it's the only one in the whole world and the decorator spent a *year* in Venice looking for it and Daddy had a *fit* about the price. Mummy will *die.* Oh, you're all horrible."

It was too dark to tell if she was crying but her eyes were too bright. Two of the boys offered to clean it up, but "That would be worse, we'd be late and you'd break everything, you'd smash it. Oh the staff will do it oh please let's just pretend it didn't happen."

THE BALL, the ball . . . it was *War and Peace* and I was Natasha.

The hotel ballroom was decorated with pine swags and tinsel angels, the round tables for eight with snowball candles and little boxed favors . . . and oh, the polished dance floor and tapping shoes and crinolined skirts and flying curls, the motley assortment of boys in tuxes, the rigged stag line, Lester Lanin's shiny teeth and swinging baton. Everything conspired to push my heart into a faster beat. I would forget none of it, not one of the jiggling and dandruffy shoulders where I placed my left glove, or the squeaky-gruff voices or scrubbed pink cheeks and early razor stubble to the right of my eyes, the polished shoes I was supposed to follow but not look at, the ballads and sambas and the suave Lindy. When it was Steve's turn, he twisted my right arm into a kind of corkscrew while my fingers crept along his shoulder and we rocked back and forth in a frozen embrace, his cheek resting on my frizzy curls as the band played "On a Slow Boat to China."

"I like the way your hair smells," Steve said. Then, huskily—"I can't wait till later."

Steve could never wait till later, even though there hadn't been, so far, much of anything to wait for. At school our meetings were closely supervised, but soon he would be at Yale, where I would visit him on weekends, where our hearts (and perhaps our bodies) would spring free.

The band played "Heartaches," and the little butter-boy—I thought it was the little butter-boy, I wasn't wearing my glasses—was coming in our direction.

"It's almost twelve," Steve said.

"Is it?"

A hand appeared and I swung off with the new partner, then another and another. I loved being a girl, I felt sorry for anybody who wasn't, and one from East Sixty-second Street, New York, in 1948. Anybody who wasn't me.

In a few minutes Steve's hand descended on the shoulder of a tall young man who had been singing, appealingly, in my ear. Who had spent the previous summer in Paris taking courses at the Art Students League . . . whose name was Chester Lacey . . . who had very sad brown eyes . . . who I mightily wanted to see again. He and I exchanged looks of mortal pain as Steve staked his claim.

"Let's get out of here," he said in my ear.

"What?"

"Let's go." He held me tighter.

"My dance card isn't finished. I promised Olivia."

"She won't care. She won't even notice."

We argued some more and then he told me how he'd been dreaming of this night for months. He began edging toward the side of the room in a roundabout path, avoiding the tables of watchdog parents. A few more maneuvers got us into our coats and out the door under the canopy.

"It's too early to go home," I said. He pushed me into the first taxi that pulled up. "I know, let's go to a nightclub."

He slammed the car door and sat very close to me. "It's too late to go anyplace but back to your house."

"But Ma might come down and join us."

She wouldn't do any such thing, but Steve didn't know that. He sagged back against the seat, gave a deep sigh, and lit us each a Chesterfield.

"All right, one drink somewhere."

He told the driver to go to the Blue Angel—an easy walk if you weren't wearing high-heeled sandals. We got out in front. The gardenia on my bunny-fur jacket was limp and brownish, my skirt dragged through the dirty snow. The familiar sign glowed and we could hear the faint thump of music from inside. The whole idea was ridiculous, we didn't even have fake driver's licenses. The friend-of-a-friend's brother who had been promising them for months hadn't come through yet. The maître d' only smiled and shook his head, blocking the entrance. There was a burst of applause as Imogene Coca or whoever it was went up to the microphone.

"We could try the Stork." I hated the Stork because it was so full of a certain kind of kids, but it was easier to get into. Steve said nothing. "Let's go to the Village, you can get in anywhere. The Vanguard. Condon's . . ."

"It's too late to go to the Village," Steve said as we got back into the taxi.

"Look at the stars. Isn't this heaven." We were in a De Soto Skyview cab and I flung my head back to see out of the top. "I feel like doing something crazy. Let's tell him to drive over the Brooklyn Bridge." The silence was deep and total. "Oh, all right. It was just an idea."

I said nothing as the cab went up Third, weaving among the el's columns, traveling along the trolley tracks in the middle or the tiny lanes outside. At our corner there was a fine layer of powdery snow on the sidewalk and the cobblestones, and the lattice of the el was etched in black silhouette so sharp that the Minute Tavern, the grocery store on the corner, the dusty bridal shop, and the Oriental rug store faded into a dim backdrop. That was the evening—fire and ice, black lattice on white.

At 204 only the hall lamps were lit. While Steve peeled off his coat and went into the living room, I stood looking in the mirror and thinking about Chester Lacey. Paris. Montmartre, *la rive gauche* . . . little cafés, accordion music, *bateaux mouches.*

"Have you ever been to Europe?" I asked.

"No, but we're going next summer." His voice, a hollow chord, came out of the darkness. "Are you just going to stand there with your coat on?"

"No." I slowly took it off. "Are you going to Paris?"

"I don't know. Why don't you ask my mother?"

"What's the matter?" I turned on the Christmas tree lights and reorganized the tinsel. The soft glow revealed his rumpled, unhappy outlines, his tousled hair.

"Are you waiting for Santa Claus?"

"No." I sat down next to him on the sofa. "You're being horrible. Didn't you have a good time?"

Well . . . sort of, but maybe I didn't understand. This was the night of his life. He'd practically flunked out of Andover thinking about me. (Flat lie, he'd graduated with straight A's.) He didn't want to mess up whatever was between us—and what was between us anyway? He'd thought I felt the same way but tonight I seemed different. Distant. He couldn't put his finger on it. Did I think about him too? Was he expecting too much? The el roared by, drowning out whatever he said next.

Cautiously he reached for my hand. I looked at his earnest eyes and low, furry brows, his lopsided bow tie, the pleated shirt coming out of his suspendered tux. He seemed to be getting farther and farther away, smaller and smaller until he was a tiny creature seen through the wrong end of a telescope. He was a good person, certainly. Honest, true blue, rock solid.

Finally he moved swiftly along the sofa, twisting and circling outward until he was a fence between me and the Christmas tree, the room, the world. His eyes closed, his earnest face moved toward mine. For a few minutes it was nice, it was even a little terrific . . . but surely it didn't come free. A conviction was building up in me, growing like a mad plant, that the price would be sacrifice—of hopes, dreams, Paris, balls, everything. He was the final curtain of a play that had barely even started. That didn't mean I wasn't as breathy as he was. I was split down the middle . . . when his chunky hand moved down the front of my dress I grabbed it, pulled it out, and gave him a shove. When he asked—still panting—what was the matter, I said my mother was going to come down, closing my eyes and shuddering at the unspeakable consequences.

"She'll absolutely kill me. You'd better go."

Steve flung himself back, eyes closed, waiting for the lump in his pants to subside, while I reorganized my rosebud top and escaping breasts. Now that it was over I didn't want him to leave. I wanted him there but docile . . . I wanted him lumpless.

"Don't go yet. Let's talk."

"We talked. Jesus Christ, I just more or less told you I'm crazy about you." He stood up. "What else do you want to talk about?"

"I don't know."

"You sure don't." He stared at me in the dim light from the tree, a blind man trying to see. "I think I'll leave. I can't just stay here all night waiting for you to get the picture."

He went into the hall and put his coat on, then his white muffler. He was leaving because I didn't make any sense. At the door he kissed me briefly.

"I had a terrific time."

He probably meant it; he had not been surprised or insulted by having been shot down in midflight. I had done exactly what was expected of me, though for the wrong reasons—not from girlish modesty but because some other, unidentified passion was crowding everything else out, growing in the same soil, soaking up all the sun and rain and nourishment, while Steve withered . . . and I didn't even know what it was about, except that its demands were like life itself.

Marion and Nunnally, Miami, 1931 or '32.

Studio photo of Marion,
early 1930s.

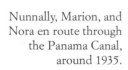

Nunnally, Marion, and
Nora en route through
the Panama Canal,
around 1935.

Nora Johnson and
Nora Sayre, around
1936.

Nana, Harold, and Nora
at Boulder Dam, 1938.

Christie, Nunnally, and
Nora, probably at 504 North
Beverly Glen, 1941 or '42.

Marion during the war, backyard at
204 East 62nd Street.

Marion in City Patrol Corps uniform
at 204 East 62nd Street.

Jo Golinkin by the
East River sometime
during the war.

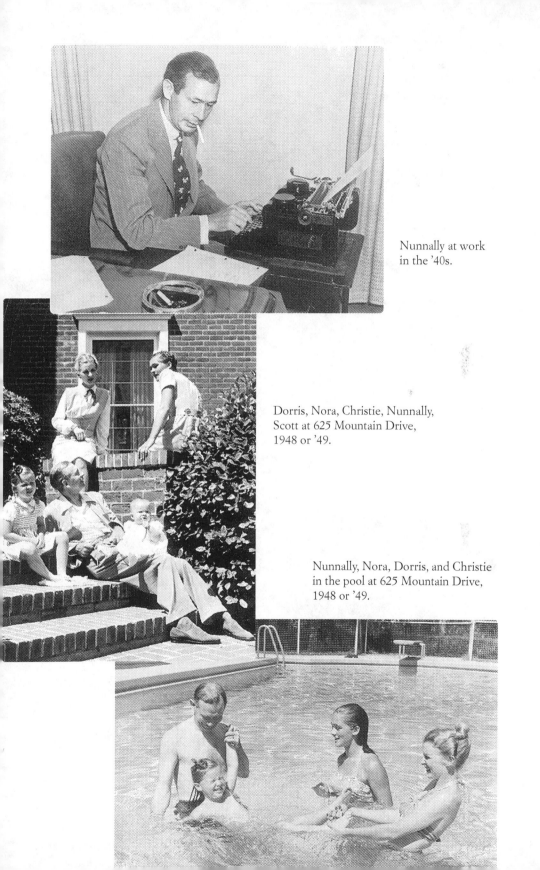

Nunnally at work in the '40s.

Dorris, Nora, Christie, Nunnally, Scott at 625 Mountain Drive, 1948 or '49.

Nunnally, Nora, Dorris, and Christie in the pool at 625 Mountain Drive, 1948 or '49.

Hjordis Niven, Lauren Bacall,
Nunnally, part of Dave Chasen,
Maude Chasen, and David
Niven, mermaid party, 1949,
at 625 Mountain Drive.

Dorris, Nunnally,
and Peter Hayes,
mermaid party,
1949.

Early 1950s.

Nora and Nunnally on a
set in the '50s.

Dorris, Betty Bacall, and
Nunnally, '50s.

Rog and Marion on their
honeymoon, 1952.

Nunnally and Marilyn,
opening of *How to Marry a
Millionaire*, 1953.

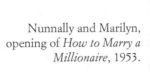

George Raft, Ginger Rogers,
and Nunnally on the set of
Black Widow, 1953.

Nunnally directing
Reginald Gardiner
and Ginger Rogers
on the set of *Black
Widow*, 1953.

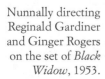

Dorris and
Nunnally,
1950s.

The Newmans
and Nunnally,
Oscar night,
1957.

Chris, Scott, Marjorie,
Roxie, Nunnally, and
Nora, 1975

THE ALMIGHTY DOLLAR

NINETEEN-FIFTY WAS, for me, the year life got a lot more glamorous.

In March of my senior year at Abbot, Nunnally took me with him to Boston for a weekend I never forgot. We stayed at the Ritz-Carlton, we went to Locke-Ober and Durgin-Park. We saw plays—one was *The Wisteria Trees* with Helen Hayes. We hung around the Ritz suite of Joshua Logan, the author of the play, with Leland Hayward, the producer, George Kaufman (I had read *You Can't Take It with You* and *The Man Who Came to Dinner*), Arthur Schwartz (I had danced to "Dancing in the Dark" and "You and the Night and the Music"), Harry Kurnitz, Kurt Weill (who wrote "Speak Low" and "September Song"). In the course of the weekend I met Ludwig Bemelmans (I had read *Madeline* dozens of times), Helen Hayes (I had seen her in summer stock and on Broadway), and her husband, Charlie MacArthur (I had read *The Front Page*), who were close friends of Nunnally's.

The Wisteria Trees, a version of *The Cherry Orchard* set in the American South, had been called "Southern-fried Chekhov" by one disgruntled critic during its brief Broadway run. Though I was only dimly aware of it then, some of the luminaries gathered that weekend were script doctors—along with Maxwell Anderson, Robert Penn Warren, and S. N. Behrman. As for the other plays we saw, Boston was a try-out town and probably they were all out-of-town runs, still in process, and all this Broadway talent was there to work on them.

Though we sat around the suite for hours while waiters came in and out with coffee, sandwiches, and whiskey, though the working-writers talk was interminable, I was never bored. I was hypnotized by the faces. The lantern-jawed, acerbic one slouched in a chair was George Kaufman; the suave, handsome, black-haired one who always smiled at me was Arthur Schwartz; the small quiet one with the accent who didn't fit in was Kurt Weill (he died within the year); the pop-eyed nervous one was Joshua Logan. The tousled funny news-paperman, the one my father seemed to love most, was Charlie MacArthur—and Helen Hayes was the tiny woman with the unfor-gettable face.

I knew I was in the presence of extraordinary people, and, at seven-teen, I knew some of their accomplishments. This was better than movie stars, this was the brains and talent that made it all happen. The astonishment was that these were my father's friends—this was the part of his life that was closed to me.

Helen Hayes's big scene was in the last act of *The Wisteria Trees.* Pop had told me that her voice was so perfectly trained that she could "speak as softly as I'm speaking to you—and it's still completely audi-ble in the back row." As her voice dropped—without ever losing its clarity—her husband, in the last row, began to clear his throat, first softly, then louder and louder into a noisy coughing spell that finally sent him out of the theater. The actors were silent until he was gone. After the curtain calls I asked Pop if he was all right, or if he might need some help. Nunnally smiled musingly.

"Oh, he does that sometimes," he said.

LONDON, SUMMER of 1950: Nunnally was there to make *The Mudlark,* the story of a small boy who creeps into Windsor Castle hoping to catch a glimpse of the recluse Queen Victoria. I was going to join him.

I had crossed on the *Queen Mary,* following Nunnally's typed instructions for ocean travel (go to the dining room and sign up for a good table, go to the Promenade Deck and get a good deck chair, don't tip till the last day). I had champagne in the captain's quarters (arranged by the agent) with Jack Benny and his radio retinue—Phil Harris, Alice Faye, and Eddie Anderson, who played Rochester. I wore an evening dress every night and was pursued by an unsuitable man and won ten pounds in the ship's pool. I got my first look at American power—when we anchored at Cherbourg, people in dinghies flocked below begging for cigarettes, and everybody threw down packages of Camels and Chesterfields to a chorus of *"Merci, merci."*

NUNNALLY AND DORRIS had taken a flat in Grosvenor Square. It was strange to see them there among the ghosts of David Copperfield and Moll Flanders, Sherlock Holmes and Mary Poppins. I had a quick impression of tall windows overlooking a leafy square and ecru rooms with suitcases and paper bags from stores and piles of packages tied with string.

In one corner of the room Nunnally's Royal portable was set up on a card table, a pile of clean paper on one side and the finished script pages on the other, an ashtray and a couple of sharpened pencils nearby. He was working on *The Desert Fox,* a story about the German field marshal Rommel. In a few days, he said, after I'd looked around some, I should get to work too—each of us in our own room with our own typewriter. From time to time he'd read my stuff, if I liked, and give his opinion or help. We would write together in this most literary of cities.

Was it possible? Everything was so different. Things in England, I saw very quickly, had a no-nonsense permanence. The bathtubs were bigger, the faucets were heavier and more faucetlike, the toilets sturdier and more thronelike. The bed linens were so heavy it took some effort to get into bed. The toothbrush from the chemist's was ivory with real bristles and the toothpaste tube had a Union Jack on it. Though the currency was said to be "soft," it appeared more substantial—the five-pound note was like a page from a tiny newspaper, the crowns and half-crowns might have come from a pirate's chest. The words that came into my head might be transformed into a similar but peculiar language.

While Nunnally was at the Shepperton Studios, Dorris and I set out for Bond Street and Jermyn Street and St. James, to Molyneux and Dunhill and Liberty and Floris and Fortum & Mason's while Dorris compared prices to those in New York and Beverly Hills. As I followed her strawberry blond coif through the halls of Harrods, my own pageboy hair, voluminous skirts, and floppy Capezios seemed worse and worse, relics of some silly peasant past. I needed a whole new look—and not that of the queen or the princesses, Meg and Lili-bet, in their dowdy tailor-mades and melon hats. A meticulously tailored suit would do it, nipped in at the waist, with a *very* narrow skirt—and kid gloves and a tightly furled umbrella . . . plus an Italian haircut. I would stroll into the lobby of the Ritz, and . . . who knows what would happen?

Shopping with Dorris was always serious and taxing, full of hard decisions and fierce triumphs and regrets over lost bargains. In London the stakes were even higher. It was the era of the Almighty Dollar, when Americans abroad could buy more, go farther, rule the world. Even those with humble budgets felt rich, and the rich felt like billionaires. That summer they were all spending like drunken sailors. Five years after the war, supplies were still limited—but what there was was *cherce.* Some might learn about a country through its art and architecture, Dorris said, but her teaching medium was the local merchandise.

At first I wasn't much interested. The Waterford crystal and English linens were for girls with hope chests. But the cashmere sweaters were tempting, and the handbags and gloves from France and Italy were pretty wonderful . . . and such is the lure of the bargain that soon certain of these items began to seem absolutely necessary.

It was easy to forget about the war until suddenly, around corners or at the ends of streets, there it would be, the bombed-out buildings and segments of walls that were everywhere, the holes in the ground with fences around them, and the rubble-strewn lots where red-cheeked children looked for treasures and sometimes found live bombs. Staring at the ruins, I tried to imagine the bombs dropping onto people's flats as they were having tea or putting their children to bed or making love. Dorris and I—and the other Americans who were beating the same path—were scrambling over the merchandise like the kids on the rockpiles, grabbing the spoils.

Still, the English chintzes and porcelains, Irish tweeds and Italian leather goods were so low in price it would be a crime not to snatch them up. American friends dropped by for a drink, to compare notes and give shopping tips. The husbands made comic protestations of poverty, though Nunnally didn't hesitate to direct them to Mr. Cleverly's Bootery, and everybody bought Liberty ties and silks and the toiletries of Floris on Bond Street, especially a scent called New Mown Hay, which my father said turned the plainest woman into a Circe you followed down the street.

A week or so after I arrived, Dorris finished her shipping and began packing to go home. Unlike my mother, who always announced her intentions ("I am making a martini! I am going to Bloomingdale's to buy sheets . . . walk around the reservoir . . . go on a cruise to Curaçao!"), Dorris forged silently ahead with mysterious plans. You didn't know what she was doing till it was too late.

Pop said she was going back because she had been away from the children long enough. Part of the idea of my coming to London—besides writing under his advisement—was to keep house for him. This was startling, because it was known that no one could feed him properly except Dorris, Dave Chasen, or Mike Romanoff.

I didn't know much beyond scrambled eggs and grilled-cheese sandwiches, but I was willing to try. It took all day. There was still rationing; you stood in lines to buy a couple of eggs and a few ounces of butter, and the chicken came complete with head and staring eyes and red feet (which I begged the poulterer to remove) and pinfeathers . . . as I plucked them out I remembered the tiny smile on Dorris's face the morning she left. The ones I missed ended up in my father's teeth.

After two inedible dinners, we went out every night, mostly to a place called the Wardroom, sometimes to the Screen-writers' Club. We always had potted shrimp and then gray meat and potatoes and a mashed nameless vegetable, with a sweet or savory afterward. It was all right with me, that was how I'd eaten at home before Ma had taken courses at Dionne Lucas and started flambéing everything. Pale bread and gluey macaroni were fine . . . but Nunnally began to sink into some netherworld, staring bleakly at his plate and the waiter—whether from deprival, or homesickness, or boredom, I couldn't say.

ONCE, DURING THE WAR, he and I and Nippy, my cocker spaniel, had crossed the country together, on an aging Southern Pacific train that strayed close to the Mexican border. There were engine problems and we kept grinding to a halt in the desert. The so-called air-conditioning broke down. The food spoiled, leaving only Spam and canned spaghetti. I wept when Pop suggested putting the dog in the baggage car, even though our compartment looked and smelled like a kennel. He finally retired to the club car where he sat drinking bourbon and glaring out the streaky window, getting madder and madder at Hitler . . . and, probably, at me.

In Chicago, with some of his friends at the Pump Room, he smiled for the first time in four days. In a few minutes he had turned our nightmare voyage into a comic Dagwood-daughter-dog adventure, which, stripped of our silent struggle, got funnier as time passed. Now the porter burst into tears, the cook took off across the desert with the can opener . . . and he later claimed I had ordered three things at the Pump Room that were on fire. It had only been one, but I loved it

145

when he made up things like that—even more that whatever had been wrong seemed to be over.

THE OBVIOUS SOLUTION for bad food and ennui was Paris.

So it was off to the Georges V and Fouquet's for *truite bleu* boned before our eyes, to Maxime's and the Tour d'Argent for *canard pressé au sang,* the Folies-Bergère, the Grand Guignol, and the Eiffel Tower. Nunnally had only the barest interest in art and music—these disciplines seemed almost to annoy him, as did all foreign languages—and the only cultural monument I remember visiting was Versailles. We went with the little group of American friends who popped up everywhere, stopping for lunch at Le Coq Hardi where we sat in the garden and were served, among other delicacies, goblets of champagne, each containing a peeled ripe peach. Here I had to go and throw up . . . I loved it but it was all too much. I remember staggering miserably through the golden parlors and ballrooms of Versailles, and Marie Antoinette's farm where she escaped when *la vie luxe* was too much for her and played at being a shepherdess.

When Nunnally left for Germany to interview Frau Rommel for *The Desert Fox,* the stylish and charming Celia Ager took me to the Louvre, to the straw market, to lunch on the *rive gauche,* to a French movie. A journalist for *Variety* and film critic on the left-wing *PM,* an old friend of both my parents, she wore tight, tailored suits with many buttons, her blond hair pulled tightly up under a pillbox hat. I liked Celia, though I wondered why she didn't have something better to do than hang around with us all the time. I remembered my mother saying, "Oh yes, Celia was always around" in New York, or Hollywood, or London or Paris, or wherever anybody happened to be—an all-purpose friend and traveling companion. She put me on a plane for Switzerland, where I was to visit family friends; she was in London when we were all back there again, in yet another pillbox hat, her bright crimson lips in a smile like a question.

• • •

BESIDES THE AMERICANS—Celia and Milton Ager, Jerry Morris (who had half-carried me through the Hall of Mirrors), Ben Lyon and Bebe Daniels, the genial Cesar Romero, and others—the people in our lives that summer fell into three or four hazy categories.

There were the *Mudlark* people—Irene Dunne and Alec Guinness (who played Disraeli), director Jean Negulesco and his wife, Dusty, and other members of the company. In my limited exposure to movie locations, the star always hid out. I saw Irene Dunne only in her latex Queen Victoria mask, sitting on the throne or riding along the Mall in her golden coach . . . as reclusive as the queen she was playing. The beguiling Mr. Guinness was much friendlier. At dinner at his home he charmed us with animal imitations, and one day he took me on a tour of Twentieth Century-Fox's House of Commons, indistinguishable from the real one.

There was Florence and her two sons and their friends, who took me to parties and pubs, cricket matches at Lord's and the cheap seats high up at the theater called "the gods." I appreciated their hospitality, because I knew the young Brits were pretty broke. Jobs were scarce; they clerked at grocery stores or picked hops in Spain.

Florence had a flat in Chelsea looking over the Thames. She had no refrigerator and the butter and milk were kept on the windowsill. When I commented she only laughed and said nobody had fridges. You shopped every day. Darling Peter slept on the chaise when he wasn't at Oxford. She'd been born American and wasteful, but she had learned how little one needed to get along very nicely.

WALKING THROUGH Green Park with Peter or taking a forbidden ride on his motorbike was one thing—but taking him somewhere in our leased Rolls, driven by one Atkins, was another. Then I became a fraudulent rich girl, borrowing the trappings for the summer. When my old friend Nora Sayre turned up on a shoestring Putney tour, remarking piteously that she hadn't had a bath since she left New York, I apologized for everything—the flat looking out over Grosvenor Square and the American embassy, the high tea brought up by a waiter, the grand bathtub and Floris bath salts she couldn't wait to use. She asked me if I was really rich and I said I didn't think so, it might have looked that way when I was around Nunnally but it wasn't so easy to get actual money out of him. I didn't think I had any trust funds or anything like that.

But . . . whatever. She and I were going to be writers, which we believed to be a solid profession you could live on, as our fathers, particularly mine, had found it to be. Nunnally and Joel Sayre, old and close friends, had given us nothing but encouragement, they made us, their Noras, feel that we could do just about anything. It was only a matter of hard work. And forget about bursts of inspiration, you had to sit there every day for two or three or four hours and get something on paper, even if you threw it out afterward. The thing was to do your best and keep up your nerve . . . and so we talked as Atkins drove us to a performance of *The Beaux-Stratagem* and to the Screen-writers' Club for dinner.

I'd hardly written a line in London. How could I, with Nunnally's Royal clicking away in the next room, turning out dialogue for James Mason? But after Nora S. left I did write a story (about an American girl visiting London) and Pop read it very carefully and told me it was pretty good, but the plot was shaky, there were too many characters . . . and generally it was better to wait longer before writing about an experience. He said to put it away for a month or so and then work on it some more. Then I could send it to Edith Haggard. She probably wouldn't send it out to a magazine, but she could give me real advice—she knew the market better.

The lease on the flat was up in mid-August and Nunnally and I moved to the Dorchester for the last weeks of the summer. London had emptied out, few people were around except Celia, and a new, frequent escort of mine, Denis . . . a sort of playboy manqué who was always available for anything that sounded like fun, except that he couldn't pay the bills. Since these two appeared fairly regularly we fell into an odd, difficult foursome, weighted down by Nunnally's loathing of Denis and his inability to avoid him.

Denis always arrived a few minutes before the appointed hour so he could check me out. "Hold still, darling—stand right there." A long appraising look. "*Almost* right—but run and get your jewelry case. Let me see . . . those earrings are better . . . I *adore* the dress, love, but let's find some other shoes." All this for a movie for which I was paying. Nunnally couldn't stand him. He was a climber, a freeloader . . . he didn't say *fairy* but he didn't have to. Never mind that Denis danced like Fred Astaire, that he was handsome and high-spirited and full of delightful gossip. When he was around, Nunnally sank into the pained, depressed silence he had over the pinfeathery chicken or when, in Paris, he had been persuaded against his better judgment to listen to a string quartet.

One evening the four of us went to the London opening of *Mr. Roberts,* a black-tie occasion. We sat in a box and drank champagne—Denis in a rented tux and a shirt with a piqué collar. Hanging over the side with excitement, he cried out the names of the celebrities passing below. The Dutchess of Kent! Rita Hayworth! The Duke of Northumberland and Lady Southwick! Tyrone Power . . . wasn't he frightfully handsome? He was—and I turned to my father to point out Denis's sharp eyes and excellent taste, only to see the stiff polite smile I dreaded. I was grateful to Celia—in a cream satin pillbox and matching dinner dress—for trying to distract him as Dorris or my mother would have done, as I was never very good at, and I realized why this delightful, exhilarating summer had been so exhausting. I was always trying, without much luck, to fulfill my assignment and take care of my father.

DENIS'S BIRTHDAY fell just before I was to leave. He wanted to take me dining and dancing. He was all too aware of the many checks Nunnally had picked up. It would not happen again; Denis had saved up for the occasion. I knew he had some depressing low-level job, and he would have paid if he could. After careful inquiry, it turned out that of all places, only the Dorchester had decent food and a band that played the kind of music we liked . . . and as the Dorchester was a favorite of Liz Taylor and Nicky Hilton, who were honeymooning in Europe that summer, they might appear. Would I mind terribly spending the evening at the hotel?

I was happy to—Nunnally would be out. And it all would have been fine except that halfway through our potted shrimp and gray meat we looked up and there, coming in our direction, were Nunnally and Celia. We all stared unhappily at each other, Nunnally looking as though his worst dream had come true.

Those were politer times, and they sat down with us. Celia's pill-box was bright red satin, and I got a whiff of New Mown Hay. Her smile was as coolly engaging as ever. She did beautifully, as always, she and Denis even got a riff going, which might have gotten very fast and funny had it not been for the unhappy Nunnally. He did badly, or perhaps he did the only reasonable thing under the circumstances—he got drearily drunk because he couldn't think how to avoid picking up the check, as I had mentioned the reason for the celebration. He couldn't let the man pay for his own birthday party. While we were dancing Denis mourned, "This is so ghastly, darling. You must hate me."

"I don't and it isn't your fault."

"I'm determined to give you a going-away present. It's been such glorious fun knowing you, and we might never see each other again." (We never did.) "We've become great pals. You must promise to come back some time." (When I did he was nowhere to be found.)

In the morning he phoned.

"There's the sweetest man crossing with you on the *Lizzy,* very smart and amusing and handsome, heir to a tobacco fortune, knows everybody, can't wait to meet you . . . and there's going to be a *very special goody* boarding at Cherbourg."

The sweet, rich, amusing man took a little nudging—I had to go rout him out—and he wasn't as perfect as Denis had said, but he was all right. And he did know everybody, and he showed me how to climb over gates on the top deck to get to tourist class, where the fun was . . . and best of all, took me to the big round table in first class where everybody on board would have died to be, where the special goody sat: Elizabeth Taylor.

She and Nicky boarded at Cherbourg, she in a gray poodle coat, holding a little gray poodle dog that matched exactly. People were almost falling over the railings and out their portholes. The young Hiltons had seventeen trunks. They had servants, maids, agents, bodyguards, hangers-on. They were on their way back from their three-month honeymoon in Europe and neither Danny, the sweet man, nor anybody else could talk about much of anything else for the whole voyage that I recall—all this during the fall when ships and planes were jammed with frightened Americans fleeing from Russians, for everyone was sure that World War III was imminent.

Elizabeth was attended by a retinue of fiercely possessive women who protected her, told her what to do, and fended off intruders—potentially everyone else on the (fortuitously named) *Queen Elizabeth.* Some of them were at the round table, along with other nameless fans, gawkers, and wannabes . . . but where was Nicky Hilton?

"He pays no attention to me at all," Elizabeth sighed, and the retinue moaned with indignation. She was ravishing, so beautiful that nothing else around us seemed very clear or important. The violet eyes and pearly skin, the dark curls, a different strapless evening dress every night. Her famous jewelry glittered, her smile threw the rest of the world into shadow.

Nicky Hilton was in the gaming room, playing poker. (The sweet man introduced me.) He looked pale and cross, and a cigarette hung out of his mouth. Somebody asked the obvious question: why wasn't he with his lovely bride? Oh—a shrug, a sip of whiskey. The trip had been . . . you know, exhausting. It had been one hotel after another for months, late nights, crowds everywhere, parties, the whole bit. He was just, well, taking things easy . . . and looking forward to getting home. He seemed to be the only person there who wasn't half-hypnotized by his wife.

"He won't even dance with me," Elizabeth murmured at the round table, sadly twirling her glass of champagne. The sweet man and three others leaped to their feet and begged to make up for his appalling neglect. She danced with them all, then came back and amused us with imitations of baby animals (oddly similar to Alec Guinness's). She told us how she loved puppies and kittens and little mice, and she put her fists, with glittering rings, together under her chin, opened her gorgeous eyes wide, and became an adorable chipmunk.

Elizabeth was friendly, but her retinue was not. And my credentials must have been either forgotten (even though Danny dropped Nunnally's name constantly) or inadequate, or my college-shop clothes not good enough, for Danny had—oddly—insisted that I wear his mother's ruby earrings just for the evening. I put them on for a while, then when somebody admired them and Danny began to explain their history, I took them off and gave them back to him. He was indignant at this lack of appreciation and then sulky. He really didn't see why I didn't want to model his family jewels.

After that he didn't pay any attention to me, but hell, the trip was practically over. When we arrived in New York everybody was almost hanging on the edge of the pier to get a glance at Elizabeth and Nicky, who were divorced four months later.

DIVINELY WRONG

AT A FRATERNITY HOUSE at Amherst I met a dark, saturnine young man who didn't look like the rest . . . who looked elusive, racy, a little dangerous.

He told me I represented a world that was, to him, a far-off glittering mirage. He spoke in riddles: He was a wandering gypsy in search of a home, a scholarship student, out of his element . . . though he had no element. Why had he come here? He gave me a puzzled smile. This was the desirable place, the bricks and white columns and red crackling leaves . . . this was the center of the circle. The elms, the Quad, the chapel. And the clothes, the chinos and tweed jackets and string ties and white shoes. The music, the references . . . where to go, what to see, everything. I must know these things by instinct.

He said my dress was absolutely correct. When we danced he told me every motion was right, though I wasn't a great dancer. But why was I right instead of beautiful, on target instead of irresistible? Why did I smell perfect instead of delicious? I was taking freshman philosophy and that week I believed there were no ethical absolutes, everything was relative. What did he keep comparing me to? I was sorry I couldn't say everything about him was right, for his attraction lay in *not* being right. He was exotic, scary, divinely wrong.

He was an eternal stranger out of Camus, always looking for a safe place. He lived with fear. In time I asked him if I didn't assuage his fear, and he said I just made it worse but in a different way. If I could ever love him it would go away . . . though it was too soon for that. We had mountains to climb, rivers to cross, we two.

If I'd been savvier I might have seen this as a vast and stylish line. But to what end? In dark rooms at the Kappa Delta house, with the requisite necktie on the doorknob, his embraces had a puzzling lassitude. Weren't we in love? Wasn't I just right, he marvelously wrong? Oh yes, that was true, but it was all too sad and hopeless. It was hard for him to really let himself go when he feared the worst. Not that I would ever be cruel. But he was very sensitive, almost fragile. He went over things I'd said, trying to pry hidden meanings out of them. And he knew things I didn't know . . . he would never push me.

I begged him to push me . . . anywhere. But only the sad, you-don't-understand smile.

In New York, during Christmas vacation, we took long walks through the snowy park and sat for hours in dark coffeehouses. He was uncomfortable at 204. Afterward he said he was sure Ma didn't like him because he was a Jew . . . and nobody liked Jews, even if they thought they did. When I told him I knew millions of Jews, he said it wasn't my fault—it was inherent in the *goyische* mind. Besides, since Nathan hoped to become a famous actor, he couldn't be sure himself that part of my attraction wasn't Hollywood. He wished my father were a postman or a life insurance salesman, it would solve so many (imaginary, I thought) problems.

Nothing could deflect this train of thought, even though, as I tried to explain, Hollywood was not a resource, even to me. Perhaps it *was* a line. But what did he want, and why was everything so fragile and delicate? Finally, driven to the end of my wits, I suggested we sleep together. He said he'd never been so moved in his life, but we both knew it wasn't a good idea. He knew me better than I knew myself—which could very well have been true, since I was never sure why I did anything. But how could he turn me down? When he finally came around, the moment was gone and I had lost my nerve.

"MA, why don't you like Nathan?" I asked.

"I like him perfectly well."

"You don't."

"Well, I think he makes you unhappy," she said.

"He drives me crazy . . . but isn't that what love's about?"

"Love is happiness."

What a touching liar she was. For her, love had been only misery. Now I was following her example—but somehow my so-called love was a trifle compared to hers.

I told her she was anti-Semitic, the worst kind because she denied it—and she only laughed. But those were the years of veiled accusations, of hidden identities and traitorous thoughts, of intolerance to anything that wasn't—as Nathan put it—inside the circle. Anybody outside was suspect or being investigated, which certainly had more dark drama than always being on target. Sometimes I even wished I were a Jew, a communist, a lesbian, a member of some forbidden group, that I had been born with some affliction that the world unfairly scorned. (Being a woman didn't yet qualify.)

AT SMITH I was surrounded by homesick girls who'd never been away from Scarsdale or Shaker Heights before, who wrote their families every night and were already talking about getting married to somebody from . . . Scarsdale or Shaker Heights. Eager girls who wanted to join things, aggressive girls who wanted to run things . . . which, since there were no males to compete with, they easily did. Dumb girls who'd gotten in because they were alumnae daughters, girls who were there to find a husband, brilliant girls destined to make Phi Beta Kappa and summa cum laude . . . country club girls, girls from the wrong side of the tracks, fervently religious girls, girls who wanted to get away from home, girls who soon transferred to a coed college, fat girls, thin girls, knockouts and monsters . . . and most of them were inside the circle. I could easily point to the ones who weren't, starting with myself. That divorce and all the rest kept me out; that I was inside only courtesy of Smith was something Nathan never understood.

Identifying ins and outs was a subtle, poisonous talent. Nathan had it, I had it. Senator McCarthy had it. My mother had it a little bit, Nunnally not at all—he made his own circle. And it had nothing to do with anything that counted.

TAKE THE GIRL in Lawrence, the scholarship house next door. Striding up the hill in her polo coat, curled up in a burning ball in Lyon Reading Room, waving her arm in the front row of English classes . . . you couldn't miss Sylvia Plath. Always bigger than life, she was a visual commercial for Smith in the days before people thought in such terms: fat bouncing blond pageboy (the kind that required sleeping on metal rollers), big, smart blue eyes, thick eyelashes, big Chiclet teeth, pink cheeks. She just missed being beautiful, and by doing so also missed being pretty. But she had star quality. When Sylvia was around you knew you were in the presence of something extraordinary.

Her hand waving in the front row presaged scholarly insights that left the rest of us a mile behind. She wasn't rude, but she couldn't help being competitive, and sometimes her pencil tapped impatiently on the chair arm when somebody else had the floor. The professors we shared—Robert Gorham Davis, Newton Arvin, Daniel Aaron—knew what they had on their hands and tactfully, kindly held her back so that the rest of us could make our paler contributions. There was a collaboration between them—she dropped by their offices or homes, we all knew, to get something straight about Melville, Joyce, Dostoevsky. She was a teacher's pet, but why not? It would be wrong—and impossible—to keep the lid on her. She was a rocket on the launching pad.

It was okay with me (though nobody asked) that Sylvia could strip-search *Ulysses* and make all the mythological connections without batting an eye, that she could dismember the symbolism of the white whale and reel off the effects of Transcendentalism on all nineteenth-century American culture. But when word got around that she'd sold a couple of short stories to *Seventeen* magazine, that was almost too much to bear.

At the same time certain flaws I'd noticed became more striking. Her camel's hair coat was threadbare—not from honorable hard wear, but from poor quality. She wore a dorky charm bracelet, her socks were too thin and short, she had pennies in her loafers, which most of us had given up in high school. She held back her lush blond pageboy with little plastic barrettes. She was outside.

But could Sylvia write?

R. G. Davis read our stories aloud to the junior-year writing class, and soon I was obsessively making comparisons. I decided that she was more skilled at using her material, but her life—growing up in boring Wellesley with her widowed mother—was colorless, and the people and things she wrote about not very interesting. Her laugh was loud and forced, sometimes ill-timed. She might have been best in class, but she lacked humor.

Our stories were published together in the *Smith Review.* Mine were purest vaudeville, full of pratfalls and what I considered clever one-liners, set in Manhattan's Upper East Side or deluxe European hotels . . . the characters were rich, outrageous, and barely believable. Now they are largely unreadable. Sylvia's characters were sedate, the settings homely, the mood dark. They were carefully crafted; she didn't get tangled up in plot lines the way I did. One of them, "Sunday at the Mintons," is solid and engaging still.

In an old issue are several of her college poems. "Admonition" advises not looking at precious things too closely; "Never Try to Know More Than You Should" speaks for itself; "Denouement" is about silent endings. She was still buttoned-up, inward-turned, polite . . . still quivering on the pad. The explosive takeoff and disastrous descent was yet to come.

And she was far beyond circles.

HOW THINGS WORK

THE DOORBELL RANG, my mother flew down the stairs. There in the vestibule stood an enormous man.

"This is Rog," she said, beaming as though she'd just found him on the beach, a perfect conch shell.

He looked very good—a shock of white hair, a big florid Irish face with a genial smile, blue eyes, blazer with brass buttons and a crest on the lapel. At six foot four, he filled the front hall. The house shrank to dollhouse size, the silver lamps and Japanese dolls quivered; when he took a couple of steps the whole house trembled. The velvet loveseat squeaked and wobbled alarmingly when he sat down. He was around 250 pounds, a square, solid column of pink flesh. My mother came up to his collarbone.

"How d'ya do."

Rog had a wide smile, a firm handshake. With his easy humor and reassuring expansiveness it was impossible not to like him. He taught at the Columbia School of Business and was financial consultant for a frozen foods company. It was all light years from what I was familiar with, but it might be just what we needed. If this courtship progressed

159

to its natural conclusion, this man could straighten us out, stop this "Oh, damn, I'm broke again."

Ma's feast-or-famine planning had been nerve-racking in Europe the summer before. We had traveled *luxe* through Italy with two friends, staying at Grands and Ritzes, buying whatever we wanted in shops, and eating ourselves bleary-eyed in a continuous Dionysian celebration. Even the CIT buses seemed first-class, with their continuous drinks and the microphone where passengers were encouraged to stand up and sing songs. We made our way to Cannes, met Florence and her sons, and after the biggest meal I've ever had in my life at a waterfront restaurant, Ma announced the money had run out and the next morning we were moving to a cheap pension until she figured out how to get some more.

Money was a covert subject in my family. My mother was a math teacher's daughter and closet left-brainer who'd been brought up believing that money, like sex, was a private matter. She managed her finances well, but the specifics remained hidden. Nunnally regarded it as a necessary nuisance. He wanted as much as possible but he didn't want to be bothered with details. For years he'd worked on salary for Zanuck—a day's work for a day's pay, predictable as his father's weekly paycheck from the Georgia Central Railroad. But now things were changing, The evolution of the movie business from the studio system to separate production companies, often working abroad, called for a financial sophistication he didn't have. It was necessary to understand capital gains, tax shelters, foreign exchange—and the short-legged men (agents, accountants, lawyers) who came into his office with papers to sign and opaque explanations only confused him more.

When I asked either of my parents for money, they threw up their hands and said I had no idea how expensive it was to run a home, raise a family, dress a daughter, live in the city, live anywhere at all . . . though they usually came through. When Ma got tired of arguing she put me on an allowance. At first I hated it, then began to like the predictability of the monthly check.

Smith didn't require a course in basic economics (which shocked

Rog), so I didn't know a stock from a bond, an annuity from a mutual fund—and taxes were a mystery. I had less sense than my five-year-old son, twenty years later, who wanted to know *where the money was* that I'd persuaded him to put in a savings account. When I said I wasn't sure, he cried, "But you told me it would be *safe!*"

"What's your major?" Rog asked.

"English," I said.

"Hmm. Well, you probably need more than that. Some history. Some knowledge of how things work, d'you see?"

"Well, I'm going to be a writer. I thought . . ."

"You have to be able to put things in context," he said.

"I suppose you're right."

He gave a big beaming smile. "Just a suggestion. Wanna go out for dinner?"

204 HAD ALWAYS BEEN a haven for lost kids, disaffected suburbanites, out-of-town culturehounds, anybody who needed a bed in the city for a few days. During the war there were friends in the service or the Red Cross who couldn't find hotel rooms, people uprooted by the war and people searching for apartments. Later on there were school friends from out of town, some escaping from indifferent parents or inhospitable homes. A few had their own keys—a courtesy that was never abused. Over holidays, boys dropped in for a visit, to collect somebody for the movies, or hopefully to get laid. But cheerful and casual as Ma was, she made it clear that there was to be no screwing at 204. Her own lovers must have come when I was away, or were hustled out before dawn—for I never saw one at breakfast.

This easygoing atmosphere seemed all right with Rog. He included a couple of my friends in his dinner invitation and we all went around the corner to Mama Louisa's, where we were greeted effusively and fed an enormous amount of food: martinis, antipasto, fettuccine, a large garlicky salad, bottles of Chianti. Then veal scallopini or steak ("Let's have some real food here!"), followed by fruit and cheese

("Let's have a couple more loaves of bread and some Gorgonzola!") and more Chianti, then espressos all around and spumoni or tortoni and then, for those who were still alive, amaretto or grappa. After hugs of farewell from Mama L. and the rest, we staggered home.

I took that evening as a generous suitor's gesture, and assumed that now he and his lady love would go their own way. But the Louisa dinners continued, other friends were swept along—the boys abashed because they couldn't ante up. Hands groped uneasily for wallets, hovered in the air till Rog waved aside even the thought. "Put it away, don't be ridiculous."

THAT WAS THE SUMMER I was going to get a job. Rog thought that was a swell idea—"It would be good for you, y'know, to see how these things work."

Girls like me were a glut on the summer-job market, especially when we said we adored literature and were dying to do "something in publishing." That some of us were actually hired on these thin credentials speaks volumes about how things were then. We were a very small generation of Depression babies growing up in an expanding economy, and the possibilities were unlimited.

But I was halfhearted, undecided, frightened. I had nothing to offer but a polite smile and a typing speed of forty words a minute, and I didn't *want* to sit in an office all day fooling with carbon paper . . . all of which was obvious to anybody who interviewed me, and I set some kind of new low by failing to find any job at all.

One day I tagged along after a friend who was volunteering at the Eisenhower campaign headquarters. After a few hours of folding and stuffing envelopes I would have left there forever except that the head of the place was Chester Lacey with the sad brown eyes, the one who had studied art in Paris. Now that was all over, and he was at Columbia Law School and working for Youth for Eisenhower. By God he liked Ike, *loved* Ike, who was the only one who could clean up the mess in Washington.

From him I heard about big government and creeping socialism and infiltrating Reds and how the country desperately needed a change. Chester knew from somebody on the inside that the White House was *literally* a mess. There were empty cans and Coke bottles all over the place and Harry Truman's old newspapers, and Bess was kind of a slob in general, and while this in itself wouldn't deliver us hogtied to the reds, it was a pretty accurate metaphor.

I followed Chester to the Chicago convention, where I wore an Ike hat and passed out buttons in the lobby of the Hilton Hotel, helped organize spontaneous demonstrations, and learned Ike songs. The best part was getting knocked down in a drunken lobby scuffle between the Taft and the Ike people. I even managed to get into the convention hall and hear MacArthur's keynote speech, which was politics at its juiciest:

". . . the party of Jefferson and Jackson . . . that party of noble heritage has become captive to the schemers and planners who have infiltrated its ranks of leadership to set the national course unerringly toward the socialist regimentation of a totalitarian state . . . we practically invited Soviet dominance over the free peoples of Eastern Europe . . . we foolishly permitted the encirclement of Berlin by Soviet forces . . ." etc.

I was admired by other campaign workers because, being nineteen and too young to vote, I must have extraordinary fervor. The Republican party was lucky to have me.

Rog approved of all this. He and Chester, being of like mind in many ways, had gotten along well at a couple of Mama Louisa dinners. But later he advised me not to hold my breath, Chester's real interest was in working the room.

"That's how some men are, y'know. This one probably won't hang around, he's a politician. You'd better be ready to cut your losses."

I didn't want to hear that . . . but I didn't forget he said it. Rog always cut to the chase. And he knew, even before I did, that I was no Republican.

STEERING RIGHT, TURNING LEFT

ALL MY MOTHER'S FRIENDS, which included Nunnally, approved of Rog. His credentials were excellent. He'd been a Deke at Syracuse, gotten his M.A. at Columbia Business School, and was currently working on his doctoral thesis about something so abstruse I've forgotten, if I ever knew, what it was. He had been a pilot in the Royal Canadian Air Force.

Much of his life had been sad. He was twice a widower. His first wife had died in childbirth, his second from TB; his infant daughter was removed from the home for her safety, to be brought up by elderly grandparents. When she was eighteen, Teddy inherited a little money from a relative and used it to flee the stern household she'd grown up in. She went to Paris where she met and married a French journalist. Rog had a framed picture of her in their Left Bank flat, a ravishing young woman with a cap of dark hair wearing a huge white tulle skirt, sprawled on a black-and-white marble floor, lighting a cigarette. (I longed for an apartment like that, a skirt like that, a face like that.)

After his second wife died, Rog moved from New Jersey to an apartment in Manhattan. "He was a sought-after bachelor, much out and about," Ma told me. "He's very fond of joining clubs"—the Union League Club, the University Club, the Dartmouth Club, the Williams Club . . . and the V.F.W. to lift a glass or two with the other old flyboys.

His health was uncertain—a month before the August wedding, most of his ulcerous stomach had to be removed. He shrugged it off and joked about his "tiny little tummy"—which could no longer accommodate Mama Louisa's five-course meals or almost anything else he liked. It made the celebratory parties rough on him. In his pastel shantung suit, he'd look forlornly at the platters of shrimp and caviar and the forbidden bottles of champagne.

NUNNALLY AND DORRIS, in town for an opening, came over one evening for a drink. When I heard this I thought I'd just go to a couple of double features, or else hide out at the corner bar. Then curiosity won. My mother was a good reporter but she'd never be able to cover *this* story.

It was a strange and interesting hour. My parents greeted each other with such barely controlled delight that I wondered, for a passing second, if this was love's fleeting flame—or if she was getting married as a favor to Nunnally, to free him from guilt and alimony payments. Rog, with his glass of ginger ale, was genial if quieter than usual. Dorris was charming; she looked fabulous in a black silk suit and Ferragamos with stiletto heels.

I can't remember if Nunnally introduced his two wives, or if they'd met before—but whichever it was, neither said "Oh, I've heard so much about you." Marion introduced Rog, and Nunnally said how glad he was to have a professor of finance in the family. Rog laughed good-naturedly, then he and Nunnally joked back and forth together.

Then Nunnally turned to Ma and said he'd seen so-and-so, and they were off on the old days . . . as I watched and wondered if they had always been so affectionate and congenial, or if it was a new mien tailored to the present circumstances. Dorris pulled her chair nearer to Rog and asked his opinion on a couple of investments she was considering. Rog's large pink face looked uncomfortable—when Dorris got going it was hard to stop her, and she was trying to learn about capital gains. Nunnally was paying far too much money to the IRS.

"No, no, you can't do that, don't you see," Rog said. "It's risky as hell, but I can't advise you about that sort of thing. You should find out more about it, y'see." Dorris asked *where* she could find out, and he jotted down a couple of book titles. Something about the seriousness of the transaction caught Ma's attention, she got stiffer and quieter, her eyes grew big and round. She looked a little overdressed in her low-cut velvet top and satin skirt.

Nunnally resorted to the comic what-do-I-know, I-leave-it-all-to-Dorris shrugs he adopted when the talk moved into certain areas, then tried to rescue the flagging discourse with stories about his younger children, then four, eight, and eleven. He wrote me about them often . . . and as I listened a familiar shadow fell on me, the one that came when I heard about life in a happy family.

THEY WERE MARRIED in the somber Collegiate Reformed Church on the West Side. The minister was a friend of Rog's; nobody had any other church affiliation. The bride—who looked happier than I'd ever seen—and groom wore pink and blue silk suits. She was, like the century, fifty-two, he was fifty-four.

I was her only attendant. My dress was too heavy for the scorching August day, and I was damp and sticky. The unaccustomed hat—with veil—was a suffocating helmet. As I followed them down the aisle, some piece of my complex underwear snapped and sagged. After the ceremony, twenty or thirty friends jammed into the Flynns' cabin on the *Île-de-France* to celebrate the new marriage. After many champagne toasts to the future, the past, old friendships, and long life, after an hour of tears, laughter, and embraces, the Flynns sailed off for a two-month honeymoon in Europe.

"WHAT DO YOU THINK of your new stepfather?" Uncle George asked at dinner, after the designated half hour for one drink and two cheese sticks, before count-the-mixed-couples.

"Terrific," I said warily. You never could tell when or where George was going to pounce. He was very smart. I liked him a lot, but that night I wasn't up to jousting with him.

"How about his politics?"

"A little right-wing."

"A little!"

"Leave her alone," Margaret said.

"I'll give her a few days," George said, his bald head shining in the lamplight, "and then she has to defend herself."

I was staying at their apartment at Ninth and University until school started and I had to stay on my toes. Every day I took the IRT to my new job at the Central Trust of China, on Maiden Lane. Unlike the high-energy commotion of the Eisenhower headquarters at the Marguery Hotel, this was a silent office where six Chinese men sat at desks, delicately clicking abacuses. What did this organization do? We were in charge of supplying the Nationalist Army on Formosa with socks, belt buckles, and other essentials. ("The Nationalist troops are in a fine state of training," *Time* magazine said, "well-fed, well-clothed, and as pugnatious as terriers . . . they would give an excellent account of themselves if the Reds attacked Formosa" [7/28/52].) I typed up lists and letters—over and over, because if they weren't perfect, Mr. Chang made me do them again. Nunnally told everybody I was working for a tong.

Every day I ate lunch with Vera, the full-time secretary, in the Trinity churchyard, then unfenced and open to the public. We sat among the historic graves eating egg salad sandwiches while Vera told me every detail of her fraught, peculiar sex life.

"He says my breasts are like Bartlett pears." Vera's voice floated over Alexander Hamilton's crypt. "He dreams about my shoes . . . what do you suppose that means?"

I had no idea . . . I was having trouble keeping my mind on things. Like most of my friends I was a technical virgin. I'd done everything except *it* —and Vera was a fount of ideas about new ways to have fun while staying pure. I tried to pay more attention.

"He says the little nether hairs are the silk of a true blond."

"No kidding."

"Mr. Chang isn't completely satisfied with your work," Vera said, "but he knows better than to be fussy about summer help."

"Tell me something I don't know."

"Don't you learn typing at college?"

"Of course not."

"Why not?"

"Because we're there to learn a lot of useless stuff and be prepared for nothing and say we went to Smith."

Vera had learned shorthand at Katie Gibbs; she transcribed Mr. Chang's letters quickly and faultlessly. But I couldn't concentrate. My mind kept drifting away to Ma and Rog in Saint-Tropez, Ma in her turquoise bathing suit with the pleated skirt and her straw gondolier hat, Rog in his madras Bermudas and shantung blazer. I imagined them at a beach café having lots of drinks and pasta and bouillabaise, laughing at everything and nothing the way people do when they're crazy about each other. I didn't follow them into the hotel room. I didn't want to dwell on a middle-aged, overweight couple making love. It was the fun they were having that I kept thinking about.

"Well, he'd probably fire you if you weren't leaving anyway," Vera said, and tears unexpectedly sprang to my eyes. "What's the matter? He's not going to. Just try not to make mistakes. Keep your mind on what you're doing. I mean, how could we be ordering six million belt buckles?"

I didn't know and I didn't fucking care.

I felt as though my past was draining away, being sucked out by some force I had no control over. Old memories kept running around in my head . . . Ma and me going down the road together. Ma picking me up at school, making *pêches flambées* in the chafing dish, crooning from above that it was time for the boyfriend to leave. I thought of shopping with her at Peck & Peck, bouncing along in the Jeep station wagon, giving the dog a bath, helping her plant geraniums in the backyard. I remembered her Alphabet Diet, insanely carried through to a final dinner of zwieback, zucchini, zabaglione, and zinfandel.

When I was away at school she broke her leg skiing and couldn't use the stairs, so she lived on the second floor and threw the door key out the window to friends who'd been consigned to bring casseroles. And there was the morning I came down to find the whole house flooded and there was Ma sitting cross-legged on the dining room table, with a cup of coffee, making a list. ("We have to start somewhere.") At the cottage on Long Island a hurricane doused the electricity and the plumbing that depended on it. For days it was candles, cold food, bottled water, singing in the dark.

I thought of her sneaking down a Swiss Alp, carrying her shoes, trying not to wake our stern, grouchy host at the chalet, down to the Parc Hotel in the village where the fun was. And Paris after the money came back, having makeovers at Elizabeth Arden's and then spending a bundle on pâté, tournedos Rossini, peaches and black grapes and Roquefort and Beaujolais. Lying half-asleep on the floor of Florence's Chelsea flat, listening to them talk about Europe in the twenties when they were young.

My head was full of her aphorisms: A lady never smokes on the street or in bed. Marriage is so interesting everybody ought to try it at least once. Alimony is as good as the man who pays it. Sooner or later, a man is going to kiss your foot. And—as she said over the Saint André cheese and the Ribier grapes—I wonder what the poor people are doing tonight?

How would I deal with disaster, or anything else, without her?

• • •

UNCLE GEORGE decided that enough time had passed and now I had to defend Rog, conservatism, the Republican Party, and Chester.

"If you approve of McCarthy in any way you're leaving my house," he said. He had a little brush-shaped mustache.

"She is not leaving anywhere," Aunt Margaret said. The maid was serving tongue with raisin sauce, a strange dish I somehow liked.

"Of course I don't but I also don't like communists and I think . . ."

"Exactly what is a communist?"

"Somebody who wants to overthrow the state."

"Wrong! Somebody who believes in a system of government under which all property is owned by the state."

I lost whatever argument we were having, and Margaret and George went out on the terrace. Little cries of glee came through the French doors as I wandered into the living room, which was two floors high and had a little balcony from the upstairs hall. Ma and I had stayed here after we'd left Nunnally and driven across the country, and sometimes in the evenings I'd stood there and sung for the adults below in the living room—"Chattanooga Choo-choo" and "California, Here I Come." I remembered their worried smiles, their hands circling their drinks, their lowered voices. I'd seen snow here for the first time. My two boy cousins had taken me down to Washington Square and thrown snowballs at me.

CHESTER WAS STILL OUT: I put the receiver back and tried to imagine where he might be: in a bar with a bunch of Ike people or having dinner with his parents in Scarsdale or with any of a dozen girls. I'd told him I'd probably be lonely after the wedding . . . but either he'd forgotten or else it just sailed past him. He really couldn't understand the things that made me miserable, and he had little patience with undefined angst.

Once in Chicago, one of the packed hotel suites had suddenly emptied out, leaving us alone amid buckets of melted ice and overflowing ashtrays, and we'd fallen onto a bed for one of those tangled fast sessions of faux lovemaking. Chester had said suddenly, during a close moment, "Why are you so unhappy?"

I stopped breathing. "What?"

Then the door burst open and three or four people came in and we had to pull ourselves together—which I didn't do fast enough. I felt as though he'd shoved my face up against a mirror.

"But I'm not."

"Forget it," Chester said. "I talk too much. Button yourself up."

Then he was back in the fray, yelling into the phone. He'd found me out—and on the fly yet, in a smoke-filled room. I didn't even know that I wasn't having a wonderful time. It was like driving some Alice in Wonderland car . . . if I steered left it went right. If I accelerated it stopped, if I braked it went faster. And wherever I was going—which I didn't know either—there were no road signs. I thought Chester knew the road signs.

DOWNSTAIRS I heard Margaret and George's voices as they came inside. Three mixed couples, pretty good. Once they'd seen seven. They only did it in the summer—in the winter they could wear coats, but it got dark early and you couldn't see skin tones clearly enough. They came upstairs and George tapped on my half-open door, saying, "Explain to me the exact difference between Ike's foreign policy and Taft's."

"Taft is much more . . . isolationist. Ike understands more about other parts of the world because of his war experience."

"That's pretty vague. Don't you want my vote?"

"You're going to vote for Stevenson anyway."

He laughed. "Of course I am. I'm trying to get you to argue intelligently. You're smart enough but you certainly go to a lot of trouble to hide it."

People always said the same thing—you're pretty good, *but.* Nothing major, I didn't have the nerve for high drama. It was more of an attitude problem. I liked the wrong things. I looked the wrong way. I couldn't steer the car.

I heard George's bedroom door close. It wasn't the first time I'd suspected I wasn't learning anything useful at Smith. I had even thought of transferring to Barnard and living at 204. I had filled out the forms, sent them in, and been accepted. Then I got a curious letter from Nunnally saying in his opinion I should go back to Smith so Marion and Rog could have an undisturbed period of peace and privacy. It would be the considerate thing to do. I told Smith I was coming back.

"HI, DOLL," Chester said. "How's everything?"

He'd almost forgotten me, my honeymooning mother and Chinese job and persistent uncle. But we went out to dinner, where he told me about how he was flunking out of Columbia Law School and his father was going to kill him and he was sure he had mononucleosis and he didn't have any money . . . but his "Clean Up the Mess" slogan was really kicking in. Next week everybody was going to go to Washington with mops and brooms to stage a big demonstration while mopping the grass on the Great Mall and dusting . . . something. What should they dust?

"The cherry trees?"

They'd probably just wave feather dusters. The press would be alerted and it would all be on television. If I wanted to come along there was still room in his car.

"I can't, I have this ridiculous job."

"My dad has threatened not to pay any more tuition and then guess what, I'd have to get a job too."

"It's not so bad. It's nice not having to ask people for money," I said.

"Oh, girls don't need to earn money."

"I'm not sure I agree."

We went back to the apartment afterward. I'd thought George and

Margaret were going to be out. But they'd come back early and George came downstairs in his Sulka bathrobe—not for duenna duty, but because he couldn't resist a good argument. He and Chester were off on the communist threat and HUAC for at least an hour, and by the time he went back upstairs, I was falling asleep.

"Uncle George is swell," Chester said groggily as he left. I'd yet to find somebody he didn't think was swell, even my Jewish socialist nutty uncle whom on all counts he should hate.

I thought how fake Chester and I were together, how completely mismatched. He only loved me when I was wearing an Ike hat and waving a pennant, jumping around and laughing like an idiot—which I only did to please him. I knew Rog was right, this was going nowhere—and I also knew I'd hang on till the phone was silent, till he finally told me to take a walk. Till then I was his.

I couldn't go to Washington, so Chester took little Janie in Pamphlets who wanted a ride. I imagined him driving along the Pulaski Skyway with a car full of cheerleaders in Ike hats. I scanned three or four papers—there was no television, my family still thought it was a fly-by-night gadget that would never last—and all I found was one wee picture of Chester buried away in the *Daily News,* mop in one hand, bucket in the other, a "Clean Up the Mess in Washington" pennant fluttering behind him.

WE WENT UP the front steps of 204 and I fumbled around in the dark till I got the key in the lock. The door was old and encrusted with black paint. I opened the two doors and groped around inside till I found the light switch.

It was the first time I'd been here since the wedding day, and I was afraid to go alone. It had taken some persuasion to get Chester to come with me. It might have made some guys feel protective but Chester only thought I was a sissy.

The crystal lamps cast dim tidal pools of light into the darkness, and I went into the living room and turned on more lights. The room looked strange, the turquoise walls made me a little seasick. It felt musty; there was a foreign leathery smell that I didn't recognize, Rog's monogrammed, matched luggage, a gift that had arrived too late to take along. Boxes, textbooks, notebooks were everywhere. The pink loveseat was pushed aside and a steamer trunk was leaning against the Ann Duffy breakfront. On the mirrored coffee table were stacks of manuscript.

"Okay, I just have to go up and get a couple of things."

I left Chester in the living room and went up to Ma's fluffy deco bedroom. Huge new shoes in the closet, enormous tweed and gabardine jackets on hangers, a rack full of ties. A shaving mug and brush, 4711 cologne and bay rum on the bathroom shelf, a large terry-cloth robe hanging next to the familiar pink negligee.

I went up to the top floor, suffocatingly hot with the windows closed. The small room—the one I'd slept in when I was little, with the prayer rug and the view of the Chrysler Building—looked the same. But the other one had piles of books, a typewriter, and a huge box saying FRIDEN, whatever that was. And a big battered desk with a green glass lamp on it, a leather office chair. I took what I needed out of my bureau and ran back down. Chester was in the kitchen, drinking a glass of water.

"What's the matter?"

"Oh, I don't know. It's just funny seeing Rog's stuff everywhere."

"I think Rog is a wonderful guy."

"Of course you do."

He said, "Listen, it's great your mother is marrying him. Suppose you didn't like him?"

"I didn't like the last one."

Chester gave me a long look and asked, "Why do you make things so hard for yourself?"

"I don't *make* them hard," I said, "they *get* hard."

"Oh, come on. People make their own lives. You gotta learn that." He came toward me in the glaring kitchen light, put his arms around me. "I know something you can make hard if you want to."

We had a whole house to ourselves, four floors, beds, sofas. No Uncle George, nobody. We could have done whatever we wanted, but we were programmed, so it was into the living room and love-without-fucking. I couldn't get into it, I kept smelling the leather suitcases.

"What's 'Friden'?" I asked, as he paused for breath—or else just gave out.

"What?"

"There's a huge box saying 'Friden' upstairs."

"That's the name of the guy inside," Chester said, as we sat up and pulled ourselves together. "I mailed him to you to take back to Smith. You'll like him, he's a lot of laughs."

Chester's long lanky torso stretched out as he hiked up his shoulders and tucked his shirt back in. When I asked if he was going to come to Northampton his shoulders collapsed, his face changed.

"You *know* I can't. You *know* I can't do anything like that . . . sweetheart. Everything's so crazy, it's a miracle I'm even here." Again I'd forgotten he was the busiest man in New York. "Listen, you should come down, it's more fun here anyway. Cabot Lodge is having a party in October. We'll go. Okay?"

"Okay." Getting kissed again didn't really do it, though it was supposed to.

"Don't look at me like that, doll. I want to see you look happy."

WALKING ON EGGS

BERLIN, 1953: That summer Nunnally was producing and directing *Night People,* a cold war story about the United States' and Russia's delicate footwork in divided Germany—using his script, from a story by Jed Harris. I was there to watch the filming, join the fun, and learn more about the world.

West Berlin was then an island in a Russian sea. Looking out the plane window on the way from London, I was sure the communist air was darker, that fear and loathing drifted upward and crept into the plane. I wasn't far wrong. You didn't fly casually over Russian territory then. Planes from the West were tracked or followed. Only five years before, the Russians had tried to starve out West Berlin by stopping all traffic through East Germany, resulting in the extraordinary Berlin Airlift.

The Hotel Kempinski in the British sector was mostly occupied by Twentieth Century-Fox people. There was a crowd of autograph hunters on the street in front at all times. Whenever the star, Gregory Peck, came through the door onto the Kurfurstendamm the crowd grew, voices rose, hands thrust out pens and pencils for autographs—

a pitch of excitement that would only be surpassed later in the summer by the king of Afghanistan.

The other actors drew milder responses. Broderick Crawford did pretty well. Rita Gam, Buddy Ebsen, and Walter Abel aroused moderate interest, as did Nunnally when he was identified as the director and an important Hollywood producer. In time the crowd dwindled, though it never completely disappeared. I became familiar with the hopeful murmur when any of us went in or out of the hotel—the searching looks, the disappointed, slightly annoyed shrugs when we were discovered to be lesser beings.

Since the fictional setting of *Night People* was the same as the shooting location, we seemed to be living the movie. On- and off-screen, the city was mostly ruins and rubble. This was before the Wall, and you could go to any checkpoint or sector border and look through the Iron Curtain (which was made of air and guns) at real Russians—or else you could look at Peter van Eyck and other actors in Russian uniform. Only a reality check distinguished Gregory Peck, Buddy Ebsen, and Casey Adams from the army of occupation.

In Berlin reality was always stretched to the breaking point. Was the major at the bar an actor or was he from HICOG (the U.S. High Commissioner's Office)? Did the Jeep belong to the military or to Twentieth Century-Fox? Was the guy in the lederhosen for real? In the back lot, the illusion was manufactured—and you always knew the difference, you could get off the merry-go-round. But here the illusion *was* the reality—as though we'd time-traveled back to Sherwood Forest to make a movie about Robin Hood.

THE FIRST NIGHT I was there I watched Nunnally direct an early, key scene called "The Snatch." It took place on what had been a residential street, now lined with bombed-out houses and piles of rubble. The private on duty at Checkpoint Charlie (not the real one) is hustled off by the commies, who, it turns out, want to trade him for a couple of West German spies. The private's ugly-American father, a corporate high honcho (Broderick Crawford) turns up and demands the immediate return of his son, and the American colonel at HICOG (Gregory Peck) brilliantly untangles the entire knot. The face-off between the two men, and the father's slow understanding of cold-war reality, is the heart of the story.

Border incidents, which took place all the time, were usually solved by similar behind-the-scenes maneuvering. The military had to pass on everything, and the Russians had to be carefully handled. There was a lot of walking on eggs. Think of the complexity of the place. We had—with justification—bombed Berlin to a pulp. So the German people weren't very fond of us, the conquerors, nor as grateful as we thought they ought to be for defeating Hitler. Now we were protecting them from the Russians, who were a seemingly worse threat. They put up with us, while they searched their souls for the reasons they'd gotten themselves into the whole mess in the first place.

DORRIS AND I went in search of cameras and watches, cashmere sweaters, gold, Henckel steel items, and funny carved wooden gadgets. Diligent searching turned up Meissen china and other antiques, which were sold privately by people in need of money. The Americans bought them up, the shipping boxes appeared again. There were some oddities around, such as cupless bras—like eyeglass frames without lenses. They were fun to try on but it was hard to understand their purpose as they failed entirely to do what a bra is meant to. They appeared to be a German joke, like nutcrackers with gargoyle faces or the mad King Ludwig's playground-castle near Munich, which we visited later in the summer.

Soon after I arrived, Dorris and I went on a sightseeing tour in the Russian sector. It was a bleak and deserted place; the streets were lined with prole-modern apartment buildings. Rebuilding had been minimal and the yellow rubble stretched for blocks. We weren't allowed out of the bus anywhere except at a couple of scary war memorials guarded by *volkspolizei* strutting back and forth with tommy guns—which they kept firmly in hand while the guide pointed out the marble statues of Stalin.

At a long, pointless stoplight—there were no cars or people around—a gang of children flew into sight and made a dash for the bus, jumping around under the windows, staring up at the *auslanders* and begging for anything we might care to give them.

Dorris knew what, she'd been here before. She dug into her handbag and came up with a secret stash of candy and cookies. The bus window was open and she threw out a few little bags of contraband treats. Then, not satisfied, she was on her feet, down the aisle, and out the door into Stalin Allee before anybody could stop her. In her Mainbocher suit, her golden hair shining in the pale sun, she handed out the rest of her treats as two *volkspolizei* in jodhpurs trained their gun barrels on her. The chocolate-faced children fled, and Dorris remained calm as the guide and the bus driver persuaded the unfriendly fellows defending their country that she was not a spy and that sometimes candy was just candy.

In the excitement afterward, Dorris ended up in another seat, next to a mournful, Nicholas Cage–looking PFC who promptly began flirting with her. And why not? Besides being the best-looking woman on the bus, she was a heroine who'd broken through the Iron Curtain. She bantered with the young soldier while I listened in annoyance. It wasn't fair. I was twenty—Dorris was in her thirties, part of the older generation. At the next stop (another monument to Stalin, where they kept Dorris on a tight rein), I sidled up to the PFC. He asked if Dorris was my sister. I told him she was my stepmother—a shock sufficient to make him drop her immediately (which she hardly noticed), and he was mine for the rest of the stay in Berlin.

I LOVED BEING with the night people.

There was a core group consisting loosely of Buddy Ebsen, Casey Adams, Rita Gam, Walter Abel, Peter van Eyck, Dorris and Nunnally, Jerry and Gerd Oswald, the associate producer, and Jim Denton, the public relations man. Others came and went—Rita's husband, the director Sidney Lumet; the Broadway producer Jed Harris; assorted friends, relatives, and curiosity-seekers. Gregory Peck and Suzette, his French companion, lived in a rented house elsewhere and rarely appeared. There were usually a few soldiers around, and there was always somebody at the Kempinski Café to have a drink with or a *Kaffee mit Schlag* or dinner and a seamy nightclub or two. At the Bassvatter or the Kit Kat I first saw (and had explained to me) a drag queen.

Besides the Iron Curtain, there wasn't much to see. Most of Berlin's monuments and museums had either been destroyed by Allied bombs or, except for the ruined, magnificent Reichstag, were in the Russian sector. The army went to some trouble to keep us amused. The brass gave lavish parties at their homes for the company, and Twentieth Century-Fox reciprocated at one of the two or three elegant restaurants. And there were cheeseburgers at the PX, drinks and dinner at the officers' mess, and amateur skits at the enlisted men's club and the immigrants' quarters—barracks where defectors from behind the Iron Curtain lived while being processed—where Buddy Ebsen danced, Casey Adams played the piano and sang, and Paducci, the PFC, and other talented nobodies did dance numbers and hoped somebody would offer them a three-picture deal.

Nunnally and Gerd Oswald, Gregory Peck, Brod Crawford, and others who worked daily weren't up to much at night. But the rest— Casey, Buddy, Walter and Rita (who had days off) and the hangers-on, Dorris, Jerry Oswald, the odd spouse or relative like me and a shifting handful of soldiers—were often out on the town. There were few places to go and the stray groups often ended up together. Sometimes Dorris and I started out separately, then met hours later in some smoky boîte, I would look across the room and see her blond head, surrounded by brass and braid. It put us, temporarily, into the same generation.

Paducci usually spotted her first. He'd gaze at her, sigh mournfully, and say, "I can't believe she's your stepmother. She sure looks good"—which didn't merit a reply.

By then he had told me he was homesick for Brooklyn, for his mother's lasagna, and for the pair of blue suede shoes in his closet that he couldn't wait to wear. The shoes dampened what small interest I had in him. I thought of telling him I was engaged to somebody at home, but every time he mooned over Dorris's youth and beauty I decided to hang onto him a little longer. He never asked whether I could get him into the movies; maybe he thought that if he just hung around with Hollywood people and performed every once in a while—twice he had grabbed the microphone at a nightclub and sung "That Old Black Magic"—that was enough.

AFTER THREE WEEKS in Berlin, the *Night People* company moved en masse to the Hotel Fier Jahreszeiten in Munich to shoot the interiors. Everything continued as it had before, including the fans outside on the sidewalk and the cameraderie.

Nunnally was working hard, and he sent Dorris and me off to Venice with Jerry Oswald, the blond, soft-spoken wife of Gerd, the associate producer. In the plane Dorris told us that Jed Harris was going to be in Venice and she was going to have some dates with him.

I'd first met the orphic Jed when I was eight or nine, and even at that age I'd felt his cobra magnetism. He both attracted and repelled. He stood out from the tangle of writers, producers, and directors that were my father's friends—though it took many years to realize what a titan of the American theater he was. Jed was the original producer and director of *Our Town,* the producer of *The Front Page* and *The Heiress,* and the director of *The Crucible.* He had a reputation for bad behavior, but Nunnally not only respected his brilliance but regarded him with enough affection to name him godfather of my young half sister. He had given Christie a tree—which stayed behind when the family moved—and, even more eccentrically, gave the nonpet Nunnally and Dorris a Doberman pinscher. They had no idea what to do with the high-strung creature, which eventually did itself in, but Pop didn't dare give it back.

In Venice Jed met us at the hotel and took us to the Danieli for drinks and dinner on the piazza. Afterward we went for a gondola ride. Plaintive *gondolieri* songs floated over our heads, as the paddle went plush-plush in the dark water of the Grand Canal. Accordion music came from somewhere . . . there were even fireworks soaring above the city. I thought I was in heaven.

Jed and Dorris sat on one seat of the gondola, Jerry and I on the other. Jed's saturnine smile glowed in the lantern light. He told stories in his Broadway voice, and we laughed and laughed as we drifted down small side canals and under tiny stone bridges. It was a little unreal, it was downright strange . . . and when we arrived at the Bauer Grunwald, where we were staying, Jerry and I got out and Dorris and Jed continued on into the night, the lantern swinging behind them.

"Do you get the feeling we're chaperoning?" Jerry asked. She and I had put in a strenuous day of shopping, and we were eating scampi at a waterside restaurant.

My eyes got wider as I looked at her over the wine carafe. It sure seemed like it. But then Nunnally had given his permission. He hadn't come with us—he probably wouldn't have even if he hadn't been working. He didn't like to walk, shop, look at statues or not be understood when he spoke English, and he didn't like pasta. Greece and Italy were "too hot and had too many steps." And he and Dorris not only traveled at different times—sometimes even taking two planes for safety—but to different places. In my world, if you were with one boy you weren't supposed to even look at another, but theirs was different. Nunnally had often written my mother letters about dates and parties with other women, and she accepted it. "Writers need experience," she said. "I didn't want to get in the way of that."

After two or three days of being gone most of the time, Dorris reappeared, just as enigmatically, saying Jed had left Venice. Jerry said she wasn't talking, even in the privacy of their shared hotel room.

In a few days Dorris went on to Rome, and Jerry and I returned to Munich. I had my father to myself for a few days. We had dinner together every night, alone or with others from the company. We went to a couple of very fancy restaurants, ordering regional delicacies and suitable wines for each course—an Austrian hock was Nunnally's favorite that summer. We had goulash and schnitzel and something called a *kaiserschmarren.* I'd come a long way, he said, from the time I had oysters for the first time (complete with a pearl, planted there by Prince Mike Romanoff) and from my early addiction to corned beef hash with an egg at the Brown Derby. We visited Salzburg and went to the castle of the mad King Ludwig of Bavaria. And I got to be an extra in the bar scene of *Night People,* for which they paid me sixty marks.

I said nothing about Dorris and Jed. Dorris was exercising her freedom—neatly, without making trouble. She had gone behind the Iron Curtain without being arrested, she had sailed off into the night with Jed without ruffling the waters. She spent a ton of money and Nunnally was still smiling. She knew how to manage things. She was a southern girl, and they always knew something the rest of us didn't.

THE SOUNDS OF HOME

DOWN THROUGH THE CLOUDS and the blue September air into Idlewild . . . the propellers slowed to a stop. Into the city in a Checker cab, up the front steps of 204. The big black door, the tiled vestibule, the dear little front hall.

Ma stood there, bright-eyed and suntanned. She and Rog had been in Bermuda. I felt a little spark of relief—she'd come back. On some level I was never sure she would. Now we were both safe. They had been married over a year, he wasn't going to leave her. Never again would I see her through the dining room window, when I came home late, eating her lonely dinner. "I'm so afraid of being one of those women eating alone in Schrafft's," she'd said.

But I had eagle eyes, the nose of a foxhound, ears like a bat. From among the familiar sounds of the house I had heard a muffled buzz-buzz-snap-rattle. When I dragged my suitcase up the two flights it got louder. There was Rog in the tiny bedroom at the head of the stairs, curled up at his desk like a baby in utero. Before him was a churning, thumping mean machine.

"My new study," he said.

"What is it?" I asked.

"It's a Friden calculator, toots."

Today a calculator fits in your hand. I have one that hangs from a key ring; you push the buttons with a pencil. Rog's was black and steel, three feet by two feet, maybe a foot high. He punched in his numbers and it took off, parts of it whizzing back and forth, the rest clanking and churning around for several minutes before producing a result on a scroll of paper. He ripped it off, scratched something down, then did it again. There was a resemblance between the Friden and Spencer Tracy's monster computer in *The Desk Set.*

My room seemed unchanged. The fireplace was set with a couple of logs and some twists of paper. My books . . . *Barbar* and *Bambi* and *The Black Stallion, My Friend Flicka, Mary Poppins* and *Nancy Drew* and *Little Women* and Somerset Maugham, Jane Austen and the Bröntes, Fitzgerald, Salinger, Isherwood and Frye, Mencken and P. G. Wodehouse, O'Neill and Hemingway. The wing chair where I'd spent hours reading or listening to *Inner Sanctum,* Jack Benny, and *Portia Faces Life* on the old RCA radio. The shelves with boxes of diaries, letters, drawings, journals, stories, and poems.

In the bathroom was the claw-footed tub with its old-fashioned fixtures, the toilet with the wall tank and pull-chain, the tiny stool I'd once stood on to brush my teeth. The medicine-chest artifacts—Dr. Lyon's Tooth Powder, Vicks VapoRub, two dusty false fingernails and a half-bottle of blue nail polish, an eyelash curler. In the hazy mirror I had detected the first chicken pox, applied the first lipstick.

Everything was small, narrow, a little cramped. It was a child's private haven, a place for teenage sleepovers. I had never made love here or done anything very adult at all. I welcomed my friends, but the first man I ever brought here was the one I was about to marry, and we only sat and talked by the fire.

Buzz-buzz, bang snap chop chop chop, the new sounds of home.

Reentry was different since Rog had joined the family. Curled up in the wing chair, I compared him and Nunnally. I imagined them both sitting among friends or family, drink in hand, legs crossed, holding forth.

Nobody could touch Nunnally as a raconteur. His touch was precise, his humor edgy but not cruel. But he had to have the floor. If a listener's attention wandered or if somebody interrupted, his blue eyes darkened, his head hung forward. A shadow filled the room until all eyes had turned back toward him.

A professor of finance might not be expected to sparkle with wit, but Rog had an Irish gift of gab, and he was fun to listen to. He produced bons mots and rhymed couplets, usually about lorn women ("Who will deflower Laura Bower?" "Still no dice for Phyllis Price," etc.) And he was sensible, direct, there was no side to him. After three drinks there was usually a switch to tits and ass, and more.

Both were drinkers, but Rog held his better. It took a lot more for him to become blotto. Both started out jolly and got jollier, leading to a joyous, joke-telling crest . . . then, like a tank emptying, they became steadily less appealing as the level in the bottle went down. Speech slurred, eyes lost focus, charm gave way to nameless gloom . . . the mutation of alcohol.

Both wanted to be pampered, but their demand styles varied. Rog cheerfully called out for more Old Fitz, more cheese and crackers, more roast beef, or something odd and supposedly good for his tiny tummy—like cantaloupe with chocolate ice cream—which his wife rushed to provide. Nunnally brooded without explaining, leaving it to others to figure out what the problem was, sending them into nameless anxiety and aimless activity.

Rog was still handsome, but now—possibly because of the sheer size of his head—there was something self-indulgent in the genial curl of his big lips and the rosiness of his complexion. Nunnally had always been "plain," as my mother put it, which never mattered to anybody but him. Rog, in his Sulka ties, his winter tweeds and pinstripes and vests, was a Brooks Brothers dream. My father wore California clothes that I didn't quite understand—short-sleeved shirts in odd shades, pleated slacks, pale jackets in mystery fabrics, pointed shoes with buckles or elastic panels, long, sheer socks with clock designs . . . but nobody noticed his clothes.

Nunnally was immaculate and finicky, wiping dust motes from his reading glasses, holding spoons up to the light and barking at people who left clothes or wet towels around. Rog wore city garb at all times—I have a snapshot of him in the middle of a Vermont field, wearing suit and tie—but I suspected he was a closet slob who fitted into the civilized world only with effort. He'd come into the hall and throw his overcoat somewhere, then hang it up a moment later—an afterthought, pasted onto him by some long-gone parent or nanny. His desk was chaotic, piled with spiral notebooks, pads of paper, bulging file folders, books sprouting markers, and strewn with desktop gadgets and ballpoint pens. The trash basket and ashtrays overflowed, the telephone rang constantly. Nunnally's desk was monastically neat, pencils lined up, ashtray gleaming, typewriter at the ready.

If marriage is about order, the right pairs ended up together. Now I had four parents.

My father continually advised all of his children. His advice to me was usually in letter form. I have letters from him going back to my childhood, continuing to close to his death—advice about boys and how their minds work, about writing, deportment, books, movies and theater, human interaction, travel, marriage, divorce . . . though nothing about being a parent. There was gossip about his friends and acquaintances, his work and the movie business and his life, stories to laugh at and stories to use if I chose. There were stories about the house and the help and tender stories about the children. I wrote back almost as often.

Rog's advice was succinct and unexpected. Some of it remains with me still, tiny semiprecious stones of solid sense I wish I'd followed. Though my mother was, in many ways, my best friend, I didn't trust her worldview—she'd made so many mistakes. So I often did the opposite of whatever she suggested. I don't recall Dorris ever giving advice—probably she thought I had enough already—but I didn't trust her worldview either.

• • •

BACK DOWNSTAIRS I said to Ma, "But what is it *for?*"

"Rog is writing his Ph.D. thesis."

"But it's so noisy."

"Oh, come on," she said.

"Couldn't Rog's study be someplace else?"

"Where?" she asked.

But I couldn't think of any place either.

NUNNALLY WROTE THAT FALL (11/16/53):

"You must remember that in a household of different affinities it is necessary to be doubly considerate and thoughtful. You may have to make concessions from time to time, and even sacrifices, but these should be done for the sake of the greater good."

This came just before Teddy's visit.

She was as beautiful as the picture I'd been looking at for over a year—better, because now you could see her dazzling smile and tall slender figure. She wasn't wearing her white tulle skirt, but a couture suit in deep red and elegant Paris shoes. Jean-François, a handsome, soft-spoken man in a vest, stood behind her, and here and around the front hall and the living room were their two baby boys and more belongings than I ever thought could be generated by such tiny creatures. There was no Nursie here to whisk things out of sight—so the stuff strewn around included diapers in all stages of use.

Ma had brought this about, in a strenuous effort to end years of poor relations between father and daughter. It was time for Rog to repair things with Teddy and get to know his grandchildren.

They were all staying on the top floor. I was at a friend's for the holiday and I would have felt dispossessed had I not been so fascinated by the French family. Teddy always wore one of her two Dior suits, even when spooning applesauce or kissing tiny feet. They had cost a fortune—but, she told me, very chic French women never spent money on cheap or mismatched pieces. One should spend on the whole outfit. If she just wanted to slop around she wore Jean-François's shirts, in which she looked almost as good. It was the first time I ever saw pale lipstick and very dark eye makeup, and intentionally shaggy gamine hair—and you could smell her Chanel all over the house.

I went upstairs only a couple of times, and each time I came down swearing I'd never have children, I'd leave my millions to the poor. Then I would sit down, take one of the babies into my lap, smell his hair and feel his silky skin . . . and waver.

Thanksgiving dinner was a chaos of weeping children, flying bits of turkey and cranberry, quarreling parents. The floor was strewn with toys and infant clothing. Rog said he was gravely ill and threatened to go back to the hospital. The caca boys, as he called his grandsons, were getting all the attention. Ma was running back and forth, serving forth string beans and pumpkin pie, trying to generate family love.

Rog looked either bored or nervous when he was handed a baby. You could tell he couldn't wait to decently unload the child. He and Teddy both drank much too much. She became strident and imperious, ordering Jean-François around and sending him up three flights for baby lotion or Gauloises; he said little, his lids grew heavier, a lock of hair flopped in his face. Any rapport between him and Rog was lost in this broken family romance.

Pre-Christmas gifts were exchanged. But Rog didn't like the hand-woven neckties that Teddy had found in the Village, and didn't bother to hide it ("I don't care for things like this, don't y'see") and her raccoon eyes became shinier, her shopping narrative more shrill. (I would have told her to go straight to Brooks Brothers.) She found her father's gift of a check sangfroid—which I overheard her tell her husband later. Ma's choices for the babies were a little off, too old or too young, and the shirts she got for Jean-François were too large, though he seemed pleased by the book of *New Yorker* cartoons.

Teddy threw her arms around her new stepmother and thanked her over and over for the presents, the hospitality, for existing. "Oh, Marion . . . you are so good . . . so wonderful to us . . . I'll never forget this visit." It was as though she had never had a gift before, a Dior-clad orphan close to tears because now she had a home.

189

• • •

MA HAD A WAY of announcing painful things. She'd come into the room and sit down, back very straight, chin aloft, hands folded in her lap. She'd tap her fingernails, clear her throat: "Rog is calling in the keys." She had to say it three times before I even grasped it.

"But he can't."

"He can and he is."

"But we've always done this."

"Things have to change."

"But *why?*" My voice turned high and tight.

"Because it bothers him to live in a hotel, he's not used to it. Last week a completely strange young woman in a tweed suit walked in on him while he was shaving." She recrossed her legs. "Besides, it isn't safe this way . . . Rog thinks. I look upon it as a security measure."

"But 204 is everybody's pit stop. What about June . . . Bobbie . . . Carol . . . they have job interviews and Pam's boyfriend is driving up from Philly and you can't tell when he'll get here and I've already told Sally she can stay here over Thanksgiving. Oh, this is crazy, the arrangements will be hell the phone bills will be awful . . ." I expanded on the unspeakable disruption of countless lives. "Anyway, Ma, I have *excellent* friends, they're polite and interesting, they have curious minds, they *love* Rog and the Louisa dinners, and they adore you and 204. Anyway, *you* like them, I know you do. Does Rog hate them?"

Later on Rog seemed a little guilty.

"You can have your friends here, you'll just have to let them in. Sorry, kiddo. You'll have to put up with my crotchety ways," he said, smiling good-naturedly. Later, after a couple of Old Fitzes, he said, "If any of them are interested in the business school, maybe I can help."

None of them were. They all wanted to work for Time-Life or Random House. He usually managed to disarm me, though not completely. My friends were nice about it but there was a tear here and there as the keys were returned. Now they had to ring the doorbell.

AT TOTO'S

SPRING OF SENIOR YEAR, 1954: They'd put a television set—
the first I'd really seen—in the dining room of Morris House so we
could watch the Army-McCarthy hearings, an investigation of supposed espionage in the U.S. Army. The national tidal wave of fear had
drawn closer: A few months before, R. G. Davis, my favorite professor, had been called to testify in front of the Velde Committee
(HUAC) for having been a communist twenty years before.

In his Twentieth-Century American Novel and his Short Story
classes of junior year, I had watched this slender, bemused-looking
man, who reminded me a little of Alec Guinness, gaze out the window, hand on chin, and say things that pushed our minds into new
and wider places. The ideas he posited didn't seem to come from
within, but rather from some passing ether of brilliance, available to
all of us if we would only look and reach out and take. "Did Sherwood
Anderson really mean . . . Does the short story form work anymore . . .
Is *anything* allowed in a novel, or should there be some rules? And
what rules?" Then a vague smile, a hopeful look around the room.

Up would go Sylvia Plath's arm. At first it was permanently up, but
she'd learned to hold back, and he'd learned to ask others first. When

she finally spoke, it was usually worth waiting for. R. G. Davis listened, head tilted to one side. He missed nothing. I soon learned not to say the first thing that came into my head, for stupidity and carelessness were gracefully shot down. Sylvia's ideas flew.

Now there was a shadow over both of them.

The news about Sylvia's suicide attempt had traveled the campus with lightning speed. I thought she had buckled under the strain of being poor, of having to sell her stories to help pay Smith's tuition of two thousand a year. And I had a moment of wicked glee that the lead horse had broken its leg—which disappeared in the baffled horror that everyone felt. If Sylvia had done this, what did it mean for the rest of us?

The Rosenbergs had been executed in June, and amid the speculation was a curious rumor that the electrocution had gone through Sylvia like lightning and made her crazy. She'd been doing a summer internship on *Mademoiselle* magazine and somebody who'd seen her around that time (she was living at the Barbizon Hotel, only two blocks from 204) told somebody who told somebody else that was when the trouble started. (Her novel, *The Bell Jar,* published years later, makes a metaphorical connection.)

I KNOW NOW, which I didn't then, how happy I was at Smith . . . if happiness is having a place where you belong. I made the customary complaints about living with hysterical girls and a housemother who smelled your breath when you came in, about spending four years gathering useless information and the absurdity of living without men—but I didn't really believe any of it.

I liked living with girls and being stopped from getting too drunk and having men around only on weekends. If they had been around all the time I would have long flunked out, so little faith did I have in my own self-control. If men had stood next to me while I brushed my teeth and seen me in curlers and zit cream, the sexual magic, the sense of occasion that my generation was so good at, would be lost.

I considered my courses—R. G. Davis's American Novel and Daniel Aaron's Political Theory, Newton Arvin's Nineteenth-Century Literature, Joyce, Yeats and Eliot—profoundly important. The novel I was writing for Al Fisher's and Mary Ellen Chase's seminars was preparation for my life's work. So was being on the board of the *Smith Review.*

If there was a measure of hysteria, it was for good reason. The future lay ahead like a black pit, and everybody was trying to maneuver the fall or at least hang onto the slippery sides. Marriage was the most acceptable solution. Now there was the twinkle of diamonds on fourth fingers, frequent screams of joy, and much talk about the church the reception the food the music and oh, the dress the bridesmaids the silver pattern meeting his parents the diaphragm to be inspected and poked (very gently) by the rest of us, you couldn't get one unless you were engaged or else a superb liar, doctors asked you the date of your wedding, the name of your fiancé, your future address and if you were making it up they knew, it was off the table and out the door.

WE SPENT a lot of time at Toto's, a coffee shop on Green Street. We sat in booths while the jukebox played Frankie Laine, Rosemary Clooney, and Patti Page . . . and then, that spring, Elvis Presley. There I read Joyce Dreiser Dos Passos Vernon Parrington Margaret Mead Reisman's *The Lonely Crowd* . . . Here we argued about Sagan and Salinger, Colette, Isherwood, Ray Bradbury. We were amused by *Catcher in the Rye* but it was Salinger's "Frannie" in *The New Yorker* that kept us up talking half the night. Why did Frannie faint? Was she pregnant? Or was it some Zen spiritual state? What did the Glass family mean? Françoise Sagan's novels were about a world where girls freely slept with men without worrying much. We brooded about virginity, speculated about who still had it and who didn't.

One evening four or five of us went to Rahar's (where we could now drink legally), had enough whiskey to loosen our tongues, then gathered in somebody's room and told our secrets. I was mortified to be part of the still-chaste minority. How could I possibly graduate in this condition?

ONCE A WEEK, a handful of us gathered in the sunny living room of the eminent Mary Ellen Chase for her senior writing seminar. I was in the final stretch of my wordy novel—full of German street-names—which both Miss Chase and my father were good enough to take seriously. There were times that year (and many other years) when I was sure writing a novel kept me sane. It was security blanket, escape hatch, conversation starter and stopper, multipurpose excuse, sometimes reason to get up in the morning. It was my best friend. I had discovered a well-kept secret.

One afternoon as Miss Chase and I were conferring, the bell rang and another member of the seminar stood at the door. I greatly admired Aggie Harding's short pieces about life in the Philippines— close-ups of creeping beasts and crawling vines and moldy bathtubs, evocative as brilliant watercolors. Aggie had won the collegewide, sought-after Prix de Paris, which meant a year working for Paris *Vogue,* learning how to edit, live, and love.

Now Aggie had come to tell Miss Chase that she was turning down the Prix de Paris because she was getting married and going to live in New Jersey. She was happy as a girl could be. She was sorry, but her fiancé wanted her to be home with him . . . somebody else would appreciate the honor more. She had come to share her joy.

I was stunned. Chase was apoplectic.

"AG-NES. You are out of your MIND," she thundered, ruffling the lace curtains and setting the Limoges teacups a-quiver. "You have no idea what you are DOING. You have not THOUGHT THIS THROUGH. You are not looking FAR ENOUGH AHEAD,"—and so forth, while Chase's companion, the distinguished medievalist Eleanor Duckett, stood in the kitchen door endlessly drying a saucer, her mouth open in a small *O.*

But Aggie was in love, she couldn't think straight—like half the class and two-thirds of the college. I probably would have been too if certain men had turned out better. As things were, I could smite my forehead in horror like the two older ladies . . . we who had true vision, who saw things as they really were. Aggie apologized, said that she might keep writing as a hobby, then she left for the road to domestic hell.

Miss Chase's swirl of white hair stood almost on end. The girl was throwing away her life choosing to live in some Jersey SLUM scrubbing FLOORS and dropping babies, and she had NEVER witnessed such sinful waste in her life. I let her believe that of course I agreed . . . though secretly I suspected I could be just as foolish.

AS SPRING CAME things got worse. The brides were flunking everything and didn't care. The nonbrides were slovenly and depressed, taking on extra work, smoking too much and getting smashed at Rahar's, sometimes having tantrums and throwing cards across the bridge table. Graduation gowns were given out in April and now a common sight was nonbrides on bicycles, like black bats, fluttering down the street to the evening courses at Northampton Secretarial School—in spite of the old saw that if you knew shorthand you would never rise above the secretarial pool.

Carrie, the girl across the hall, became engaged to a Harvard medical student. Did I care, would I have wanted him? Oh no, not ever . . . but why did I feel a dull ache every time she came twittering into the room, when she fell onto my bed babbling about the rabbi, the temple, the honeymoon at the Caribe Hilton?

A bacteriology major in my house had been visited by representatives of Boston and New York firms offering her jobs at incredible salaries, seven and eight thousand a year. She smiled, dawdled over making a choice, and then turned them all down and became engaged to a boy she'd known since she was seven. I was her bridesmaid.

A brilliant Indian girl named Rani something, Honors and Phi Beta

Kappa and everything else, was offered a complete postgraduate scholarship to Johns Hopkins and turned it down because she had to go home to a marriage being arranged by her parents to a man she'd never laid eyes on.

Another girl I knew had expressed the wish, at the end of sophomore year, to leave college and marry the love of her life . . . until her father tried to dissuade her with the promise of a European honeymoon and other perks. She assumed her fiancé would of course scorn this base bribery. But he thought the trip and the perks were a better idea and preferred to wait. She married two days after graduation—and I was her bridesmaid too.

In those days, if you got married without telling the college, you got kicked out. If you got pregnant without being married, you were kicked out and you were a slut besides. You could be married while you were at Smith, you could even be married and pregnant—but in neither case could you live in your college house, seemingly because you were privy to too many secrets of the nuptial bed, which you would pass on to your ignorant friends. You had to live with your husband somewhere in town, and everybody stared at you as you came into classrooms. I knew of only one such marriage, a noisy, frizzy-haired girl in jodhpurs who had captured an Amherst Phi Psi I'd had my eye on.

There was a girl down the hall who was secretly married. Everybody knew, but nobody told. Another one went down to the Draper Hotel in the afternoons with a series of shady undocumented males and did it and got away with it and wasn't sorry about anything. A girl from the Quad had been seen coming out of the dean's office with her tight-lipped mother, weeping, pregnant, expelled.

Then there were the two who were thought to be lesbians, and later both married and had children . . . and then there were the real lesbians that nobody knew about, and they were miserable.

There were the girls who'd had only one boyfriend ever, and they got married and lived happily ever after—and girls who never had a date. We were all sort of desperate, but some girls were *so* desperate that they married the first Mr. Wrong who asked them. There were girls who were so confident that they continued to play the field up to the very moment they accepted somebody's proposal . . . but they belonged to my mother's era.

If you did it, you would get pregnant and have to choose between a baby you didn't want and a back-street abortion. Or you might catch syphilis or gonorrhea or worse, and/or be punished by never finding the right man because you were such a slut. Even if you found him and he didn't mind your damaged condition, you'd be punished in some other terrible way—and in any case how could your mother ever face her friends?

And *it* didn't sound like that much fun—certainly no more than the high-style, fancy petting we did. It couldn't be movie-style spontaneous. Before anything happened you had to somehow get a diaphragm or he had to get the much riskier condoms, which he might not want to do—but worse yet if he had them already tucked in his wallet. And it sounded like it hurt, that it was all about the boy having fun—and we were too worried about ourselves to think much about him. At the very best it sounded immensely complicated, one more thing to learn. Both people trying to come at the same time, one miserably holding back, the other desperately trying to relax enough to get there.

MAUREEN BUCKLEY, sister of William F. Buckley, the author of *God and Man at Yale,* was a classmate. (I had once been persuaded by her to take the conservative side in a library debate about the congressional investigations—only to find, in midspeech, that I didn't believe a word I was saying.) Now another Buckley sister, a past graduate, came to address us along the family lines.

Speaking in John M. Greene Hall, she warned us that the Smith English Department was riddled with communists—naming most of my professors—who should be removed from the faculty. And Harvard was just as bad, and certain other Ivy colleges too . . . and this didn't even address atheism and other matters of great seriousness. It was her duty to speak out because the Buckleys believed alumni/alumnae had the right, even the obligation, to direct the course of education at their alma maters, and until all this was taken care of, nobody should donate any money to Smith.

Everybody turned to look at Maureen, who sat among the other Young Republicans. Her face was calm and firm. But so were the faces of the prosecutors on the TV screen—and the wretched accused had become the faces of the professors we saw every day in class. The notion that their lectures on Emerson and Hawthorne, Poe and Dreiser and Hemingway, were embedded with heresies was incredible, almost funny—though nobody felt like laughing.

Benjamin F. Wright, Smith's president, took the stand and said he wasn't going to fire anyone, he would stand by his faculty to the end. And he did—though we didn't know that a mini-investigation, launched by the Commonwealth of Massachusetts in response to Ms. Buckley's alarum, would soon take place in Northampton to further examine the mind-bending techniques of the five accused professors.

R. G. Davis had already testified before HUAC that Harvard and Smith did not indoctrinate students, in fact ". . . we [colleagues who were communists, ex-communists, Marxists, fellow travelers, etc.] had a lurking feeling that it wasn't quite good sportsmanship to try to influence young people." Could any serious indoctrinator have stated the case with such suave and graceful humor? Years later I wondered why I had heard so little about the literary radicalism of the 1930s from my courses under those experts—and later realized that of course, they had steered clear of the subject.

Offended as most of us were by the Committees's continuous attacks on civil rights, we were not the political animals our professors had been at the same age. We took it all pretty tamely, and did little beyond sighing and shaking our heads and wondering exactly what evils a communist could commit in this country, and how bad was it to be one, and why did anybody think it mattered twenty years later? We didn't know, we didn't get it. If only the ones who knew had not been afraid to tell! And we dropped our voices in Toto's because there were many around who thought McCarthy was on a noble crusade.

IT WAS GOING to happen soon and it was going to be at the Sheffield Inn. I'd suggested it, assuming that such an event should be arranged ahead of time. But from the expression on Willy's face I saw I'd been dead wrong. He looked stunned—not a very good beginning.

I'd met Willy through the friend, now graduated, who'd led me to Ike. She'd found a Republican husband; this was his brother. Blue blood coursed through the husband's veins, Willy's veins . . . the family went far, far back. Did that mean they had different ground rules about sex? Willy was thirty and had had affairs with other women. I'd thought he'd be casual and knowing.

Willy lived in the city when I met him, but very shortly he became what my mother called a boniface. He went home to help his *Mayflower* parents run the Sheffield Inn. It wasn't too far from Northampton and I drove back and forth in Ma's Buick—you were allowed to have a car for the last part of senior year if you had at least a B average. It was rather glamorous, I thought, driving to an assignation that would take place . . . sometime. If things went well, I'd talk him into moving back to New York.

The inn sounded appealing. I'd imagined another Wiggins Tavern, fireplaces and ceiling beams and waitresses in aprons, a cozy bar, four-poster beds and hooked rugs. My friend had warned me, but I refused to believe it till I saw it. The Sheffield Inn was ill-lit, oppressive, and mostly empty. There were yellowing antimacassars on the chairs and dark portraits of leather-faced ancestors on the walls, dim little lamps and corner whatnots full of china tchotchkes, cracking photo albums full of forgotten people. Everything looked shaky and there was a smell of mold and old closets.

Willy hadn't mentioned the general age of the clientele. White-haired ancients rocked on the porch, wobbled through the sitting room, and there was no bar at all and no liquor license. Willy bought a bottle of Cutty Sark and we sat in a chilly back pantry and drank it out of jelly glasses, but not for long because—since he and the senior bonifaces did most of the cooking—he (which meant we) had to get back to the kitchen and do the salads.

Willy and I had our first difference over the salads. He said I wasn't cutting the carrots into tiny enough pieces, and I should shred the iceberg lettuce. I said if he must have carrots they should be in little sticks in a separate dish with olives and celery and cottage cheese and currant jelly, the way Wiggins did it. Willy's smile was studied.

"They have weak teeth," he said.

The three bonifaces and I had dinner at a separate table in the dining room. Everything was very soft and easy to chew. Mrs. Boniface didn't like me, she had my number. I'd never be any good here and she'd be sure Willy knew it.

I didn't care as long as it didn't interfere with my project.

There are few men alive who don't want to get laid, and Willy was essentially agreeable. Everybody was asleep. We were rolling around on a dark mildew-smelling sofa in the back parlor.

"Let's go," he said.

"You mean now?" I'd thought it took planning.

"Well—isn't that what you want?"

"I was hoping *you'd* ask."

"Oh—I see," he said. "You surprised me, I didn't know. And I'm really thrilled. I thought we were waiting." For what?

I followed Willy up the creaky stairs and down dark hallways into a deserted wing. He led me into an empty room where he turned on a tiny wobbly lamp, closed the curtains, and pulled back the bedcover, giving it a couple of shakes ("Everything gets so dusty here").

Then he left me and went to get "something," which I fervently hoped was some device to prevent pregnancy. It took forever. I had never felt so exposed, so vulnerable, so annoyed. It was cold and dark, and Willy had showed me the bathroom, indicating that I should undress—unless he wanted to do it himself. If wedding-night lore applied here, I understood the bride who spent the whole night in the bathroom and was found in the morning asleep on the floor in her new negligee.

Willy returned (with a condom) and I wished I was in the Buick on my way back to Smith. Surprise had become lust; he was ready to go—and if I backed out now not only would I still be a virgin, it would probably be the end of Willy too. I didn't know how to vote no without quitting.

So we did it, and I was as worried and fretty as I'd known I'd be. The memorable moments were so hateful—Willy sitting there unwrapping the condoms and fitting one on what seemed like an unnaturally large erection. The pain while he grunted and groaned . . . then when it was over (of course I didn't come) the gush of blood when I stood up, which sent him into a frenzy of wiping-up with Kleenex because I was standing on an important braided rug . . . his crouching white back in the gloom, his moving arm and shoulder, the wadded tissues . . . and beyond his knee, the little drooping balloon.

NOW HE HAD ME, he owned me.

I had put myself in an ideological bind. If I really cared about him I would love the Sheffield Inn too, and if I didn't I was a slut. He assumed the best—and carrots moved on to Waldorf salad, tapioca pudding, and other applied arts. There was instruction about the inn's antiques and he even tried to teach me to shoot his rifle—which knocked me backward to the ground. The rabbit scampered off and Willy picked me up undiscouraged and patient. And somehow his politics slid rightward with the gun and the country; he didn't entirely disagree with the Buckleys. After a couple of rapidly escalating arguments, he said if he wanted to save what we had, we shouldn't talk politics.

What did we have, what did he want with me? I was a city girl, we had almost nothing in common. I wasn't even very good in bed, I always thought I was pregnant . . . was it all worth it? The sex would have had to rival Lady Chatterley's, and it didn't . . . and I began to wonder why I had come up this road, and how I could make a U-turn.

GRADUATION WEEKEND.

Nunnally came. Ma and Rog came. Willy came. Dorris didn't come—because, as Pop said, the possibilities were simply too droll.

The three men were a strange trio. Willy had gone country in a not very cute way—local-barber haircut, corduroy jacket and Frye-like boots before they were fashionable, awful socks knitted by me. He drove over in the family truck. That was good, because he took Nunnally back and forth to his hotel in the next town, the only room I'd been able to find because I had waited till the last minute. God knows what they talked about. I never asked, they never told. Had I actually invited Willy? Did it matter?

It was inevitable that we were together for all the events, though sometimes we were insulated among crowds, and sometimes I was obliged to be elsewhere. But from the daisy chain to the party at Morris House to the dinner at Wiggins to the ceremony itself with the address by Alistair Cooke, it was necessary that we all get along.

In Wiggins's dark bar with the maple tables and chairs, Willy talked boniface lore—what Wiggins did wrong, how they did it at the Sheffield Inn, how much things cost and how much you saved by ordering in bulk, addressing this to anybody who would listen—with an occasional little nudgy remark about how much I was learning about innkeeping. I wouldn't have cared if it were only Ma and Rog, but the notion of Nunnally being subjected to this deadly and misleading chatter made me want to die. Hell on earth, to me, was my father being bored.

I knew how neurotic this was. Ordinary girls were happy to see their fathers, they did not feel obliged to provide continuous amusement. I had suffered similar anxiety some months before at Smith's Father's Day Weekend. I'd told Pop he needn't come, he probably wouldn't have any fun. Not only did he come but he seemed interested in everything—even the three-legged race. And he saw things I never did, he asked questions I couldn't answer. I'd forgotten his newspaperman's curiosity—this was discovery. He'd stayed late in the hotel bar with the divorced, unloved father of a friend of mine, heard curious things, and hinted later that there might be a picture in all this. (The closest he came was *How to Be Very, Very Popular.*)

Though I always struggled—still do—to put my father into words, on some nonverbal level I usually understood his behavior. He had been severely tested by a few rides with Willy and I knew he was running out of ability to be a good sport. Fortunately, at Wiggins, Rog caught his interest and they seemed to get along well, lifting martinis together and exchanging stories and jokes. Willy, shut out of the boys' club, pulled his chair closer and draped his arm over the back of my chair.

"Did I tell you we're going to renovate the barn?"

"I don't think so."

"I'm going to put in a Ping-Pong table and maybe a television set."

"Wonderful."

"Maybe you could help decorate it."

This was an ordinary man I'd given myself to, this was what I'd thought I wanted. How wrong I'd been: the truth was I was hopelessly fixed on my father and his unachievable world.

We were in a sea of normality. All around were the kind of families we were pretending to be; proud dads in tweed jackets, scarlet-lipped moms in perky hats and white gloves. Breathless seniors in Ann Fogarty dresses, pink-cheeked boyfriends in chinos, little brothers with cowlicks—a preppie Norman Rockwell scene. The place was deafeningly noisy, the air full of smoke. Bubbles over our heads read: *What are you going to do next?* And *Do you have any plans?* And *Well, you deserve a rest, but when you're ready, give me a call—I know a lot of people in publishing/advertising/on Wall Street/on Broadway/on the Coast/in Washington/anywhere.*

"There's some old porch furniture that just needs a coat of paint to look really spiffy. When you come over next weekend we'll paint it."

Pop was talking about joining the Savannah Hussars at seventeen and fighting the forces of Pancho Villa at El Paso.

"I had those spiral leggings that unwound and were constantly trailing after me. God, it was awful."

Rog was chuckling. "Did you see any action?"

"We charged with swords—but I got in some real hot water when I lost a mule."

"Wow, I never knew that," I said.

Then Rog was off on flying whatever he flew in the RCAF, as Willy said in a low voice, "And there's a couple of rooms in the back that we could fix up just for us, there's even plumbing in that corner, so we can have more . . . privacy." Wink, nudge.

Ma, in a navy blue suit and a new hairdo, was in her element, at first. Here she was with her two men, her graduated daughter and eager beau. But she got quieter and quieter, eyes downcast, plucking at her pearls.

"What's the matter?" I whispered, gratefully turning my back on Willy.

"I'm a little tired. I might go to bed."

"The lobster hasn't even come, Ma."

You had to have lobster at Wiggins—broiled, with a lot of bread crumbs on top. And fries. And coleslaw . . . and lots of martinis, and of course the relish tray. And a few extras. ("Let's have a coupla extra vegetables and salads, how about some blue cheese dressing . . . and fill up the bread basket again.")

"I'll stay just a little longer." She was smiling at me. If only she'd known how to take my hand, to put her arm around me, but chill Gobbie hadn't taught her.

"Don't go," I whispered. "What's the matter anyway?"

She glanced at her two men. "I'm very uncomfortable."

"So am I. Please stay." Oh, help.

"Well . . ."

"*They're* perfectly happy," I whispered. "Don't abandon me."

I got through the dinner by making Willy change seats and talk to her while I hung onto the sleeves of Pop and Rog. But it didn't work. When I tried to get her eye she smiled blankly and unhappily at the wall behind my head. Finally she told Rog she was going back to the room they'd reserved two years before. Rog understood the realities of graduation weekends.

"Have another drink, sweetie," Rog said. "The kid's made it through—made Dean's List—won a prize." I'd gotten the Alpha Award for writing, which, if fate hadn't intervened, would have gone to Sylvia Plath.

Pop took my hand. Willy had been holding the other one and I snatched it back.

"Oh my, I'm so proud," he said. His smile was loving. He had never gone to college. "It's a long way from a certain Latin grade I remember."

"What was that?" Willy asked.

"Well, I'll only say that if Julius Caesar had come to town, Nora would have only understood forty percent of what he said."

We all laughed on cue. But Julius Caesar was too much for Ma. She picked up her bag and stood up.

"If you'll excuse me."

She was firm. In a few minutes they left and I wanted to die.

Willy said to Pop, "I was just telling Nora about the old barn behind the inn we're going to fix up."

"Really." He looked at me, then at Willy. "Why don't you tell me on the way back." He dug in his pocket, then threw down some bills. Oh, thank you, I thought. Thank you, thank you. You're all leaving and now I can go hide under the bed.

MA AND ROG didn't turn up for coffee and sticky buns at Morris House the next morning.

"You mean you're just sitting in the hotel?" I screamed on the phone. I was in a hallway of excited girls lugging suitcases out of their rooms and dragging them downstairs.

"It's too hard for me to be with both my husbands at the same time."

"But they like each other. How can you desert me?"

"Oh, heavens. Graduation's over. Rog and I are going to the movies. We'll see you after Nunnally has left."

I began to cry. "This is horrible. Why did you even come? Why can't you deal with it? Why aren't you setting me an example of *politesse* for when I have a couple of husbands?"

After a tiny pause she said, "Rog is feeling a little off, it's been a busy weekend."

When Pop arrived I told him what she'd said. Nothing in my B.A. degree had taught me how to deal with this.

"That's okay," he said. "We'll have breakfast alone, just the two of us."

"Where's Willy?"

"He had to leave," Pop said. "He sent his apologies. Seems like a nice fella." With a glance.

"Oh, he did." I hung on his arm and said, swallowing hard, "Oh, I don't know . . . but I feel sick to my stomach and I haven't the faintest idea what I'm going to do with my life. Maybe you'll tell me over breakfast."

BELLA AND ME

COULD IT BE? Gregory Miles, waiting for American's Flight 3 at Idlewild . . . sitting in a chair reading *The Hollywood Reporter.*

I hadn't seen him in years. I knew that he'd inherited millions when his father died in a car accident on the 405, driving home after a wild party. When I got closer he put down the magazine.

"I hear you graduated from Smith. I should offer congratulations."

"Don't bother if it's a nuisance."

"I've seen Smith, Nora. Northampton is charmless and blue-collar—nothing but beer joints and B movies."

"People don't choose schools for the architecture, for God's sake. Who cares?"

"Well, they should. Ugliness isn't instructive. You should be surrounded by beautiful things."

As usual he had a point. "It's fun to see you, Greg. You haven't changed a bit—except maybe sartorially."

His outfit was almost comic. Gangster suit, black shirt, yellow tie, Stetson hat, pointed boots, flowing white aviator's scarf. Was he George Raft in Texas? Lindburgh in Hollywood? Oh, who knows? It all looked very high-style and expensive.

On the plane he told me he'd gone to Princeton for six months, but he wouldn't say why he'd left.

"But you're so smart. You're bad and brilliant."

His face, better-shaved than before, looked wistful. "They want people who fit in, darling. Who love sports, who aspire to things I don't aspire to."

"What do you do all day?" I asked curiously.

"Whatever I want. Go out . . . stay in. Everything and nothing."

"Pop told me you're filthy rich."

"I can't believe how rude you are. You should *never* say that to anybody."

"Oh, I can say anything to you," I said. "Having any louche affairs these days?"

He laughed. "Actually I'm thinking of getting married."

I didn't want to hear about it. I needed him to always be on trains and planes when I got on them. Over the Appalachians I asked him why he'd gotten himself on my flight.

"It was chance."

"The seat next to me?"

He was peering across me to see out the window. "Well . . . I wanted to see how you were."

"Just suddenly, after three years?"

"That's right." He stared at me from under furry eyebrows. "It's something about being from the same tribe. The same planet."

That was it. He was my brother, my occasional brother—that was why I didn't mind being picked on by him. Every once in a while he appeared out of nowhere and checked me out and scolded me and bossed me around. There was almost nothing we agreed about, but it was okay, he was family.

We were in one of the early jets like a dolphin, with a lump on top that housed a little bar. We went up the stairs and ordered martinis, which came in miniature bottles. A bronze-faced, white-haired man in a white suit was sitting opposite. At the sight of us he jumped to his feet and came over to pump our hands.

"Spyros," Greg said. It was the trip celebrity—Spyros Skouras, head of Twentieth Century-Fox.

"Hello, hello, hi. You charming children of the Business. Coast to coast again. What do you drink?"

More martinis appeared and then he and Greg were off on intramural matters. I wondered if Greg was faking his seeming command of the subject, but since I didn't know much myself, I couldn't tell. Spyros went along with it, throwing me a couple of puzzling Greek compliments. Then in a moment the joviality disappeared. He put down his drink and went back down the tiny staircase.

"He has work to do." Greg gazed moodily out the tiny window. Then he asked, "Why aren't you engaged?"

"Well, I *could* be engaged," I said, "but he wanted me to help run his inn. And milk his cow. And shoot his rifle, and get along with his mother."

It hadn't been easy, turning Willy down. I was afraid nobody would ever ask me again. But I couldn't see myself as young Mrs. Boniface. I had books to write, worlds to explore. I was going to go up the Nile in a felucca; watch the sun rise over the China Sea.

"How often have you been in love?" Gregory asked when we were back in our seats.

Nobody had ever asked me that. "Twice."

"Was one the boniface?"

"No."

He lit a Black Russian cigarette. "It's nice not to have to think about money."

"How rude you are!"

"Nunnally will probably settle something on you when you're twenty-one, then you can take your time about things."

"I was twenty-one in January," I said. Greg looked surprised.

A glassine curtain slid back, revealing other small moments in the past months—remarks of friends I'd paid little attention to. "I met the accountant the other day . . . Daddy and I had lunch with the trust people, I have to read all these books . . . I'm getting my money-bags next month and I'm terrified . . . It will be mine eventually, but I don't really have any control over it till I'm twenty-five." My friends were becoming men and women of property before my eyes. Some were—or had been—close friends. It was embarrassing to realize that I thought I'd be among them. But my birthday had come and gone and the message was clear.

"I don't need anybody else's money," I said. "I'll earn my own."

"Oh, Christ," Greg said.

He wrapped his face in his aviator scarf and went to sleep while I brooded. No man, no money. I was as naked as though I'd been shot out of a cannon, flying into the future with nothing but three hundred pages of raw fiction in my suitcase. I had friends who had trust funds *and* boyfriends—and great hair, too, and actually all those things seemed to go together; either you had it all or you had nothing.

When I was seeing Nathan, the object of everybody's disapproval, Nunnally had written me that I should think of myself not as Schrafft's but as "21." From the looks of things now it was going to be Nedick's. I looked out the window at the black mountains below, the occasional sharp peak traced with snow. Gregory was snoring through his white silk. I grabbed his arm.

"We're going over the Rockies. Wake up, I'm scared." He moaned and grunted. "Do you remember that first time we went together on the Chief?"

"Oh, grow up," he muttered, turning his back to me.

NUNNALLY'S OFFICE AT Twentieth Century-Fox was a big bright room, all beige and buff and ivory. There was a pale, deep-pile rug on the floor and a green leather sofa. The enormous desk was of tooled leather, with silver-framed family photographs and children's clay pieces, a leather-bound blotter, silver scissors and letter opener, and little alabaster bowls for paper clips and typewriter ribbons and Scotch tape. The big Royal electric hummed, a virgin ream of paper awaited. It was unassuming by mogul standards but I thought it was magnificent.

I was there to rewrite my novel, *The Unloved City,* in his office, under his tutelage. I was very wary of this project, suggested by him, especially since Ma had behaved as though I were going on the haaj. "Oh—to work with the master!" she'd cried. Was she over him? No. Since she was married to somebody else, the old sparks had become hero worship. And what about the good long rest I needed after all that hard work? Time for that later—this opportunity mustn't be missed.

Every morning Pop and I drove to the studio together. He went to the set and I walked down the long carpeted hall to the office to work, or pretend to work. Betty Baldwin, Nunnally's secretary, smiled encouragingly as I came in and offered coffee. "Pick up the phone if you want anything," she told me. In her adjoining office she typed up my pages as they were finished, just as she did his.

It took half an hour every morning to believe where I was, another hour to look everything over. The ashtrays sparkled, the cigarette box was filled. There was a bushy green palm right outside the window. But why were there two pictures of Roxie (my younger half sister, named after *Roxie Hart*) on the desk and only one of me? And where were *my* clay ashtrays . . . and the blue glazed bunny rabbit I'd made him in kindergarten? Christie's yellow chicken was there instead. What were all those scripts for, these notes? The inscriptions on framed photographs of stars he had worked with hinted at vast areas of Nunnally's life that I knew nothing about.

It was like trying to work in the middle of a circus. Walking around, eating lunch at the commissary, standing around smoking, were clowns, knights, New York cops, ladies of the court, cowboys and Indians . . . stars in full makeup, hair in fat rollers under a scarf. Nunnally was directing *How to Be Very, Very Popular,* and sometimes the stars—Betty Grable, Sheree North, and Robert Cummings—came by our table at the commissary. The story took place on a fictional college campus with little resemblance to Smith, a place where the students wore heavy makeup and baby blue caps and gowns at all times. Even I seemed to have a little news value—an item appeared in a local paper explaining my presence on the lot.

I told Pop I was so dazzled by it all that I couldn't concentrate. He said writing was the same at Twentieth Century-Fox as it was at Toto's, hard work at any level. I should ignore the glitter and take the opportunity to work with a kind of comfort and service writers rarely have. I didn't add that I was so overwhelmed by his attention that I could hardly think straight.

In the evenings, after dinner, we worked on the story together. We talked about my derivative characters and incredibly complicated plot. He was tactful. He told me the story was more important than the five- and six-page ruminations my characters were so fond of having, and he advised throwing them out and showing their feelings through their actions. He said scenes in a script were usually around three pages long and it wasn't a bad idea for a novel too. (Mine went on for twelve or fourteen pages.) He said if I removed half or two-thirds of the plot, the rest would be stronger and more interesting. And it was not necessary to tell the characters' entire life histories—only what was necessary to push the story along.

At first I couldn't bear to change a word. He was turning it into a script! When I hinted that Hollywood might ruin my art, Nunnally was quick to point out that since Hollywood had paid my bills from the day I was born, the schools I attended, the roof over my head, the clothes on my back, the food I ate, it would be more becoming not to think along those lines.

Sitting in the office, I struggled to adapt his suggestions to the Kurfurstandamm kidnapping scene and the Tiergarten love scene. In the next room I could hear Betty typing up my revisions. *The Unloved City,* so tangentially mine at best, was slipping away, becoming a Nunnally Johnson production. The story was based on what happened during the making of *Night People,* the characters were taken from the movie or the people making it. Now I was revising it according to his ideas—at his desk, in his studio, with his secretary. But what else did I know?

THAT SUMMER I heard a lot about Bella Darvi, a Polish ingenue who made her unpromising Hollywood debut that year in *The Egyptian*. Nunnally didn't think much of her. Even her name, he said, was derived from that of her lover, Darryl Zanuck, and his wife, Virginia.

Nunnally had worked for Zanuck since 1934. He had spent a few years at Universal in the forties, then returned to Fox after turning down a lucrative offer from MGM. Back with Zanuck, he made a string of solid successes, including *Three Came Home, The Mudlark, The Desert Fox, My Cousin Rachel, Night People,* and *How to Marry a Millionaire* (1953)—the first picture to be made in CinemaScope.

At that time Hollywood was in a downward spin. Television was catching on as important entertainment and business was sinking. The increasing number of independent productions, among other factors, was slowly weakening the entire studio system, which had suited Nunnally so perfectly, as well as diminishing the power of the studio chiefs. It was said that Twentieth Century-Fox made half as many pictures in 1953–54 and that they were at least twice as big and half as good. Zanuck was convinced that CinemaScope was the way to lure audiences back to the theaters, but Nunnally didn't share his enthusiasm. When asked if he altered his writing technique for the new wide screen, he replied, "Not at all—I just put the paper in sideways."

The boss's other obsession was Bella Darvi. She had charmed both Zanucks in Paris some years before, and been invited to visit them at their home in Santa Monica. A screen test arranged by Zanuck confirmed a remarkable lack of talent. But he cast her in *The Egyptian* anyway and so continued the spectacle—not the first one—of a movie magnate besotted by a young starlet, this time one who had moved in and become part of the family. Virginia Zanuck endured it for a while, and then she threw the girl out. Bella went back to Paris, and Zanuck followed her. It was the beginning of the end of the marriage . . . and, as Zanuck later said, of his marriage to Hollywood as well. Not only was Zanuck's power ebbing away, but his attention was elsewhere—either in Paris or in his home projection room, where he watched old Bella Darvi films over and over.

Nunnally said, "For God's sake. Can you imagine, that's how he spends every night of his life? *Zanuck?*"

I'D NEVER LAID EYES on Bella Darvi, but in some ways we had a lot in common.

We were both waifs—Bella authentically so, because she came from Poland and had spent time at Auschwitz—about which she never spoke. Even though I wasn't Jewish I could imagine ending up in a concentration camp. It wasn't likely, but I was beginning to find out that life was full of surprises.

Bella and I both longed for a family—and were taken in by kind Hollywood people, on whom we were financially dependent, who encouraged us to use our talent and earn money. We were showered with opportunities but we screwed up—she had her *Egyptian,* I had my *Unloved City.* We both loved, in different ways, Twentieth Century-Fox royalty. Then, thankless creatures that we were, we proceeded to make trouble. Bella coldly broke up a marriage, and I somehow upset Nunnally's house in subtle ways when I was here, because I wanted to be part of the family. I knew Virginia was happy to say good-bye, and I suspected Dorris was too. And I knew that something was gnawing at Bella, as it was at me.

ON MOUNTAIN DRIVE, we had dinner in the dining room every night. There was still a cook and butler, but the food wasn't very good, and the butler was awkward and forgetful. When they left, Dorris would do the cooking, and the family would eat in the breakfast room.

I was getting reacquainted with the children, now twelve, eight, and five. Christie, the oldest, was like Julie and me at the same age, when we suffered deeply because we didn't look like Rita Hayworth. Scott, the fetching five-year-old, asked me if I was writing a book, and I said I was.

"Can I read it?"

I said of course. He had big blue eyes—we all had blue eyes, that was something. My parents, all the five kids. Later all my kids. I considered this when I got married. "Are you my sister?"

"Yes."

"But you live in New York."

For a moment—longer than a moment—I wished I didn't.

Nunnally was listening to this exchange. I knew how badly he wanted us to get along. When I caught his blue eye, I saw that we both wanted exactly the same thing—to somehow mend this broken family. It was the catalyst for a lifetime of letters to me about the younger children, and reportage to them about me—all toward an end that never came.

Suppose I had lived here? Suppose—after an argument with Ma—I'd packed a suitcase and gone down and boarded the Twentieth and then the Chief. I'd have arrived at 625 Mountain Drive and explained to Nunnally and Dorris that I wanted to move in for a while. Suppose, rather than looking horrified, they'd welcomed me with cries of joy.

How different my life would have been! I'd have slept in the room with the horse lamps and the evening jasmine. I'd have certainly had a car, maybe a little Mustang. Between novels I'd have worked for the studio writing scripts. And the people I would have known! Probably I'd have been dating Monty Clift or Rock Hudson, and Liz Taylor would have been one of my best pals.

For years Nunnally had written letters about the fun I was missing. The mermaid party on the patio, Nunnally's grand birthday party at Chasen's, innumerable small dinners and openings they seemingly went to the minute I left town. The most painful of all was the evening of the opening of *How to Marry a Millionaire*, when the movie star of the decade, the idol, the icon had actually come for dinner. I'd almost memorized Nunnally's letter of November 1953.

> . . . when I told the children that Marilyn [Monroe] was going with the Bogarts and us to the opening . . . Scotty began immediately to chant "Best undressed woman in town!" . . . the two girls began to writhe like belly dancers. . . . Mary, the maid, and Jane, the cook, were just about as excited. What this girl does to people is almost unbelievable. She was late, of course, and when she rang the bell the door was opened by three children, two in Oriental kimonos and a small boy in his finest dressing gown. [They served] the hors d'oeuvres with such gaping awe that she was lucky not to have got most of the stuff in her lap, which would have been a major disaster, for the studio wardrobe and make-up departments had been at work on her since shortly after noon. She owned nothing that she wore. The fact is, she doesn't own anything anyway. She told a girl reporter at the studio that the only thing she wore that she owned were her underpants. I was informed later by Dorris that she wasn't wearing any. That's all I know about that. (Dorris later said that she had been called upon to assist Marilyn, who was sewed into her dress, in going to the bathroom.)
>
> . . . [at dinner] we found that the cook was serving too. She was taking no chance on being stuck back there in the kitchen and not getting a look. . . . . I may add that when Marilyn came in she asked me for a very big drink, Scotch on the rocks. I gave her a tremendous one straight, and she had another just before we went in to dinner. When we went out to get in the car, Dorris came to me with a paper cup and said Marilyn wondered if she could have another one to drink on the way to the theatre. . . . The next morning when I talked to her on the phone, she complained that she had a hangover and said in some surprise that she was

quite tight the night before. Since she had certainly behaved herself very well I assured her on that point. Then she said, "that's the first time I ever tasted Scotch, you know." And it was. She never drinks anything but a little Dubonnet. But she was so nervous and scared she said she thought she needed it that night . . . she of course looked stunning and the rest if us were ignored by everybody.

Stories like these might have been mine . . . if only I'd been invited.

OFTEN AFTER LEAVING THE STUDIO I'd drive up the Coast Highway to Malibu, circling the bay as the breakers crept in like tiny fringes of lace in the gray water. Sometimes I parked and walked on the beach. It was windy, and a fine sand blew around. The air was damp and sticky on my skin. It was too cold to swim, and the beach was so wide that by the time you'd gotten to the water you didn't want to go in; the thing was lie very still on the sand and warm up. The ocean was vast and gray, and the waves were breaking half a mile from shore, and I could see a few surfers in wet suits. It was a wild, cold place, but back on the road where the car was parked it was burning hot. It was pure California.

Sometimes I went over the mountains, my hands icy on the wheel as I crept around tiny, close curves high above the Valley. I'd open the window and breath the hot fragrant wind. There was something evocative about the smells of the West and the grainy light . . . even the Mountain Drive house, the rose garden, and the turquoise pool, and the hot concrete, and the smell of jasmine crept into me like a second self.

The Sweethearts had moved a couple of years before and dozens more houses had been built up in the hills where Pop and I had walked in the evening. I thought if I could find the magic canyon again I might understand certain things. I went to what I thought was the right place, but an entire mansion had appeared on the spot, and I didn't see the culvert with the red flowers in it or hear the water dripping and the pebbles falling.

I drove slowly around the flats to the house on Bedford where my parents had lived when I was born, the one on Beverly Drive when they were still together, and Camden, where they tried again, and Beverly Glen, the first one with Dorris. I went to Julie's old house where I used to go once or twice a week, every summer for years. Now it had new facing and the yard was replanted with topiaries. But when I parked in front they seemed to disappear and the old lemon trees and hibiscus were back, and the window to what used to be Julie's room was open and I heard the slushy love songs she'd played on her Victrola. Lying on the grass was the ghost of Benny's baseball mitt.

Everything had gone wrong for them. There was a messy divorce, the money disappeared . . . young Irv never came back from England. Then Lola had taken them back to Oak Park with the blanket covers and the knife props. Once it would have blown Julie away to hear about the Marilyn evening, but I didn't know if she was still interested in these things. The last I heard from her, she said she was trying to forget Hollywood—though her therapist said she shouldn't; everything had to connect or she'd be like a string of sausages, everything tied off from everything else.

I'd always been good at tying things off; I'd done it twice a year. But now I wondered if it was such a great idea. Julie and I had been dealt a certain kind of Hollywood experience: not the cataclysmic ups and downs of the powerful, but a kind of sidling up to the back door and catching glimpses of things. It was tantalizing; it could be heartbreaking—until you learned to appreciate its intense, unique clarity, like the view though a pinhole camera.

UNDER THE MEXICAN MOON

ON THE WAY BACK from California I spent a week with a school friend in Mexico City. She and her family lived in a house with fifteen rooms and thirteen servants, or else the other way around, in the elegant section called Coyoacan. Each morning a maid brought breakfast in bed and took whatever I needed pressed or polished for the evening. The tennis and riding parties, teas, cocktail parties, dances, and nightclubs were nonstop, and my friend had an endless stream of boyfriends she was happy to share. We never got to bed before three, we slept till eleven, then got up and rushed off to the next lunch or brunch. I thought I was in heaven. I had a great time . . . too great.

"I don't know what it is about coming down here," my friend said as I left. "People think it's off the map or something, they do things they would never do at home." So-and-so had tried peyote, another girl had disappeared with a Spanish boy and her family raised hell. She turned up later in Rio. I told her she was too good a hostess, people lost their heads.

"Thank God you behaved." She laughed.

I earnestly hoped she was right. There had been a couple of pretty wild nights, one particularly—I had done some rolling around in a car with a Canadian boy who worked down there, both of us full of margaritas. He disappeared after that and I never saw him again. It was all pretty hazy and I wished I knew exactly what had happened. I told myself that nothing could have in a front seat with a gear shift, and that the whole episode was finished.

On the plane I kept worrying about it. Keeping control of my life was much harder since I no longer had my virginity to defend— exactly what I'd been afraid of. By the time we'd landed and I was in a taxi, I was feeling pretty low.

At 204 there were some unnerving changes. While I was gone the living room had been turned into a study. Rog's giant desk replaced the pink loveseat, dominating the room, and all around were files, books, and boxes of papers. There was a new telephone line in open defiance of Ma's lifelong ban on phones in living rooms. On the desk was the Friden, big as life, playing its merry tune—zonk-bippity-boppity-zonk.

Ma was wearing a starched cotton dress and a ruffled apron with polka dots—a page out of *Ladies' Home Journal.*

"You'll love what I've done with the back porch."

"Sorry, toots. I didn't fit upstairs." Rog smiled genially from behind the desk. "The house is small, d'you see. This is the best we could figure out, at least till the thesis is finished."

The thesis had been in process for ten years and I was betting on another ten. That was okay, it might be fun to endlessly write something . . . but did it have to be in the living room? But what else could be done? He *was* too big, he *didn't* fit. It would have been inhuman to insist, like forcing him to wear clothes from the college shop.

"Why not put the desk down here?" I asked as Ma and I went downstairs.

"It gets too cold, he'd have to wear an overcoat." I said nothing. "Oh, come on, sweetie. Rog lives here, you're away most of the time." Not a trace of guilt in her voice.

"But I'm here now."

"Of course . . . and now you have your top floor back." She smiled, looking very pretty with her dark hair and blue eyes. "I'll make you a martini."

Good, good—that was how we handled things around here. And some onion-soup-and-sour-cream dip would solve everything.

The back porch was behind the kitchen, a cool, tiled area jutting out into the backyard. The long wall was all windows looking out at the bushes and the tree of heaven, and a window over the couch looked into the kitchen. There were new burlaplike slipcovers on the bamboo sofa and chairs, some bright pillows, and a few new plants and pictures—signs of recent attention, attempts to distract from the treachery she'd wrought in the living room. She'd gotten tips from Dorothy Draper's *Decorating Is Fun*.

But there were serious flaws. The toilet in the wooden stall rendered the merest tinkle too audible—enough to send anyone with normal privacy needs up two flights to a conventional bathroom. And there was nothing to do about the icy drafts because we were renters, and the landlord wouldn't pay to have it winterproofed. Nor would he sell 204, though Ma had often told him she was interested. (He wasn't so dumb—the three corner houses would come down in the next couple of years to make way for a high-rise, and the owners would make a bundle.)

No wonder I'd had the creeps in the taxi.

"I have rotten news," Ma said, pouring gin into the silver shaker. "My sister is leaving George."

"That's terrible!"

"She's over sixty. She'll never find anybody else."

After thirty years of marriage my aunt Margaret had pronounced her husband too neurotic to be tolerated any longer. Since he said the same thing about her, it was impossible to tell who was leaving whom or how it had all got started. Margaret admitted that he didn't drink, beat her up, or insult her friends—and that they shared the same interests and liberal passions they always had. But he had actually said that he didn't believe her to be always right, all the time . . . which of course was ridiculous. Ma thought there was more to the story but she'd found in her lifetime that there were secrets in all marriages the world never knew. She wasn't going to pry any further.

I stared into my white-gold martini, with its two little white onions like eyes, while she went into the kitchen.

"Now tell me about you, sweetie," she trilled through the window. "I want to hear all about everything."

That's exactly, I thought, what you are *not* going to hear.

Maybe something *had* happened in the car. I'd been pretty drunk. Maybe we'd done it. Maybe I was pregnant . . . but it was too soon to know. Maybe I'd caught something from whatever-his-name-was, Perry or Terry—or maybe he'd told everybody and my friend would hate me because I was like the other girls who lost their heads under the Mexican moon.

I watched her trot up the couple of steps into the backyard with a two-inch-thick porterhouse and some beefsteak tomatoes the size of melons. Everything was growing larger to suit Rog. There were some new double old-fashioned glasses the size of small ice buckets. He couldn't stand our eggcups and pickle forks, and his heavy overcoats threatened the wobbly newel post. He was Gulliver among the Lilliputians, Was he still growing? Would he expand until he completely filled the place, like Alice in the White Rabbit's house? She had kicked as hard as she could and Bill the Lizard had flown out the top. Rog would kick, and I would fly out and sail through the sky, over the roofs of the East Sixties and into oblivion.

MA SET THE umbrella table with new daisy place mats and linen napkins. The salad was in an unfamiliar bowl—part of what Rog called his "dowry." He was in the process of selling his three houses in New Jersey, and their contents were slowly crowding out our old ivy plates and aluminum pots. Every time I came home something else was gone or different. The silver had disappeared two years before—

she'd sold it, she admitted later, because she'd needed money. Now we were using Rog's silverplate and china with pictures of shepherds and unfamiliar cut-glass wineglasses.

Rog came out the door in a pale green shantung suit. Hanging around his neck was his sphygmomanometer, a word he and Ma not only knew how to spell but threw around as casually as you please. Hypertension was no fun but it was a novelty to take your own blood pressure, and Rog loved being on the cutting edge. He took not only his but others' too. By the time the steak was *bleu,* Ma and I had been checked and found within the normal range.

What else could the sphygmomanometer pick up?

I would have given anything—my soul—to know, to undo what—if anything—had happened in the car that night. But since I couldn't, I'd thought I had a solution. Aunt Margaret, a longtime employee at the Margaret Sanger Institute, knew all about birth control and unwanted pregnancies. I'd thought I'd approach her. But it did not bode well that her marriage was falling apart and she was deep in confessional mode, possibly with shaky judgment.

Ma gave the charcoal briquettes a stir and pronounced the steak done. Wasn't that the man's job? No—the man was writing his thesis.

"Get a good rest, toots?" Rog asked.

"Wonderful."

"Thought any more about the business school?"

Not for two seconds, which made me feel bad. For graduation Rog had given me five shares of W. R. Grace stock, worth $25 a share at the time. It was better than the watch, the money, the pearls. It was serious, it would grow, it might split . . . it would teach me something. My heartfelt gratitude had somehow made Rog think I had a hidden aptitude for finance.

"You know, I'm not sure I think . . . I think I'd rather . . . maybe I should."

"Well, just an idea. You have plenty of time. You gotta start out on the right foot. If you don't it's harder to change later on."

What was the right foot? Change to what? They were starting to worry about me. Consider the investment: the East Side address, the clothes from Saks and Best's, an Irish nanny, the best schools, orthodontia, piano lessons, dancing school, summers in Hollywood and Europe, exposure to bicoastal society, cultural opportunities—and for what? There had been a little promise—a prize here and there, a few kudos from generous professors, a mediocre novel. A job could be hoped for, or even—God willing—a husband. But forget all that now. I—and my baby—were going to be a permanent liability.

I spent most of my time on the burlap bamboo couch. I had a pad of lined paper and a couple of ballpoint pens, and the telephone had a long cord that stretched almost all the way through the kitchen. I made a lot of coffee in the electric coffeepot.

I counted my assets. I had the Grace stock and $4,000 I had inherited from my grandmother. There was the remains of the trust fund that had paid for my education. It was supposed to have lasted a few more years but what with one thing and another, Smith's tuition rise to $2,000 a year, and other unpredictables, there wasn't much left.

Ma didn't pull any punches.

"You aren't rich," she said. "You have to work."

"A lot of my friends have private incomes," I said.

"Well, you don't."

I'd heard this before but while I was still in school it didn't seem real.

"I want to go back to Smith," I said.

"Do you want to go to graduate school?"

"No—what for? I want it to be freshman year again, and for us to go shopping at Peck & Peck, and to Rumplemeyer's for hot chocolate with whipped cream, and for it to be four years ago. Or six or seven. I want to be getting ready for my first date."

"Well." She wasn't in a mood for whimsy.

"Maybe I'll get married."

"To whom?"

"Does it matter?"

She was fingering some fabric swatches. "I'm thinking of gingham curtains for here. What do you think?"

I looked at them. "Nice. Café curtains?"

"Exactly—all the way across, edged with pom-poms. I think I like the blue." She was making a list too. List makers, Ma and I were. "Are you sorry you turned the boniface down?" Her pen hovered in the air. Was that going on the list too?

"Oh no. What are we having for dinner?"

"Roast beef."

It was part of the deal, she said—Rog wanted steak or roast beef every night, but she told him it was too expensive, he'd have to have it cold sometimes.

"Is marriage always kind of a deal?"

"Well . . . I guess so, in a way."

"It sounds weighted in his favor."

"Well . . . I have many advantages."

"You don't have to eat alone at Schrafft's."

"I'm very contented," she said. "I have two boxes of strawberries. I think I'll make a shortcake."

SOMETIMES my friends dropped by. Some were working, some were married, some were job hunting or looking for apartments. They wore sleeveless linen sheaths, high-heeled pumps and little white gloves, double strings of pearls and harlequin sunglasses. They talked bosses, three-flight walk-ups, sex, money . . . we discussed *the problem.*

It was before you could buy pregnancy tests at the drugstore. There was only a doctor's examination and a rabbit test—your urine was injected into a hapless rodent who either lived or died depending on the level of your hormones. It all took forever. Somebody said that the first sign with a lot of women was tender breasts. I took to sitting with my arms tightly crossed so I could continually prod my nipples to see if they felt funny.

"How late are you?"

"Eleven days."

"What are you going to do?"

"I'm going to jump off the Queensborough Bridge."

"Ridiculous. You can get rid of it."

"But how?"

"A girl in my office has the same problem, I'll ask her."

I had everybody running around asking questions but nobody could find an answer—because there wasn't one. I couldn't think straight while this was happening. Why had I ever? Life had been simpler when I was a virgin. I'd loved to have blamed Willy for ruining me but it had all been my idea; he had intended to keep me pure until I was his legal property. And by now some of my linen-sheathed friends were fucking their brains out and loving it.

I COULD TAKE my money and go to France and Italy and Greece and Persia and India and Egypt. A writer needed experience. I'd keep an extensive journal, get an abortion somewhere along the way—other countries couldn't be as unreasonable as this one. I needed mystery, bead curtains, the strum of stringed instruments, dark eyes in the night, the scent of sandalwood. Maybe a whole new look—flowing saris and toe rings and an armload of silver bangles. I'd grow my hair down my back and wear lots of kohl and purple lipstick.

I worked out a complicated itinerary through several countries, traveling by boat, plane, train, and bus. I went to a travel agent where I picked up a lot of folders that I brought home and put on the sofa.

A friend wanted to go along. She had a Persian boyfriend who recommended Tehran highly. Ali would show us around and take us to exotic parties and introduce us to the best people. Maybe we should even live there, they loved American women. It was cheap if you had dollars. We could probably rent a house and have maids to dress us and houseboys and a cook to make whatever they ate there, hummingbirds' wings and halvah and things with mint and rosewater.

Four thousand dollars would last a long time . . . when it ran out I'd come back and get a job.

The revised version of the Berlin novel arrived in the mail, a clean copy of around half the original length. Pop wrote and said I shouldn't be startled by its lack of heft. The other version had been so marked up that he'd asked Betty to retype it.

Everything about it was different, everything shorter and snappier. I hardly knew what I thought of this other book. The original version—almost a year in the making, okayed by agents, rejected by a couple of publishers—was gone. The new one might sell . . . though I didn't care one way or the other, it was a novel by a stranger. Pop had done his best with it, he had pretended it was worth the trouble because then he could teach me something. He had. After twenty or thirty pages I stopped reading.

MA DECIDED TO run up the café curtains on her sewing machine, which Dorothy Draper said was easy. I helped her, then painted the end table the same blue. It came out so well I decided to paint my bureau to match the pale pink walls of my bedroom.

We'd always had wallpaper but Dorothy Draper was all for paint— she even painted antiques to make them more modern-looking. Paint in beautiful colors and yards and yards of gaily flowered chintz were the key to everything—you could transform your world with color. A cherry-red carpet, dead-white walls, a sky-blue ceiling . . . or how about a shiny black ceiling, a white fake-fur rug, and rough white fabric slipcovers?

Take Miss Ash, in one of the thumbnail case histories. She met Mr. Right the moment she moved into her apartment, before she'd decorated, and foolishly invited him for a glass of sherry! What to do? Fortunately the walls had been painted a pale soft green, so she pulled her ugly sofa up to the fireplace and flung yards and yards of gaily flowered chintz over it. She spent on accessories—clear glass vases of Easter lilies and pussy willows, a huge glass ashtray and cigarette box, a sherry decanter and glasses. The lamps were hideous so she put dozens of candles around and when the lucky man arrived she plumped him on the chintz before the crackling fire and he thought he was in heaven.

SANDING TOOK FOREVER, and after I'd rubbed a large ruinous patch on the top of the bureau, I began to feel nauseated and awful, as though a hundred little cap guns were going off inside me. My hands shook, and tears trailed down my cheek and landed on my bare knees.

"What's the matter?" Ma asked.

"Ma, I think I'm pregnant," I said.

The silence was terrible. I'd persuaded myself that it was going to be okay, that she would be understanding and sensible, that we'd go to Aunt Margaret and figure out how to get me out of this mess. The two sisters might even be a little amused—perhaps it had happened to one of them, these jazz babies who loved to talk about their flirtations and their conquests.

But she stared at me as though I'd turned green and shiny. Her eyes went from cerulean blue to inferno black.

"*What* makes you think so?" She had a whole new voice, Joan Crawford through an empty pipe. It was like the night I got drunk at the Christmas party.

In a quavering voice I explained.

"*Oh my God,*" she said. "You mean you don't remember?"

"Say something nice," I said. "I didn't kill anybody."

"*I am astounded* . . . horrified." She had a double standard, like Nunnally, who believed that it was okay for men to sleep around but not women. *She* could have a naughty girlhood but I couldn't. It was a kind of ethical Ponzi scheme, the last guy in the lineup got screwed.

"I think I'd better have an abortion."

Her eyes closed as though she'd been stabbed. I was hitting all the wrong keys: that one had landed on her girlhood Catholicism. She closed her eyes, dropped the pieces of gingham . . . opened her eyes and stared again. *"Oh my God."*

How right she was. Back alleys, grim-faced people locking doors, windows taped up to keep the light out, like during blackouts. No anesthetic; they gave you a rag to chew on and it hurt like hell, that was for sure. I'd heard it was the worst pain ever.

"All right." She got businesslike. "When did you last have the Curse?" I'd taught her the term to replace Falling Off the Roof and Going to the Country. "Are you nauseated? Do your breasts hurt? Anything in your panties?" and so forth. I felt better that I'd told her, no matter how hysterical it made her. She was still Ma. I reported all real and imaginary symptoms. Then—"I'll tell Rog."

"What?"

"I don't know what else to do. He knows people—doctors and lawyers and judges."

Oh, horrible, horrible . . . but what else was to be done? None of my friends had come up with anything better. There were a few grim days while Rog, avoiding my eye, made a few phone calls and came up with the name of an allegedly understanding gynecologist.

Ma and I went to the office, and I went into the examining room, which was painted death-row gray. The first doctor, a woman, was silent and not friendly. The second one—male—was stern and businesslike. When they'd finished examining me we all sat down to hear the pronouncement: No sign of pregnancy though it was still too early to tell.

"But what if I am?" I gasped.

"In cases like this we advise the young woman to have the baby."

The woman said it. *She* wasn't about to break the law and lose her license. I looked into her granite eyes and those of her gray-haired colleague and found no mercy. They suggested I put the baby up for adoption. I thought I was going to faint, but fortunately I didn't. Those two would have left me on the floor and stepped over me as they left the room. I could hear them talking: The slut. She deserves it.

Will they never learn? Ma would chime in, Rog would take them all to Louisa's for dinner while I stayed home locked in the bedroom.

Ma and I crept out of there in silence.

"I don't know what we're going to do," she said in the taxi.

We went home and had a martini.

THEN THERE WAS lonely Isabel, who had a dreary one-room apartment. But she was bright as a copper penny. She painted the walls and ceiling pale lemon yellow and turned her bed into a sofa, then bought yards and yards of gaily flowered chintz and ran up some curtains and a slipcover on her old sewing machine. She painted all her furniture to match the walls . . . and before you could say boo people were fighting to drop by.

I began to understand Ma.

There was the young couple who left the city and bought an old barn for a song and installed six bunk beds and painted everything bright blue and now people were fighting for invitations. There was the widow who suddenly hated her drab house so she threw everything out and did you-know and now she was giving luncheon parties every week.

Then one day I went into the stall toilet and there was blood, lots of blood.

Ma called the doctor, who told her that fear and anxiety could cause the Curse to arrive late—which Ma and I didn't know. Any advice? Well, chastity was always the safest road. Hopefully I had learned my lesson. Girls were better off married.

ROOM AND BOARD

AUGUST 1954. The city was baking hot and empty, the sky was a glaring blue-white.

One afternoon I called Chester. He wasn't there, but I left a message with his roommate. Three days later he called back and I invited him over for a drink.

Then, like little Miss Ash, I flew into a panic. What had I done? The living room had been taken over by Rog and the Friden. There was only the porch with its pom-pom café curtains and the public-spirited toilet and the nest I'd made on the sofa. I cleaned up mightily and the day he was coming I went out and bought two large ferns in pots and some white candles. I spent two hours making cheese sticks from scratch. I arranged all this attractively, along with a bottle of Dry Sack, put on my best toreador pants, and when Chester came, I brought him down and plumped him onto the sofa among the yellow pillows.

Chester was stiff and formal as well as suspicious. In his crew cut and cord jacket he had never been so attractive, and he had never seen through me so clearly.

"So what have you been doing?" he asked.

"Trying to face the future. Hoping to hear from you."

"I thought it was clear that wasn't going to happen." He had dumped me ages ago.

"Nothing is ever clear with you, Chester."

"I was always straight with you. You were more serious than I was, I told you that."

"I wasn't serious at all. I was anything but serious."

"You know what I mean. About our relationship."

"Well, of course I took you seriously, Chester. Would you rather I'd made fun of you?"

He sighed. "I'm moving to D.C. in September."

"Terrific! Working for Ike?"

He looked grave. "I'm getting married."

"Oh my." Oh shit. "Who is she?"

"Janie McIntosh." He looked up slowly. "You might remember her."

"Not Janie in Pamphlets."

"That's right." He put one cigarette out in the accessorized ashtray and lit another one. "Small. Blond, with a dimple in her chin."

"Janie from Pamphlets. So all the time we were . . ."

"It just started at the end. Come on, nothing was going on with us."

"Nothing. So that was nothing. Did you take her to the Cabot Lodge party?"

Pause. "I was perfectly clear about how I felt. You were always the one who . . . wanted to be serious."

Why had I called him? "That's what you want to think."

"You were depressed. Clingy. You expected me to spend more time with you than there were hours in the day." I'd crowded him, which Janie never did. She was cheerful and she didn't make him feel guilty. She had money and great hair and a dimple.

"I hope you're very happy, Chester. It's true, I'm not right for you at all, now that I think about it—which I never have before. I never dreamed you had marriage on your mind. I certainly never did." This would have been a good tack if I hadn't started to cry. He was distantly comforting and after a few minutes he got up and went toward the door. He kissed me on the cheek.

"Have a happy life, Nora."

I watched him as he walked to the corner and waved for a taxi, wishing he'd have a heart attack. He probably would by the time he was forty but he wouldn't die, he'd just linger and be incontinent and Janie would have to take care of him. Had little Miss Ash thought of that?

I THOUGHT I would probably not live another week. But so resilient is the spirit at twenty-one, so quick to change direction, that one week later I was not only alive but at a portal I never dreamed I'd enter—25 West Forty-third Street, the offices of *The New Yorker* magazine, on my way to a job interview.

They had called and asked me to come. Why me? Some feeler, sent out by somebody, had sprung a root. Of course it was ridiculous. They would see through me soon enough, unless I could fool them for a while. I had to get off my heap of lists and itineraries and *Decorating Is Fun* and do something with myself.

I sat and waited in a dim hallway until a small white-haired lady, Miss Daise Terry, came out to look me over. Where had I gone to college, what was my major? How fast did I type? There were two kinds of jobs, receptionist and Miss Terry's typing pool, and my erratic peck-and-hunt must have served me well because she offered me the receptionist job on the eighteenth floor. The hours were ten to six, the pay sixty dollars a week. The job was to take phone messages and tell visitors where to go. Occasionally when she was overwhelmed Miss Terry might send down some copy for typing. The rest of the time I could sit there and write stories or whatever I did. Later I learned that the magazine liked to hire English majors for low-level jobs, hoping one or more of them would show some talent.

• • •

I HAD THOUGHT OF the *New Yorker* staff as a tight fraternity of brilliant, silver-tongued people who together generated and guided the cultural life of the city. But if this was true, the evidence was well hidden. Of three silent, bleak floors of offices, I seemed, at first, to have landed on the dullest. My desk, set in a doorway, looked down a long empty hall where by-line writers were said to work behind closed doors.

At first I saw only an occasional furtive ghost darting toward the elevator. Then slowly the shades became flesh. At the far end of the hall were three reporters—Whitney Balliett (music), John Brooks (finance), and Audax Minor (the track). In the middle, Faith McNulty (Talk of the Town stories) and Sheila Hibben (About the House), and behind me Lois Long (fashion), whose nom de plume was "Lipstick."

"I knew your father," she said, erasing any notion of anonymity I might have. My father had not been a *New Yorker* writer, but many of his cronies—James Thurber, Joel Sayre, Sid Perelman, John Mc-Nulty—had been, and he felt a connection.

"What was he like?" I asked.

"An adorable bastard."

She knew everyone. She had been married to the cartoonist Peter Arno, who drew old guys with walrus mustaches and bimbos with big tits. With her fluffy hair and eye-catching hat, her modish clothes, she was the twenties personified. Nunnally was a bastard! I didn't dare ask why but didn't need to—by then I knew there were many Nun-nallys, most of which I would probably never see.

Lipstick sparkled, chattered, and joked—her peal of laughter flowed down the silent hall. I'd thought writers were morose and pre-occupied. But Lipstick was lively and gregarious, Technicolor footage in a noir landscape. All day, her typewriter clattered behind my back, her voice poured into the phone, her assistants came and went with ex-citing finds—a turban, swatches of Italian silk, a pair of marvelous shoes. I took it all in: Ann Fogarty and Clare McCardell were still strong, Haymaker shirts were out. Linen sheaths cried out for dusters—plaid was everywhere, even for evening—stoles were all right for summer but they weren't going to last. A-line coats were new and terrific, especially the ones with dropped shoulders and pushup sleeves that required elbow-length kid gloves. ("The coats from both sides of the water are magnificent," Lois Long wrote.)

Hats—Sally Victor, John Frederics, Lilly Daché—should be either good or heads should be bare. "Such an odd feeling," she wrote (8/28/54) "to see so few veils and other flutter in the fall showings. Refreshing, like a good clean wind from the sea, it is." She could be stern—"the new French hats . . . look like something you might have lifted off a tray of petits fours, profiteroles and napoleons stuck somewhere on your head with a bit of Duco cement. Very, very cute, but I maintain that they just aren't Millinery" (10/9/54). Fashion, she believed, was for real people, and the clothes around that time were not only wearable by all but very pretty too with their narrow shoulders, small waists, and pronounced hips.

Mrs. Hibben, as she was always called, approached household lore with the stern purpose of a general going to battle. From the beginning she misread my function in the office. Her door opened, her pale face and brown hat appeared.

"Miss Johnson, be so good as to get Vendôme on the phone."

But she *had* a phone, I had no switchboard—if there had been one I wouldn't have known how to use it, and wouldn't have been hired in the first place. If one of the writers got a call on my phone, which occasionally happened, he or she took the call at my desk. It seems primitive even for fifty years ago—I don't recall any buttons on the phones, but then, as now, anything that went on in these hallowed halls was beyond criticism, and nobody questioned the arrangement.

I told Mrs. Hibben I didn't have a switchboard.

"You don't . . . oh dear." After a moment of thought, the door closed.

The next time it happened her tone was peremptory: "Miss John-son, be so good as to get Mr. Otis at Sloane's lamp department on the line."

"I can't, Mrs. Hibben. There's no connection between your phone and mine."

"There isn't . . . goodness. All right."

The next two times she was increasingly frantic, and her tone became cross. "Get the Bloomingdale's food department . . . the Dover Delicatessen . . . customer service at General Electric." Her own phone was ringing as were others, typewriters were clicking away—as close to chaotic as the place ever got. "Now, please hurry, I have to leave very shortly."

"But Mrs. Hibben . . ."

"*Please* just do as I ask."

"But I . . ."

"I have *no time to argue!*"

Her tone was fierce—there were deadlines to be met. I was getting the idea, time was everything. So I did the only thing I could think of—went into her office, dialed the number on her phone, and handed her the receiver. She thanked me and took the call, and that became part of my job—dialing Mrs. Hibben's phone and handing it to her.

In her "About the House" pieces, she was a *grand dame* suddenly discovering the secrets of downstairs. The servants had fled, but she didn't complain—she was grateful, even awestruck, at the new wonders before her:

"—I assumed that I knew all there was to know about Fiberglas, and this deplorable lack of open-mindedness has delayed a report on a group of fabrics that proved to be, when I finally got around to looking at them, among the most exciting I've seen in quite a spell." (9/11/54). And "Until recently, I fear, I have been sadly out of step with all those efficient women who have presumably laid the spectre of domestic drudgery [to rest] for all time by turning things over to what are known as the major household appliances. Now, however, I have done some intensive investigating of new electrical contrivances, and far from being bashful about speaking up for the good life on such short acquaintance, I am positively eager to testify, like the reformed sinner at a revival meeting, to the blessings I so stubbornly overlooked" (9/18/54). On to the GE portable dishwasher, the Philco automatic refrigerator, and the Amana freezer.

The household arts were coming into their own. As Lois Long brought a silk scarf or gloves into the office to show around, Mrs. Hibben brought a chopping knife or a tin of pâté—apologizing to it for being so slow in her appreciation. The war was over, the men had their jobs back, the servants were gone. Housework, now unavoidable, was becoming respectable. The housewife was the heroine of the day.

AT FIRST I'd been disappointed at being among practitioners of the feminine arts instead of the editors and reviewers upstairs. But the atmosphere had its effect, and after work I walked up Madison, peering into Vendôme and Nils and Georg Jensen and Bonnier and Scalamandré, furnishing an imaginary dollhouse, imagining spectacular parties. I detoured through Bloomingdale's, admiring the Dutch ceramic pots, the Chemex coffeemaker, the copper chafing dish that put the battered aluminum cookware I'd grown up with to shame. *The New Yorker* seems an odd place to have found my *yin* . . . though I suspect I would have found it anywhere.

MY MOTHER AND ROG were thrilled about my job. They had thought I would never rise again, they would have to do something with me for life.

But one evening:

"Sit down," Ma said.

"I hate it when you use that tone."

"Rog and I have been talking. This is a big house . . ."

"I thought it wasn't big enough."

". . . and it requires a lot of upkeep. The landlord will only do so much. Everything is expensive." She put a dab of Camembert on a cracker and recrossed her legs. "Your trust fund has almost run out; you'll get the rest but it isn't much. A thousand or two. But thank God for *The New Yorker.*" I didn't like the way this conversation was going. "Anyway, we think it's only fair to ask you to pay for your room and board."

We eyed each other over the martini pitcher while many violent things flew through my head.

"*We* shouldn't decide—*you* should decide." But as soon as I said it, I knew that now it would always be *we.* "You could always afford me before, why not now?"

"Oh, I was always short of money. Then Nunnally's support stopped when I married Rog, of course." She had an answer for everything. "Oh, come on now, sweetie. It isn't fair that Rog should pay your expenses. Anyway, you won't be staying long—you'll get an apartment with a girlfriend, or you'll get married."

I felt slightly sick. Was she right, was she wrong? She'd given her life to me, now it was her turn. But what was my problem? I didn't want to leave 204. She'd made the place too good, too enticing. If I'd had a home like some of my friends, I'd have been out the door like a comet.

She suggested twenty dollars a week.

"Well, Ma, what with lunches and carfare now I'll be so poor I won't be able to buy clothes or go places to meet men, and I'll be so frantic about paying bills I won't be able to write, which might augment my income."

"You'll manage."

Had I a bad character? If it had been just she and me, and if I knew she needed the money, I would have been glad to contribute.

"To tell you the truth, we might be moving in a couple of years anyway," she said. "Rog needs a real study, and he needs to be nearer Columbia. He's thinking of teaching another course."

Oh, God. That didn't bear thinking about. I said nothing to Rog, he and I got along by sidestepping troubling matters. And in most ways he'd been generous to me. Maybe they just wanted to be alone.

"POP," I said on the phone, "Ma is charging me to live here." Maybe he'd invite me to live with him and Dorris.

"How much?"

"Twenty a week."

"It could be worse."

"But I'll starve."

"I doubt it. Your mother's a very good cook."

"I think they really want me to leave."

Long pause. "Perhaps they do."

"But why?" I felt about four years old.

"It's the same as when you wanted to go to Barnard. They want to be alone together."

He said the same thing he'd said then about making her new marriage work. What he really meant was that if it didn't, she'd be alone again and somehow he'd be responsible for her.

"They're always alone together."

"I've talked to her about this, honey. There are certain things you've got to understand. A house is an expensive venture. When the children grow up people want to scale back their way of living. Dorris and I talk about selling this house all the time."

"Oh, please don't," I said.

Now I would never live with him. What was the matter with them, all of them? They went to endless trouble to provide children with happy homes, to create memories—Christmas festivities, birthdays, pool parties, pajama parties, Easter-egg hunts, teenage dances—then suddenly it was off to the real estate agent. They were like those people from the Himalayas who made elaborate, beautiful patterns out of colored sand that they wrecked the minute they were finished. It was the hateful process over product.

One evening I'd heard Rog barking into the phone while Ma lurked nearby looking pained but supportive.

"No, you can't, d'you see," he was saying. "It just won't work. There isn't room, we aren't set up for it." He looked upset. "You can't expect that of us, it's time you learned some consideration. And there's my health to consider."

"What?" I asked her in the hall.

"Oh. It's Teddy." She pulled her earring worriedly, then dropped her voice. "You can hear what he's telling her. She just thinks she can come any time she wants."

"But can't she?"

"Of course not. She takes him completely for granted. Anyway this isn't the time, her marriage is in trouble."

"Oh, no."

"They've had problems all along. She's a very spoiled, difficult young woman."

"But don't you want to see the children?"

"They're much bigger now and we can't accommodate them, crashing around and breaking things. And she wants to bring her au pair. She thinks of nobody but herself, and it's high time Rog put his foot down."

From the living room Rog's voice was heavier and raspier. "There's no need to bring all that old stuff up. Stick to the present. You can't get around me with that, d'you see? I've spoken and that's final. You can stay at a hotel."

"It wouldn't be just a visit," Ma said in a low voice. "They'd move in. She wants to leave her husband and come here and have Rog support her, and he simply can't and won't." The phone slammed down. "She upsets him, his blood pressure goes up. She won't quit picking over past injustices."

"Sweetie," he called, "bring me some ice, will you? I think I need a drink."

Off she trotted, down the stairs to the basement.

I HEARD THE
BRASS BAND PLAY

IT HAPPENED ON the west side of Fifth, somewhere in the Fifties. I was on my way to Berlitz for an Italian lesson. *Per che?* So when I couldn't stand *The New Yorker* any longer I could go to Rome and live in a flat on the Palatine Hill and write belles lettres. Or something. It was pretty vague. I was having the one-on-one lessons and the teacher wouldn't allow a single word of English. If you wanted to go to *il gabinetto* you had to say so in Italian.

October 1954. A bright and sparkling day . . . the breeze was blue as the sky, fresh as the sea. My hair blew around, my high heels tapped on the pavement, silvery with mica. Lipstick like my raspberry wool dress. In the mirror of a store window, I looked pretty dishy. The world was mine . . . and I saw possibilities rolling out in front of me like a red carpet.

It was before anybody'd thought of glass ceilings. The women I knew did what they wanted. Look at my parents' friends, Ann Duffy and Edith Haggard and Emily Hahn and Edith Asbury and Gertrude Sayre and Celia Ager and all the other professional women, look at

Lena Horne and Rita Hayworth and Helen Hayes and Betty Bacall and Liz Taylor and Claudette Colbert and the other actresses of stage and screen. Look at my sister Marjorie and the other film editors, look at Aunt Margaret and suffragette Gobbie and Miss Gorgon and the City Patrol Corps and the women doing war work, look at Jinx Falkenburg and Eleanor Roosevelt and Wallis Simpson for whom the duke gave up the throne. And the headmistresses, Millicent McIntosh of Brearley and Marguerite Hearsey of Abbot, Mary Ellen Chase and other inspired teachers at my single-sex schools, and Sylvia Plath and a few other peers who seemed headed for immortality. Look at Lipstick and Mrs. Hibben and Faith McNulty and all the *New Yorker* writers, Jean Stafford and Rumer Godden and Mary McCarthy and Nancy Hale . . . look at Dorothy Draper.

You could say that for each of these there were ten like Aggie Harding or Ina the ex-bacteriologist or Rani who went back into purdah. But I had always been told to aim for the top, never to underestimate myself. Ma had said I could have it all—a career, marriage, children, money, loyal friends, travel, a home like 204, a talent for party giving, a fashion sense, and swingy hair. If your mother tells you something again and again, no matter how ridiculous it is, you start to believe it.

That was when I saw the brass ring shine, heard the brass band play.

COMING ALONG FIFTH in the other direction was Len, a man I'd met at a party and gone out with a couple of times. He looked very good—dark wavy hair, glasses, a tall athletic build, well-tailored gray suit, and diagonally striped tie. His office was nearby; he was probably going to lunch. He liked me, he was ready to set something in motion. I was wavering. I thought about him sometimes—sometimes I thought about other things. There were a couple of others guys around.

We looked, we spoke not a word. He grabbed me by the arm, sprinkled pixie dust on me . . . then steered me around the corner and down the side street to a small dark French restaurant where we had a bottle of wine and coq au vin or escargots or cheese soufflé. I blew off the Italian lesson and he went back to his office an hour late.

I floated back to the eighteenth floor. I was a little drunk but that was all right—those were the days of three-martini lunches, and people came back to the office popping breath mints. I was humming tunes from *Kismet* and from *Fanny,* which was playing on Broadway that fall . . . the music from the side street.

LEN AND HIS FRIENDS worked for Aramco—the Arabian American Oil Company, based in Saudi Arabia. They'd been living in the desert, the hostess had told me sotto voce, and now they were earnestly seeking the company of American women. They were tall, suntanned, and good-humored, with a foreign, exotic air. They spoke fluent Arabic, they mentioned Cairo and Beirut as casually as I mentioned the West Side or the Village. Had they galloped across the dunes on camelback like T. E. Lawrence, had they made love to veiled Scheherazades with liquid eyes? Did they sleep in tents, dine on loaves of bread and jugs of wine . . . were they in search of Thou?

At the party, Len and I had sat in a corner and talked about life. Tragedy. God. Allah. The afterlife. Dostoevsky. Baseball . . . he'd asked if I liked it, and I didn't say no (the first lie). He was grave— there wasn't much lightness about him, but that was all right. I'd had enough airheads. He was eleven years older than me and he knew the world was a serious place.

Len was Catholic. He had grown up in a Polish section of Chicago, his father was a butcher, his mother a cook. The family's store and savings had disappeared in the wake of the 1929 crash. One of three children, Len had put himself through Northwestern by publishing a small local newspaper. He spent three years in the army at the end of World War II, then went on to the Johns Hopkins School of Advanced International Studies. He was recruited by Aramco and sent to Tübingen, Germany, and to Cairo for cram courses in Arabic, then to the company's enclave in Saudi Arabia.

I thought I detected some similarities to Nunnally, whose parents could not afford to pay for college. After high school he'd applied to West Point, and when he didn't get in, he went to work on the Columbus *Enquirer-Sun* . . . all of which I thought gave him and Len a potential bond. Self-made men must instinctively understand each other.

I LOVED RESTAURANTS, and I loved sitting around in bars drinking and smoking. Len couldn't stand sitting for too long—he had to walk or move around or play tennis or volleyball. I read novels, he read only detective stories. He had been to extraordinary places seen by few Westerners, but he didn't describe them in a way that lit them up or brought them to life. He had seen no elves in the Black Forest, no Pharaonic ghosts in the Valley of the Kings. Theater he could take or leave, and we liked different kinds of movies.

But we were immensely attracted to each other, which made everything sparkle. We were on an enchanted voyage. It almost didn't matter what we did. I wanted time to stop during one of those fall twilights when the lights were going on and music leaked into the air, as we came out of a restaurant and walked hand in hand, heads together , , . when every patch of sidewalk and bare slender tree, every lighted window and shadowed doorway, the whole city, existed for our pleasure.

On the bamboo couch, among the yellow pillows, our lovemaking was very much like what had gone on pre-Willy. At first I'd thought this had to do with logistics. Even if Ma had lowered the bar, habit was too strong, the whole house was permeated with nursery rules. At first I didn't care, I was just as glad to fall back into old habits and not worry about getting pregnant and all that. But before long I began to tire of retro sex—I wanted a real love affair. Very shyly I'd suggested we do more grown-up things, take it up a notch. If not here, how about going to his apartment?

Len puckered up his mouth. His blue Slavic eyes looked brooding and I was reminded of Willy at the same juncture. What did I do to bring on these precoital pauses? It turned out that Len wasn't anxious to move things ahead. Not yet, he said. It was an important step, not to be taken lightly.

I explained that the purpose of losing my virginity was so I could stop worrying about losing my virginity. I'd *had* an affair . . . but he didn't want to hear about it. He changed the subject, paced around the porch, even went into the too-public bathroom.

"But why shouldn't we sleep together?" I cried as he came out.

"The time hasn't come," he said cryptically.

The balkier he was, the more determined I became. Possibly backdrop was the problem—the right place would engender the right time. I led him through possible venues like a real estate agent trying to make a sale.

His ground-floor apartment at 58 East Eightieth—described by a friend as "Len's black-and-gold sex nest"—was the obvious choice. With its Danish modern in stark colors, the black sofa that turned into a bed, it had a striking, slightly decadent look. I persuaded him to cook dinner for me—he'd mentioned some specialties. After martinis and schnitzel and a bottle of Tavel, I kicked off my shoes, sprawled on the black sofa, and dropped some heavy hints.

"Not here," said Len, with a gesture of dismissal.

"Why not? It's perfect—I love it."

A shrug. The weeks he'd spent shopping for lamps and curtains and four place settings of everything and pots like his mother's, the hours sanding and staining beautiful planks for bookcases, all this was relegated to the ashheap of unimportant things. The client didn't even like his own home.

The top floor of 204? One evening I led him up the three flights to my room. I lit a fire in the fireplace, we curled up on the bed with childhood picture books—and one thing might have led to another if the front door hadn't slammed below and the Flynns—who'd been out to dinner—came in, and that was the end of it.

All right—a hotel room, a place unconnected to things that

reminded us of other things. No, no! That was for people who sneaked around. Anyway we both had perfectly good places to go, both of which had been rejected. I should be patient. He hinted at a solution, a surprise that was coming before long.

Then he asked me if I was "really married" to New York, to my job, to my family, to my friends. I said I was pretty fond of them all. He described Dhahran, Aramco's desert enclave—weekly movies, air-conditioning, a swimming pool, tennis courts. The hostess had said that Len was now a permanent resident of Manhattan, but how wrong she'd been. He liked it there, he was going back to the field early in the new year. Which he had to do or quit. Which he didn't want to do, because he loved his job hobnobbing with the local sheikhs and emirs.

It was to Len's credit that he had such engaging friends. They were clever and well-spoken and good-humored about Dhahran's short-comings and peculiarities. By making fun of it all, they did a better selling job than Len, whose sense of humor tended to dry up when crucial things were at stake. To him Dhahran was close to holy, not to be defiled. Was this because he was Catholic? No—so were many of his friends. This was because he was Len.

Len sprinkled more pixie dust and popped the question at the Hotel New Yorker where we'd gone for dinner and dancing.

I said I didn't think I could deal with living in the desert. Len said if I loved him I'd be happy to go anywhere with him. What did it matter where we were? My prejudice against Dhahran would disappear when I saw it—or after a few days or weeks. But my job, my friends, my city! Oh, I could write anywhere, I was bored to death at *The New Yorker* anyway. And my friends were all getting married and leaving. It was time I left 204, I was a big girl.

I told him I was going to live in Rome or possibly Tehran—my rest-less friend was again anxious to flee. But Len had been there, Tehran was a dump and Rome wasn't so easy. What kind of life was that, going to some strange place all alone without even speaking the lan-guage? And a single woman could never break into the expatriate colonies—too threatening to the wives. I'd hate it, I'd be back inside a month.

It was my second proposal and it was just as bad as the first. I told him I needed a few days. He said I should decide as soon as I could, because he had to be back in the field by the end of February and there was a lot to do.

I submitted the problem to my friends, expecting to be told to forget the whole thing. But they sighed, looked down, said it was up to me. One of them said she'd do it in a minute. The way they saw it, Len wasn't the problem—it was Dhahran. Intense questioning had pried out some fearful truths: it went up to 120 in the summer, there were blinding sandstorms that went on for days. There were no stores, or certainly not the kind I was used to. There was no alcohol in Saudi Arabia—you had to make your own in a pressure cooker with copper coils and black curtains over the windows so you wouldn't get arrested. There was more I didn't find out till it was too late.

"Oh God," I said to Ma and Rog. "It isn't fair."

"Who said anything's fair?" Rog said over an outsized Old Fitz on the rocks. "You'd better check out his religious beliefs, d'you see. You don't want to have a baby a year."

"Babies! I don't want any babies."

"Well, you might change your mind about that," Ma said.

"You might have to talk to a priest," Rog said. "Len might want you to convert." He seemed to think all this was funny.

"No! No!" I cried.

NUNNALLY WAS IN NEW YORK around that time, and he and Len and I had dinner together. It seemed to be all right, though I was so nervous that I couldn't tell if any serious bonding was going on, or if it even mattered. Pop asked questions about the Middle East, particularly the chances of being shot at or blown up, and Len said there were six thousand Americans there who had never felt a moment's unease.

Nunnally knew about the pending decision, and back in California he wrote:

"I found him intelligent and attractive and easy to get along with . . . thank God he is an adult [Len was 32]. Boyish charm is pretty well lost on me . . . Len . . . struck me as having the kind of confidence that comes from having found a field of his liking and competence in that field . . . you will be spared the frantic hopes and despairs of a husband still wildly groping for a rope to climb up . . . God help the poor bride who has to go through it." He said he had complete faith in my judgment, adding "there is no guarantee on any marriage . . . Does he love you? Has he any understanding of people? Is he fun? If you can satisfy yourself on a few fundamentals you would be wise to take a chance on the rest . . . the odds are greatly in favor of success."

He made it sound so easy, my thrice-married father.

AND WHAT WOULD my life be if I said no? The eighteenth floor, dialing for Mrs. Hibben, cooing over Lipstick's hats. A three-flight walkup with a girlfriend, tuna-fish casseroles, going to bars every night looking for men. I'd end up a Jean Rhys heroine. Even the idea of staying at 204 was losing its glow. The Friden dominated the living room and Rog was drinking more and more Old Fitz every night and edging more toward Irish charmlessness. The smorgasbord of life had dwindled to a few dreary half-eaten dishes.

"I can't stand it," Len said among the yellow pillows. "Are you going to make me happy forever, or plunge me down into hell?"

If I say yes we can sleep together, said a little voice from within. We can have a long engagement and I can persuade him to move back to New York. Or we can go to Dhahran for a couple of years, travel a lot and then come home. There were other companies to work for.

I said yes.

· · ·

I TOLD MA FIRST and she sighed and smiled and looked distressed at the same time. She asked me the same questions I'd been asking Len, such as how would I live in such a place without losing my mind. I said we were in love and that was going to take care of everything. After I said it for the fifth time, I began to believe it myself. It didn't take much talking—she was too much of a romantic to be bothered for very long by facts. She wished I wasn't going eight thousand miles away, but she knew that was selfish. She was behind me whatever I did, wherever I went.

Announcing the engagement was like turning the switch that lit up the whole amusement park. Ma and I flew into action. We were going to do it right, straight down-the-line *Vogue's Book of Etiquette*. Tiffany's for the engraved invitations, the Carlyle for the reception. An engagement party at 204 around Christmas. Shopping for a trousseau.

Len produced a diamond ring. And a daunting list, and an Aramco booklet. We had to shop for the whole two-year contract and Aramco would ship it all to the field. The booklet was full of gentle mysterious reminders such as, we should think ahead to what we wanted to give the children a year from Christmas—and there were no curtain rods at all in Saudi Arabia—and nobody ever brought enough shoes—and if I had some unique hobby such as origami or playing the psaltery, I should bring the wherewithal along because hobbies were strongly encouraged.

By then I'd met some of the Aramco wives. They were ten years older than me and very savvy about living in exotic places.

"I suppose I should bring lots of suntan lotion," I said to one.

She gazed at me with a bemused expression. "Well, you can. But I don't think you'll want to sunbathe much."

We were having drinks at Delmonico, across from the Aramco office at 505 Park. Georges Feyer was playing cocktail music. I was wearing a cream-colored wool dress and a black A-line coat like Audrey Hepburn's in *Sabrina.* On my finger was the diamond ring, which I wiggled around to catch flashes of light. They were talking about a man they knew who brought his wife to the field where she completely failed to adjust. She sat around all day in her bathrobe drinking spiked coffee and then she began coming on to the other husbands, and it ended up in a messy divorce, and he resigned and went to work for the State Department . . . and what a waste it was for the company. I wasn't really taking it in, I was purring because everything was so wonderful. My head was full of shopping lists and party menus.

JENSEN'S had the most beautiful silver. I wanted the cactus pattern, Len wanted the acorn.

"But the cactus is so perfect for the desert."

"There isn't any cactus," Len said. "It isn't Arizona."

Down went another fantasy. And didn't I get to choose? Len wanted to share everything . . . it was the age of Togetherness, a concept dreamed up by the editor of *McCall's* magazine. What the hell— I liked the acorn almost as much. I could give in on the little things, because I was going to win on the big one. Anyway when I quit my job I could shop full-time and Len would still be working and decisions would be presented as a fait accompli. I picked out the Rosenthal china and the lovely cloudy glassware from Bonnier's to be registered for wedding presents.

Then Ma and I went to Bloomingdale's housewares and bought every single thing for the kitchen and bathroom either of us could think of, plus sheets and towels and blankets and table linen and God knows what else. I have no idea where the money came from, from one or both of my parents or from me, but it seemed infinite. We had a marvelous time. Everything that looked even potentially suitable— scissors, lightbulbs, padded coat hangers, shoe trees, whisk brooms, flashlights, hairbrushes, a sewing box, tennis balls, boxes of candles, decks of cards and board games, a do-it-yourself mosaic kit—we grabbed with little cries of joy. It was all sent to a shipping address for Aramco to take care of.

Even more fun, if possible, was buying the clothes.

"This will be perfect for your first luncheon party," Ma said, pulling forth a little linen outfit. "And this for company banquets"—a svelte dinner dress. There weren't any, but we didn't know that. Drip-dry and wrinkle-shed outfits for travel, casual skirts and blouses for around the house, pedal pushers for bicycle riding and driving into the desert. Cotton dresses for barbecues and trips to the local Arab towns. Makeup and toiletries—even things I never used. Who was to say I wouldn't want to try mascara and stick-on beauty spots in a year or so? Creams and lotions to fight the desert dryness, lingerie and frippery for the boudoir . . . a lacy nightgown and peignoir and satin mules. We were to honeymoon in Cuba, and there had to be beachwear and dresses for dancing under the stars in Havana. When we came back we'd live at the Dover Hotel on Lexington and Fifty-eighth for three months before leaving for the Middle East.

After each shopping binge Ma and I went to the Veau d'Or or Charles à la Pommes Soufflée for another celebratory lunch. And why not? We were fulfilling our ordained purpose, we were Bride and Mother-of-the-Bride. We drank wine and giggled, then took the boxes home in a taxi and I tried everything on all over again.

Len's smile was patient and bemused. His attention was on the basics: we had to buy a washing machine and a dryer. Susie A. and Janet B., Aramco wives of impeccable authority, advised Blackstone. We should check it out.

In spite of Mrs. Hibben, I hardly knew what a washing machine looked like. I thought you called the laundry the way you called the liquor store. Every week or two at 204 we flung a sheet down on the living room floor and we and/or the maid tossed the dirty laundry on it, then knotted it up and the laundryman picked it up. Nobody counted it—if anything disappeared Ma either didn't know or care.

I would do the same in Dhahran. There must have been a laundry—and somebody had mentioned houseboys. The houseboy would do it.

Len looked grave at this chatter. Wives were supposed to do laundry. It was a shame I couldn't sew or darn—which he'd discovered when he dropped a pile of holey socks and a darning egg into my lap, and I suggested he throw them out and buy new ones. And he seemed to expect me to iron—the hidden downside of owning a washer. I said I was sure we didn't need one. There had never been a washer at 204, the maid rinsed the undies out in the sink . . . We argued, I sulked, Len sulked. We bought the washer and dryer.

One of Len's errands was fun—a trip to a certain drugstore on Lexington that catered to Aramco employees. They sold restaurant-sized pressure cookers and copper coiling and hydrometers and other equipment for distilling. You made the mash (water, sugar, frozen orange juice, yeast) in huge glass crocks rescued from some stage of the petroleum refinery process, available in the field from secret sources. For weeks it bubbled and bubbled, then you set up the still, closed the black curtains, and turned it on. I shouldn't worry, the husbands took care of it.

IN THE ARAMCO PACKET was a scale map of our future apartment. Ma and I cut out tiny chairs and tables and beds, as Dorothy Draper suggested, and moved them around the rooms. We painted the walls and discussed fabrics. Then Len said there was a choice of only three colors for the walls, as there was for the upholstered furniture supplied by the company (mustard, liver, and spinach), and everybody used it, it was silly to take furniture out there. By then I was actually relieved. I was getting what Phyllis McGinley called "spendsickness." It was all spinning around. I didn't know what I wanted anymore.

AS SOON AS it was legit I had gotten fitted for a diaphragm. But Len—who was starting to be a problem—still wanted to wait.

"Wait—why?" I'd spent half an hour in the bathroom getting the damn thing in.

Probably it was sentimental and corny but he wanted a traditional wedding night that we would remember forever. Didn't I want to walk into the bedroom in my new lacy peignoir? I said I would do that anyway and if I were really a virgin that would be one thing, but I wasn't and this was not only ridiculous but fraudulent. We started to argue till I realized that on Judgment Day, when all accounts were settled, I didn't want this particular line of argument on the record. (She Fought for Sex and Lost.) So back we went to faux lovemaking.

WE TALKED TO Father O'Brien of Saint Ignatius Loyola, Len's church, where the ceremony was to be. ("My gracious, Saint Ignatius," Rog said.) Len gave me a booklet for non-Catholics marrying into the mother church. A quick read showed that my presence was disturbing, if not downright dangerous, to the believers—I had to be reminded to keep my place. The ceremony would not take place on the high, main part of the altar, but on the less-holy ground just below—what Pop, who was following all this with interest, called "some kind of Jim Crow section of the church." He told me the story about Groucho's son going into the country club pool only up to his waist because he was half-Jewish. And there must be an understanding about birth control.

On this issue I was utterly terrified. I imagined Len ripping a hole in my diaphragm or burying it in the sand, and of course I wouldn't be able to get another in a place where everybody was either Muslim or Catholic. Every nine months I would be pregnant, I would come back from Arabia with two children and another on the way. I'd be wearing Arab robes, my ankles fat and my feet bare, my hair in long dirty tangles, communicating in grunts. I lay awake at night worrying about this, and when I brought it up, Len, according to his evolving technique for dealing with knotty problems, looked agonized and wouldn't discuss it.

I talked to a couple of Catholic friends who told me to agree with everything the good Father said but to keep my fingers crossed and out of sight. This was good advice, for I had to have two instructive sessions about how I should never interfere with my husband's faith and if there was a disagreement, he was the automatic winner . . . and I would never use any contraception except nature's way. My fingers were twisted in knots in my lap. Len never asked me what Father O'Brien and I talked about and I never brought it up. Neither he nor Father O'Brien ever mentioned converting.

WE PUT an engagement announcement in the *Times*—which brought Miss Terry to my desk, newspaper in hand.

"It says here you're going to Saudi Arabia."

"Yes, Miss Terry. I would have told you but things have been a little unsettled." Not too unsettled to call the *Times.* "So I'll be leaving before Christmas." I was surprised that she seemed to care—she even looked a little annoyed. Wasn't I infinitely replaceable? I told her I had a friend who was interested in the job; if she liked I'd ask her to phone.

"What's she like?"

"She's like me," I said. "She can probably type a little."

Helen was an English major. She'd work out very well. She'd stay on the eighteenth floor for a while, then gradually work her way up to doing some Talk of the Town pieces. She'd get to know people, eventually review books or movies—become a staff writer—she'd end up replacing Mr. Shawn. I was voluntarily leaving all this. I'd be in Arabia, again on the delivery table, and Helen would be editor of *The New Yorker.*

I told them all good-bye, answering all their questions about Saudi Arabia. I told them they'd taught me all I knew about lares and penates, which were going to be the center of my life. Mrs. Hibben still didn't really know who I was, but Lipstick did—I was the daughter of the adorable bastard.

•   •   •

WHEN LEN called home to tell them the news, his mother's first question was "Is she Polish?" and her second "Is she Catholic?" Then a silence—which Len pretended there hadn't been.

We drove to Chicago in Len's car that he was selling to somebody before we left. No, we didn't want it anymore, nobody had cars in Dhahran. (They did.) We stopped at a motel for the night. I was so frightened of meeting his family that I got drunk in the motel dining room and, on the wan hope that Ohio would prove irresistibly erotic, again made a move on Len—for which purpose I'd brought my diaphragm. No, he said, there was only a couple of weeks (around eight) to go. It was a scene straight out of *It Happened One Night*. He hung his raincoat—on a hanger hooked onto the light fixture—in the middle of the room as a symbol of apartheid. I told him he was crazy—he said I'd be glad someday. I got furious and he became sphinxlike and went to sleep.

There were a lot of people living in the two-family house—Len's parents, his married sister and her husband and their three children—and I stayed at a hotel. They didn't quite know what to make of me. Len's brother and his family and all the aunts, uncles, and cousins who lived within a few blocks dropped in to look me over, bringing delicious offerings of plum tart, kielbasa, cucumber salad, pierogi. They were all very proud of Len for his success, and he looked happier there than I'd ever seen him. His mother and father barely spoke English—he was a big oil man. I was the wife that came with the American dream.

BRIDE-TO-ORDER

"LET'S LIVE IN A TENT," I said to Len.

We were at the Henri IV on Sixty-fourth Street. It had red-and-white checked tablecloths and Chianti bottles holding dripping candles. It was dark and quiet and cheap. The menu was always the same. My friends and I had hung out here for years. I was going to miss it terribly.

"Tents don't have plumbing," he said.

"Well, maybe not an actual tent. But why not live in a local town . . . with Persian rugs on the floor and brass lamps and incense. We could be closer to the people."

Len looked at me with the bemused expression I was seeing more and more. "You wouldn't like it, darling," he said.

"But why?"

"It's primitive, it's dirty—and the people don't want to be close to you."

I was picking strips of wax off the candle. "Are there any restaurants?"

"Not like this. People eat at home."

I felt like crying.

"So we'll be living in a prefab just like everybody else's with puke-colored furniture and no martinis and no movies or theater or books or restaurants and no Bloomingdale's. Why do you like this place?"

Len looked furious and grim and sad all at once.

"That isn't the point. Of course it isn't perfect but that's where my job is and I *like* my job and my job is going to support us. Oh, you know all this. Life isn't perfect or even near perfect. It's just what it is—that's all."

That was the difference. To me life was something to be questioned, explored, improved if possible. But we had come this far . . . I would widen Len's vision, deepen his sensibilities.

The Aramco wives told me about a man who was transferred to the New York office for the usual two-year term but failed to find a wife. He went back to the field and became something of a predator, chasing the few single Western women in Dhahran and then finally the unthinkable—getting involved with a young Saudi woman from Al Khobar, the nearby Arab town where I'd suggested living. All hell broke loose. Her family had a fit and the company tried to protect him but couldn't, and he ended up in jail and there was a rumor the girl had been stoned to death.

Embedded in this sad story was more cause for alarm.

"Do you mean Aramco assigns its single men to New York *for the purpose* of finding a wife?"

The women exchanged a look. "Well, pretty much."

"For the *sole* purpose?"

"Of course the real work is out there. It's make-work at this office. Didn't you know?"

"I guess I don't know much of anything."

They exchanged more glances. "It makes perfect sense. It's hard to be single there. The whole thing is about adaptation. They try to weed out the bad apples—they run a CIA check on everybody."

"On me?" I screamed.

"Well, of course. Didn't Len tell you?"

"No."

"Not that it makes any difference. You'll never know about it, unless you've been smuggling arms or drugs or something." They laughed merrily. "Anybody want to go to Bonwit Teller?"

I was a corporate bride-to-order!

I TOLD LEN I was afraid that if I did something wrong I'd be stoned to death or beheaded. Len said shari'a law didn't exactly apply to Americans, or not most of the time—and anyway Aramco had a whole law department to protect us. What was my problem? A lot of people lived in strange places. He hadn't thought I was so provincial.

"NUNNALLY HAS OFFERED the services of Twentieth Century-Fox," said Ma with complete inaccuracy.

"For what?"

"To help plan the reception."

This exchange shows how crazy we were. I believed this peculiar statement and told Pop that we didn't need or want their help, to which he replied:

> . . . I must admit that you hurt me by a certain loftiness of attitude toward the company I work for, and indirectly Hollywood and my business . . . When you say that Fox might be called on for assistance if it is able to remember its place, there was a suggestion that the colored folks would be permitted to pitch in and help provided they understood they were not to mingle with the white guests . . . a suggestion of contempt which is common enough but which I hope my family will never share . . . in any case . . . Fox wouldn't have the slightest interest in the task . . . Just keep your head . . . In dusty corners of the world it is still fashionable to be politely contemptuous of American movies, just as it is fashionable in certain quarters to be ignorant of certain idols of the masses, but I'm sure

as you grow older you will find such affectations to be no
more worthwhile than [here he mentions the daughter of a
Pulitzer Prize–winning friend] who is ashamed of her father
because he is neither Dylan Thomas nor a rich stockbroker.
(undated letter early 1955)

But that wasn't exactly it. I had been brooding over the guest
list, the bizarre mix that was coming to our reception at the Hotel
Carlyle—Helen Hayes and Charlie McArthur, Jed Harris, the
Irving Berlins, the Bogarts, the New York newspaper and magazine
crowd—and a group of Polish people who cooked and carved for a
living, went to mass every Sunday, who danced the polka and read the
Polish paper. It might epitomize the American dream but I was in no
mood for breaking down barriers, I just wanted the damn party to go
off well, and all I could imagine was the Carlyle's Victorian Suite
starkly divided like the motel room with the hanging raincoat. I
wanted the Hollywood element to be unobtrusive so Len's family
wouldn't be further terrified.

Still, there was a shred of truth in what my father said. I must have
gotten it from Ma and her old grudge against the place where she'd
been unhappy, or from my own Ivy education in and out of circles.
Deep in my heart I thought Hollywood wasn't really respectable—
with the notable exception of Nunnally. There was something tacky
and superficial about it. It might have been sour grapes, because I'd
never belonged there, or else an attempt to protect against the eleven
thousand miles that would soon separate me from it. It fed into the
feeling of wrong that was piling up inside.

Every fruit had a little poisonous seed. I liked the cactus better than
the acorn. I didn't want to get married in the mother church. Some of
my friends were talking about renting a house on Fire Island in June
and I wanted to go. Len could be sanctimonious and I didn't like his
short-sleeved shirts. Helen was going to be editor of *The New Yorker.*
When I confided all this to a couple of friends (not Ma, she was too
happy) they said I had pre-wedding jitters. Sure—Len might snore,

we might be attacked by crazed revolutionaries on camels. And you could get hit by a bus on Lexington Avenue. Why didn't I go hide under the bed for a few years?

I THOUGHT OF other men I'd left along the way because there had seemed to be something wrong with them at the time or because I just didn't want to bother. Some that I hadn't thought about for years now seemed winsome and appealing—even Gregory Miles, who appeared on planes. Other men, other lives flashed by like seductive previews of wonderful movies I'd never see. I brooded over my flawed character. I was superficial and frivolous, a dragonfly adept at skimming surfaces but blind when it came to looking at my own reflection. God knows what opportunities I'd missed.

One evening Rog said over an Old Fitz: "Be sure you know what you're doing. Don't go out there thinking you'll divorce him if it doesn't work out. You'll ruin his career, d'you see."

He said it sotto voce, when Ma was out of the room. It was kind of an opening.

I told Len he could get out of the whole thing if he wanted, it was okay with me—I didn't want him to feel trapped. He looked as though I'd driven a stake through his heart. Then I thought of something that must certainly give him pause.

"We haven't really talked about money," I said. "It looks as though I'm rich with Hollywood and everything else but I'm *not*. Pop loves to get his daughters off the payroll. I *needed* that *New Yorker* salary," which I was proud of earning.

Len said, "I've never expected money from you."

"I should have brought it up before. You can't be indifferent to what I have. Or don't have."

He broke into a loving smile, then got a little huffy. "I've always expected to support you, for God's sake. I'm very touched but it's a matter of pride to me that I can take care of a wife."

"If you want to call it off I'll understand perfectly."

No—never! He didn't care if I was poor. He'd be making twenty-five thousand a year plus the living allowance, and no U.S. income taxes. And—didn't I get it? He was in love!

The man was a saint. There was no way to get out of this.

FEBRUARY 19, 1955.

In my long satin dress and Juliet cap, holding my train, I climbed the stairs of Saint Ignatius. Behind me was the limo, ahead in the vestry among the holy-water fonts were the half and whole members of my family. On the sidewalk were a couple of photographers popping flashbulbs.

Never had I been so alone, never would I be so alone again.

Everyone was there: Len's parents and the rest of his family, Dorris in an elegant suit, Rog magnificent and genial. Ma with her mink stole and little hat, Nunnally in his tux, my half siblings in their finest attire. I felt like a mummy—laced into a merry widow, an undergarment that nipped in the waist, kept the tits aloft, and held up the stockings. I felt hot and jammed into my clothes, overly made-up and frizzy-haired. On this great occasion, I didn't feel beautiful as I had the day I'd met Len on the street.

The organ was playing as the procession moved down the aisle—the maid of honor, the bridesmaids, and Roxie, the flower girl. The others entered in the manner prescribed by *Vogue* for dismembered families—Dorris sat in one pew, Ma and Rog in another. The handsome Aramco ushers escorted everyone to the correct seats.

I took my father's arm, and six-year-old Scott, in a little white suit, picked up my train. We moved toward the entrance. When I looked into the church I caught my breath. On one level (if not all) I would have been an easy convert—the incense, the candles, the vibrant tones of the organ, the way the eye swept upward all made my heart beat faster. Saint Ignatius was a magnificent space lined with marble columns and arches, and rows of hanging lanterns lighting up the frescoes, the marble statues, and the stained-glass windows. The tones were muted like those of an ancient tapestry. In the back were the confessionals, and beyond, the little group of flickering candles to be lit for the dying and the dead. It was a holy place.

What was I doing here? I had choked out a halfhearted yes to a man I barely knew and this was the result—a major rite of church and state, an extravaganza, the unnatural gathering together of one family that had never been under the same roof before and another family who wished they were back in the Polish hall in Chicago. Limousines were parked in front, wedding presents were piled at 204 or else in boats on their way to the Middle East . . . and it was all going to be in the paper the next day.

I had no idea if the drive behind all this was love or lust, intensified by Len's insistence on legal sanction—or if I even knew the difference. And I felt blackmailed by the force of the disciplines that were going to rule my life—the Catholic Church, corporate ethics, shari'a law. They all contradicted each other. What I understood about them I didn't much like, and I was supposed to honor all of them, or else pretend to.

I wanted to rip off the veil and run out of the church, down the steps, and into a taxi—straight to West Forty-third street and back up to the eighteenth floor. I'd explain that I'd made a terrible mistake, beg for my job back—Helen would surely understand. We'd send back all the wedding presents, I'd pay them back for the reception out of my paycheck. I'd start looking for an apartment and a roommate and prepare for my Jean Rhys future.

Len would be upset, but it wouldn't last long, he'd find somebody else. Aramco would let him stay in the New York office till he found a wife. How about one of the bridesmaids? This time he'd look more closely at what he was getting. It took more than just passing the CIA check. She'd have to be able to fit into the round hole that I knew I wouldn't, like I knew I was alive.

At the end of the long, long aisle Len stood with the best man and Father O'Brien, Len with a broad and happy smile. How it would fade if he knew what was going on in my head! He had done nothing wrong—nothing except hang up his raincoat between us and buy me a washing machine. I couldn't think of a single reason to get out of it.

I suspected he was not the love of my life. But in my small experience, great loves caused great pain. How much happier Ma would have been if she'd found Rog in the beginning! I was taking a shortcut past the years of misery my parents had gone through, before Nunnally pulled himself out of it and married Dorris. Why not find the solid long-term companion right off?

We were there. My father lifted my veil up and kissed me, with a smile of utter love and trust. *I have complete faith in your judgment.*

I'd make it work. Hadn't Ma told me I could do anything?

INDEX

Aaron, Daniel, 193
Abbot, 140, 242
Abbott and Costello, 96
Abel, Walter, 177, 179, 180
Academy Awards, 1
Adams, Casey, 177, 179, 180
"Admonition" (Plath), 158
Ager, Celia, 146–47, 148, 149, 150,
    241
Ager, Milton, 147
Alexander, Shana, 29
Alice in Wonderland (Carroll), 33
American Sporting Scene, The
    (Kieran), 74
Amherst College, 153–54, 196
Anderson, Dottie, 64
Anderson, Eddie, 142
Anderson, Maxwell, 141
Andover, 126, 137
Anti-Defamation League, 131
anti-Semitism, 97–98, 102, 154, 155
Arabian American Oil Company
    (Aramco), 243–44, 246, 249,
    250, 251–52, 257–58, 261, 262
Army-McCarthy hearings, 191
Arno, Peter, 234
Arrowhead, Lake, 79
Art Students League, 135

Arvin, Newton, 193
Asbury, Edith, 59, 241
Asbury, Herbert, 59
Auschwitz, 97, 214
Automat, 57

Bacall, Lauren, 13, 14, 29, 36, 70,
    111, 112, 242
Baldwin, Betty, 211, 212, 227
Baldwin, Faith, 66
Balliett, Whitney, 234
Baltimore Sun, 58
Barbizon Hotel, 192
Barnard College, 172, 239
Beaux-Stratagem, The (Farquhar),
    148
Bedtime Story, A, 1
Behrman, S. N., 141
Bel-Air Bay Club, 42, 116
Bellamy, Catherine, 59
Bell Jar, The (Plath), 192
Bemelmans, Ludwig, 140
Benchley, Robert, 2
Benny, Jack, 2, 142, 185
Berger, Teddy (Flynn), 164, 188–89,
    240
Berlin, 176–81

Berlin, Irving, 259
Berlin Airlift, 176
Berlitz, 241
Beverly Hills Hotel, 27, 77, 106
Biltmore Hotel, 91, 92
Bloomingdale's, 6, 237, 250, 257
Blue Angel, 136
Bogart, Humphrey, 13, 14, 29, 70,
    111, 112, 114
Boston, 140–41
Brearley, 57, 242
Brecht, Bertolt, 2
Brooklyn Daily Eagle, 32, 65, 123
Brooklyn Navy Yard, 61
Brooks, John, 234
Broun, Heywood, 66
Brown Derby, 2, 12, 183
Buckley, Maureen, 197, 198
Buckley, William F., 197
Bulldog Drummond Strikes Back
    (film), 2
Burns, George, 2
Byrnes, Gobbie (grandmother), 131,
    204, 242

California, University of:
    at Los Angeles, 43, 217
    at Santa Barbara, 78
Carlyle Hotel, 89, 249, 259
Carmichael, Hoagy, 99
Catalina Island, 35
Cavalcade (film), 1
Center Island, 121
Central Intelligence Agency (CIA),
    257–58
Central Trust of China, 167
Chang, Mr., 167–68
Chase, Mary Ellen, 193, 194–95, 242
Chasen, Dave, 111, 144
Chasen, Maude, 111, 112
Chasen's, 2, 12, 215

Château Marmont, 26
Chicago, 145–46, 163, 170–71, 255
Chinese Nationalist Army, 167
Chrysler Building, 24, 92, 174
Churchill, Winston, 24
CinemaScope, 213
Ciro's, 26, 40
Citizen Kane (film), 67
City Patrol Corps, 64, 242
Cloisters, 57
Coca, Imogene, 136
Cohn, Harry, 13
Colbert, Claudette, 128, 242
Collegiate Reformed Church, 166
Columbia University, 238
    Business School of, 159, 164
    Law School of, 163, 172
Columbus Enquirer-Sun, 244
communism, 85, 96, 98, 99–100, 102,
    116, 170, 173, 176, 191, 197, 198
Cooke, Alistair, 202
Country Doctor, The (film), 28
Crawford, Broderick, 177, 178, 180
Crucible, The (Miller), 181
Cukor, George, 15, 17
Cummings, Robert, 211

Dachau, 97
Daniels, Bebe, 147
Darnell, Linda, 2
Darvi, Bella, 213, 214
Daughters of the American Revolu-
    tion (DAR), 133
Davis, Bette, 79–80, 128
Davis, Robert Gorham, 156–57,
    191–92, 193, 198
Decorating Is Fun (Draper), 221, 233
Delmonico, 249
Denis (London friend), 148–51
"Denouement" (Plath), 158
Depression, Great, 1, 59, 67, 162

Desert Fox, The (film), 142, 146, 213
Desk Set, The (film), 185
Dhahran, 69, 246, 247, 248, 251, 255, 257
Dimples (film), 2
Dinner at Eight (film), 1
Douglas, Kirk, 29
Dover Hotel, 251
Draper, Dorothy, 221, 227, 242, 252
Duckett, Eleanor, 194
Duffy, Ann, 58–59, 64, 174, 241
Duffy, Eddie, 58–59, 67
Dunne, Finley Peter, 66
Dunne, Irene, 147
Dust Bowl, 1

earthquake (Los Angeles), 1
Ebsen, Buddy, 177, 179, 180
Ecstasy (film), 2
Egyptian, The (film), 213, 214
Eisenhower, Dwight D., 162–63, 167, 170, 171, 199, 232
Elizabeth, Princess of England, 143
Equus (Shaffer), 56

Falkenburg, Jinx, 54, 242
Family Circle, 59
Farmers Market, 2, 31, 43
Faulkner, William, 2
Faye, Alice, 142
Feyer, Georges, 249
Fisher, Al, 193
Fitzgerald, F. Scott, 2, 67, 69
Florence (mother's friend), 65, 67–68, 147, 160, 169
Flushing High School, 65
Flynn, Marion Byrnes Johnson (mother):
    character and personality of, 19, 30, 31–32, 38, 64, 111, 129,
144, 160, 161, 169, 188, 190
    childhood and adolescence of, 32, 65, 160
    family and religious background of, 24, 65, 133, 160, 228
    Hollywood life of, 1, 2, 39, 130–31, 259
    jobs of, 32, 65, 66, 123
    lovers of, 3, 22–24, 31, 127
    motherhood of, 5, 21–24, 30, 118
    Nora's relationship with, 5, 21, 23–24, 30, 31, 39, 55, 88, 122–23, 128–33, 155, 160, 169, 170, 184, 187–88, 204–6, 228–30, 250–51, 263
    Nunnally Johnson and, 2–3, 11, 19, 30, 32, 33, 38, 39, 40, 49, 65–68, 75–76, 123, 124, 130–31, 164, 165–66, 182, 216
    physical appearance of, 19, 23, 38, 55, 74, 128
    Rogers Flynn and, 159–67, 168, 172, 174, 184, 188, 190, 202–6, 220–21, 222–23, 225, 237–40, 261, 263
    summer residences of, 63, 121, 122–23, 127, 129, 169
Flynn, O. Rogers (stepfather), 159–67, 168, 172, 174
    character and personality of, 159, 161–62, 184–90, 248
    flying experience of, 164, 204
    health problems of, 165, 223
    Nora and, 161–62, 163, 173, 187–88, 190, 220–21, 239, 260
    physical appearance of, 159, 186
    teaching career of, 159, 238
    widowerhood of, 164–65
Fogarty, Ann, 235
Fowler, Gene, Jr., 111, 112, 123–24
Fowler, Marjorie Johnson (half sister), 33, 111, 112, 123–24, 242

Front Page, The (Hecht and
    MacArthur), 140, 181

Gable, Clark, 128
Gam, Rita, 177, 179
Gangs of New York (Asbury), 59
Garland, Judy, 71
George, Uncle, 131, 167, 170,
    171–73, 175, 221–22
Georges (chauffeur), 22–24
Georgia Central Railroad, 160
God and Man at Yale (Buckley), 197
Godden, Rumer, 242
Goldwyn, Samuel, 107
Golinkin, Joseph, 74–76, 121–24
    character and personality of, 61,
        74, 76, 123, 129, 131
    Marion Flynn and, 3, 60, 61, 76,
        122–23, 124, 129, 131
    Nora and, 76, 123, 129
    painting career of, 59, 74–75,
        122–23
    wartime naval service of, 3, 61, 65,
        68, 75–76
Grable, Betty, 211
Grand Central Station, 5–6, 128
Grapes of Wrath, The (film), 2–3, 28
Graumann's Chinese Theatre, 26
Great Dictator, The (film), 96
Griffith Park, 35
Guinness, Alec, 147, 152, 191
Gunther, John, 54

Haggard, Edith, 20, 59, 64, 148, 241
Hahn, Emily, 59, 241
Hale, Nancy, 242
Hamilton, Alexander, 168
Hammerstein, Oscar, 2
Hammett, Dashiell, 2
Harold (chauffeur), 40, 46

Harris, Jed, 176, 180, 181–83, 259
Harris, Jimmy, 39–40
Harris, Phil, 142
Harvard University, 195, 197, 198
Harvey, Fred, 7
Hayes, Helen, 140, 141, 242, 259
Hayward, Leland, 140
Hayworth, Rita, 36, 110, 149, 215,
    242
Hearsey, Marguerite, 242
Heatter, Gabriel, 24, 63
Hecht, Ben, 2
Heiress, The (Ruth and Augustus
    Goetz), 181
Hempstead, Avery, 59
Hempstead, Eleanor, 59
Henri IV restaurant, 256
Hepburn, Audrey, 249
Heyn, Ernie, 65
Heyn, Ethel, 59
Hibben, Sheila, 234, 235–37, 242,
    248, 251, 254
Hilton, Nicky, 150, 151–52
Hiroshima, 76
Hitler, Adolf, 1, 60, 68, 145, 178
Hollywood Hospital, 1
Hollywood Reporter, 207
Holocaust, 97
Holy Matrimony (film), 28
Horne, Lena, 6, 9–10, 12, 14, 15,
    16–17, 242
Hotel New Yorker, 246
House of Rothschild, The (film), 2
House Un-American Committee
    (HUAC), 82, 95–96, 100–101,
    173, 191, 198
How to Be Very, Very Popular (film),
    203, 211–12
How to Marry a Millionaire (film),
    213, 215–16
Hubbel, Mrs., 133
Huston, John, 15

Île-de-France, 166–67
Ingrid (domestic), 45, 47–49, 52–53
Iron Curtain, 179, 180, 183
It Happened One Night (film), 128, 255

Jesse James (film), 2, 50–51, 93
Jessel, George, 2
Johns Hopkins University, 196
    School of Advanced International Studies at, 243
Johnson, Alice, 16, 66, 123
Johnson, Christie (half sister), 181, 211, 215
Johnson, Dorris Bowdon (stepmother), 142–45, 178–83
    character and personality of, 31–32, 124–25, 144, 179, 182–83
    film career of, 2–3, 32
    Nora's relationship with, 30, 35, 36, 39, 49, 77–78, 124–25, 143–44, 178–79, 187, 239
    Nunnally Johnson and, 2–3, 27–33, 37, 52, 68, 75, 82, 87, 96, 124–25, 142, 165–66, 182–83, 214–15, 239, 263
    physical appearance and clothes of, 30, 35, 111, 124–25, 165, 217
    pregnancies and children of, 32–35, 95, 98–99, 117–18, 124, 166, 214–15
Johnson, Nora:
    abortion considered by, 225–30
    boyfriends of, 86, 87–93, 120–21, 123, 132, 133, 135–39, 153–54, 162–63, 170–75, 199–206, 260
    California life of, 1–2, 26–53, 93–109
    childhood and adolescence of, 1, 3, 5–206

children of, 45, 161, 215
coast-to-coast travel of, 5–17, 30, 46, 125–28, 145–46, 170, 207–10
college graduation of, 202–6
courtship and marriage of, 244–63
early writing of, 27, 142, 148, 157, 193, 194, 211–13, 214, 215
education of, 3, 22, 29, 30, 55–56, 75, 131, 140, 155–58, 160–61, 168, 172, 191–206, 224, 259
European travel of, 140–45, 146–52, 160, 176–83
financial assets of, 223–24, 260–61
first novel of, 211–15, 227
first sexual experience of, 199–202, 245
half siblings of, 32–35, 95, 98–99, 111, 112, 123–24, 166, 181, 211, 214–15, 242
jobs of, 162–63, 167–68, 172, 233–37, 238, 241, 246, 254, 260
New York life of, 2, 5, 18–25, 36, 54–68
relations of domestic help with, 21–22, 24, 45–53, 63, 64, 94–95
social debut of, 132–39
trousseau of, 45, 249, 251
youthful friends of, 6–17, 27, 30–31, 34–44, 55–56, 77–110, 113–21, 124, 125–28, 147–48, 207–10, 215–18
Johnson, Nunnally (father):
    character and personality of, 16, 17, 29–30, 31, 46, 49, 67, 68, 70, 82, 95–96, 97, 124, 145–46, 160, 185–87, 228, 234
    combat experience of, 204
    drinking of, 113, 131, 150, 186
    early writing career of, 65–67, 123, 244

Johnson, Nunnally *(cont.)*
  education of, 244
  fatherhood of, 5, 7, 12–13, 16,
    27–28, 32–35, 123–24, 166,
    187, 215
  film directing by, 76–81
  film producing by, 2, 71, 176–81,
    183
  finances of, 2, 122
  humor and wit of, 12–13, 133,
    145–46, 186
  Nora's relationship with, 16,
    27–28, 29, 30–31, 36, 38,
    39–40, 49, 53, 69–73, 75–76,
    94, 95–96, 128, 140–46,
    148–50, 172, 183, 187, 202–6,
    209–10, 211–12, 215–16, 227,
    247–48
  physical appearance of, 29, 49,
    186
  scriptwriting of, 1, 2–3, 12, 28, 29,
    43, 50–51, 71, 93, 133, 141–42,
    146–47, 148, 176–81, 203,
    211–13
  social life of, 28–29, 110–14,
    130–31, 140–41
  southern heritage of, 75, 133, 160
  wives of, *see* Flynn, Marion Byrnes
    Johnson; Johnson, Alice; John-
    son, Dorris Bowdon
Johnson, Roxie (half sister), 211, 261
Johnson, Scott (half brother), 215,
  216
Johnson, Van, 29

Kahn, Otto, 55
Katie Gibbs school, 168
Kaufman, George S., 140, 141
Kerr, Deborah, 29
Kerr, John, 56
Kieran, John, 74
King Kong (film), 1

La Brea Tar Pits, 35, 42
Ladies' Home Journal, 220
Lake Arrowhead, 79
Lamarr, Hedy, 2
Lanin, Lester, 134
Lassie Come Home (film), 43
Last Tycoon, The (Fitzgerald), 69
Len (husband), 242–63
  army service of, 243
  character and personality of, 243,
    244–46, 248, 252–53, 260–61
  education of, 243–44
  family and religious background
    of, 243, 246, 247, 253–54, 255,
    261–62
  oil company position of, 243–44,
    246, 249, 250, 251–52, 257–58,
    261, 262
  physical appearance of, 242
Lenin, V. I., 102
Lewis, Sinclair, 67
Life, 29
Life's Choice (drawing), 75
Logan, Joshua, 140, 141
London, 65, 141–45, 146, 147–50,
  217
Long, Lois "Lipstick," 234–35, 237,
  242, 248, 254
Los Angeles, 26–44, 69–73
Louvre, 146
Loy, Myrna, 128
Lucas, Dionne, 145
Lyon, Ben, 147

MacArthur, Charles, 140, 141, 259
MacArthur, Douglas, 163
McCall's, 59, 250
McCardell, Clare, 235
McCarthy, Joseph, 156, 170, 191, 199
McCarthy, Mary, 242
McDowall, Roddy, 43–44, 78
McGowan, Ada Ruth, 59

McGowan, Anne, 59
McGowan, Frank, 59, 65
McIntosh, Millicent, 242
McNulty, Faith, 234, 242
McNulty, John, 234
Madeline (Bemelmans), 140
Mademoiselle, 192
Malibu, 217–18
Mama Loves Papa (film), 1
Mankiewicz, Herman, 2, 66, 67
Margaret, Aunt, 131, 167, 170,
    171–73, 221–22, 223, 228, 242
Margaret Rose, Princess of England,
    143
Margaret Sanger Foundation, 131,
    223
Martindale's bookstore, 71, 93
Marx, Groucho, 2, 13, 14, 253
Marx, Karl, 102
Mason, James, 111, 112, 148
Mason, Pamela, 111, 112
Mayer, Louis B., 13, 15, 29
Mayflower, 133, 199
MCA, 6
Mencken, H. L., 96
Mendl, Lady Elsie, 29
Mercer, Ginger, 29, 111, 112
Mercer, Johnny, 29, 111, 112, 113–14
Metro-Goldwyn-Mayer (MGM), 12,
    15–16, 107, 213
Metropolitan Museum of Art, 57
Mexico City, 219–20
Minor, Audax, 234
Miss Lonelyhearts (West), 1
Monroe, Marilyn, 216–17, 218
Montana, 61
Montgomery, George, 29
Morris, Jerry, 147
movies, 69–73
    blacklisting and, 96, 100–101
    directing of, 71, 76–81
    dubbing of, 70
    independent productions and, 213

musical scores of, 70
production of, 70–73, 213
rushes of, 72
sets of, 69–70, 72
studio system and, 160, 213
"talkies," 1, 13
television and, 213
war, 63–64
Mr. Peabody and the Mermaid (film),
    29
Mr. Roberts (Heggen and Logan), 149
Mudlark, The (film), 141–42, 147, 213
My Cousin Rachel (film), 213
My Friend Flicka (film), 43

Nanny (nurse-maid), 22, 24, 40, 63,
    64
Nash, Ogden, 2
Nathan (boyfriend), 153–56, 210
Nazis, 63–64
Negulesco, Dusty, 147
Negulesco, Jean, 147
"Never Try to Know More Than You
    Should" (Plath), 158
New York, N.Y.:
    Chinatown in, 57
    department stores and shops in,
        20–21, 24, 54, 57, 131, 169,
        189, 224, 237, 250
    hotels in, 57, 89, 91, 92, 246, 249,
        251, 259
    in 1920s, 66
    restaurants and nightclubs in, 3,
        54, 57, 66, 136, 161–62, 184,
        210, 249, 251, 256
    skyscrapers in, 24, 57, 92, 174
    Third Avenue el in, 21, 54, 57,
        127, 137
    204 East 62nd Street, 18–25,
        58–61, 64–65, 74, 86–88, 122,
        128–29, 137–38, 161, 172,
        173–75, 184–85, 188–90,

New York, N.Y. (*cont.*)
220–21, 231, 237–39, 242, 244, 245, 248, 249, 251–52
wartime, 62–65
New York *Daily News,* 173
New Yorker, The, 59, 65, 67, 189, 193, 259
Nora's job at, 233–37, 238, 241, 246, 254, 260
staff and writers at, 234–37, 242, 248, 251, 254
New York *Evening Post,* 66, 67
New York *Herald Tribune,* 66
New York Times, 59, 254
Night People (film), 176–81, 183, 212, 213
Niven, David, 111, 112, 114
Niven, Hjordis, 111, 112
North, Sheree, 211
Northampton Secretarial School, 195
Northwestern University, 243
Nursie (nurse-maid), 45, 47, 48, 94, 95, 98, 113, 124

Oberon, Merle, 29
O'Brien, Father, 253–54, 262
O'Hara, John, 2, 67
"One for My Baby and One More for the Road" (Mercer and Arlen), 114
Oswald, Gerd, 180, 181
Oswald, Jerry, 180, 181–83
Our Town (Wilder), 181
Oxford University, 147

Paramount Pictures, 1, 79–80
Paris, 67, 135, 137, 146, 162, 164, 169, 213–14
Parker, Austin, 67
Parker, Dorothy, 2
Parsons, Louella, 39–40

Pearl Harbor, Japanese attack on, 3, 60–61, 63
Peck, Gregory, 176–77, 178, 180
Perelman, Sid, 234
Perkins, Berry, 56
Perkins, Tony, 55–56, 57
Photoplay, 118
Pied Piper, The (film), 28, 43
Planetarium, 57
Plath, Sylvia, 156–58, 191–92, 205, 242
Plaza Hotel, 57
PM, 146
Power, Tyrone, 50–51, 53, 70, 149
Preminger, Otto, 29
Pressman, Joel, 128
Prisoner of Shark Island, The (film), 2, 28
Prix de Paris, 194
Prohibition, 1
Psycho (film), 55
Pulitzer Prize, 58, 259

Queen Elizabeth, 150–51
Queen Mary, 142

Red Cross, 65, 86, 161
Republican Party, 163, 170
Rhys, Jean, 248, 262
Ripley, Mr., 57
Ritz-Carlton Hotel, 140–41
RKO, 37
Road to Glory, The (film), 2, 28
Robinson, Edward G., 29
Rockefeller Center, 57, 66
Rogers, Cam, 67
Rogers, Ginger, 13, 36, 70, 75
Roman Catholic Church, 24, 65, 228, 243, 246, 253–54, 255, 261–62
Romanoff, Mike, 144, 183
Romanoff's, 3, 13, 116

Romeo and Juliet (Shakespeare), 68
Romero, Cesar, 50, 147
Rommel, Erwin, 142
Roosevelt, Eleanor, 54, 242
Roosevelt, Franklin D., 1, 24, 60
Rosenberg, Ethel and Julius, 192
Rose of Washington Square (film), 50
Ross, Harold, 66
Roxie Hart (film), 211
Royal Canadian Air Force, 164, 204
Ruby, Harry, 2

Sabrina (film), 249
Sagan, Françoise, 193
Saint Ignatius Loyola Church, 253,
    261–62
Saturday Evening Post, 13, 66, 67
Saturday Review, 59
Saudi Arabia, 244, 247, 249, 254,
    256–57
Savannah Hussars, 204
Sayre, Gertrude, 59, 64, 241
Sayre, Joel, 59, 65, 148, 234
Sayre, Nora, 59, 147–48
Schoenberg, Arnold, 2
Schwab's drugstore, 44
Schwartz, Arthur, 140, 141
Screen Writers Guild, 1
Seawanhaka Junior Yacht Club, 121
Selznick, David O., 36
Seventeen, 157
Shawn, William, 254
Sheffield Inn, 199–201, 202
Shepperton Studios, 143
Sherman, William Tecumseh, 75
Shirley (friend), 80–81, 85, 98
Silver Screen, 6
Simpson, Wallis, 242
Sixty-second Street Association, 54
Skouras, Spyros, 70, 208–9
Smith, Harrison, 59
Smith College, 155–58, 160–61, 168,

    172, 175, 191–206, 207, 212,
    224
Smith Review, 157–58
Song of Russia (film), 96, 101
Southern Pacific Railroad, 145
Stafford, Jean, 242
Stalin, Joseph, 179
State Department, U.S., 250
Staten Island Ferry, 57
Stevenson, Adlai, 171
Stewart, Don, 2
stock market crash of 1929, 243
Stork Club, 136
Street, Julian, 67
Success Magazine, 66
suffragettes, 131, 242
Sullivan, Frank, 66
"Sunday at the Mintons" (Plath), 157
Super Chief, 3, 5, 6–17, 42, 49, 210, 215
Syracuse University, 164

Taft, Robert, 163, 171
Taylor, Elizabeth, 150, 151–52, 215,
    242
Tea and Sympathy (Anderson), 56
Temple, Shirley, 2, 41–42
Terry, Daise, 233, 254
There Ought to Be a Law (Nunnally
    Johnson), 67
Three Came Home (film), 213
Thurber, James, 66, 234
Time, 167
Tobacco Road (film), 93, 133
Todd, Ann, 29
Tracy, Spencer, 16, 185
Transcendentalism, 157
Trinity Church, 167–68
Trocadero, 26, 40
Truman, Bess, 163
Truman, Harry, 163
Turner, Lana, 44
Twentieth Century, 3, 5, 8, 215

Twentieth Century-Fox, 31, 69–73, 147, 176–77, 180, 209, 210–12, 213, 214, 258
Twentieth Century Pictures, 1
"21," 3, 57, 210

Ulysses (Joyce), 157
Universal Studio, 213
Unloved City, The (Nora Johnson), 211, 212–13, 214, 215, 227

Variety, 146
Versailles, 146
Victoria, Queen of England, 142
Villa, Pancho, 204
Vogue, 261
Vogue's Book of Etiquette, 249

Walker, Stanley, 66
War and Peace (Tolstoy), 134
Warren, Robert Penn, 141
Weill, Kurt, 140, 141

West, Nathanael, 1
Wiese, Otis, 59
Wiggins Tavern, 199, 200, 202, 203
William Morris Agency, 5, 6, 46, 63
Winchell, Walter, 3, 63
Windswept, 122–23, 127, 129
Wisteria Trees, The (Logan), 140, 141
World War II, 60–65, 68, 75, 121, 132, 144, 145, 161, 243
    fall of France in, 23
    Pacific theater in, 3, 65, 75–76
    shortages and rationing in, 39, 62–63
Wright, Benjamin F., 198
Wylie, Philip, 2
Wynn, Keenan, 29

You Can't Take It with You (Kaufman), 140
Young Republicans, 198

Zanuck, Darryl, 1, 50, 160, 213–14
Zanuck, Virginia, 213

ABOUT THE AUTHOR

Nora Johnson was born in Hollywood, California, the daughter of Nunnally Johnson and Marion Byrnes Johnson. Her parents divorced when she was a child, and she moved to New York City with her mother. She went to prep school and college in the East and spent summers in Beverly Hills. She has been a writer all her life; in 1958 her first novel, *The World of Henry Orient,* was a great success and was subsequently made into a film starring Peter Sellers and Angela Lansbury and a Broadway musical called *Henry Sweet Henry.* She has written novels and nonfiction books, as well as short fiction, articles, and essays for various periodicals, such as *The New Yorker, Atlantic Monthly, McCall's, The New York Times Book Review,* and the *Los Angeles Times.* She's been married twice, has three children, and has lived in Saudi Arabia, Larchmont (N.Y.), and New York City, where she currently resides.